You Are (Not) a Fı

A Scientist's Guide to the Imposter
Phenomenon

Marc Reid

You Are (Not) a Fraud

A Scientist's Guide to the Imposter Phenomenon

Marc Reid

ISBN 978-1-7398243-0-3

For a list of all ways to share this main book and the journal resource accompaniment, scan the QR code below:

https://linktr.ee/reid__indeed

For Amanda, Adaline & Lachlan.

Contents

Credits

Publisher: NullaFraus Publishing (Marc Reid Ltd)

Editor: Kirsten Rees | Book Editor & Author Coach
Proofreaders: Kirsten Rees & Dominic Pattison
Fact-checking and final proof-reading: Holly Moore
Formatter: Leanpub
Contact: *See **Contact the Author** section at the end of the book.*
Book social media hashtag: #YouAreNotAFraud

Author's Note

From the moment I first scribbled down my own thoughts of feeling like a fraud, and during the entire course of preparing this book, I collected many books, notes, blogs, videos, lectures, diaries, and journal publications on the Imposter Phenomenon. Wherever possible, I have tried my utmost to acknowledge the original sources.

It is also important to note that my thoughts, assertions, and interpretations described herein are (except in the case of particular acknowledgements) entirely my own. But make no mistake, I share it all to help you manage the imposter experiences that might be holding you back. I offer you my story with absolute sincerity, and I am in no way attempting to represent a particular institution or public body. I don't wish to lay blame or point fingers at anyone for anything that you are about to read.

This is all on me. For you.

Preface

My one promise to you in this book is to show you the hidden stories, dark data, and actionable tools that will help you manage your imposter experiences. Allow me first to take you on the scenic route through my own reasons for writing this book.

On a map of the world, Italy is the infamous geographical version of a long-legged boot. Just above the knee of the boot, in the north of the country, the city of Bologna represents an architectural haven for lovers of the Middle Ages and the Renaissance. Among the sea of ragu-red rooftops reminiscent of the region's famous pasta dish (this is where Bolognese sauce comes from), Bologna hosts its most enlightened claim to fame, the Università di Bologna: the oldest university in the Western world. For almost a thousand years, since 1088, the university's crest has boasted a proud motto reminding the world of what a university should be:

"Alma mater studiorum" or *"Nourishing Mother of the Studies"*[1]

If you leave Italy and head northwest on the world map, you eventually reach the University of Cambridge in the UK, home of the 500-year-old Cambridge University Press. On its crest, this publishing house displays an image that conveys another message of the university ideal. The alma mater – or 'nourishing mother' – stands tall, proud, angelic. Her maternally curvaceous body is the centre of the Press's crest. From a wreathed crown on her head rises a castle. Waist-length locks of hair meet a pedestal that the mother stands behind. She holds a chalice in her left hand to represent spiritual fulfilment. Her right hand cradles the sun, shining bright for intellectual enlightenment. And surrounding the crest, the motto:

"Hinc lucem et pocula sacra" meaning *"from here, light and sacred draughts."*[2]

Go still further north to Scotland, and you see the coat of arms for the University of Glasgow. The crest bears a Book of Learning sitting in the highest position as a font of knowledge atop the crest. This book is placed at the peak of a hierarchy of symbols depicting the story of Scotland's largest city.

Since their beginnings, universities have been designed and perceived to be places where knowledge and progress could move with untainted ease. Regardless of whether you're in Bologna, Cambridge, Glasgow, or another university town, universities have been modelled as places of discovery for those seeking to understand Nature and all that she possesses. Places free from political strife, free from apathy, free from mundanity, universities were born to be fertile grounds from where knowledge could grow without restriction. But fast-forward to modern universities in the 21st century and there is a parasitic weed growing on the crisp green grounds of utopian university life. There's a discussion topic that has been somewhat swept aside, out of sight but not out of mind. And it's no longer taboo.

Rather than universities providing nourishment for the mind, an ever-growing literature is showing that university culture is in serious danger of becoming the insidious centre of a tragic mental health crisis.

That darkening stain on academic life is manifest in higher-than-average reports of poor wellbeing, troublesome work-life balance, and debilitating stress. Sometimes it has even gone so far as to have life-threatening impacts on mental health.[3] Students[4] and staff[5] alike have used suicide as the only means of escape. The utopian perception of the university haven is being recast as a survivalist gauntlet. Moreover, social media is driving new behaviours and university cultures that misguidedly protect students from difficult and debatable ideas that might cause offence.[6]

There is a worrying string of reports on both student and staff[7] mental health problems in the higher education sector. These reports are scattered but nonetheless convergent, and they all crystallised in 2017.[8] A mental health review commissioned by the Royal Society and the Wellcome Trust – two of the most respected and trusted bodies in the UK's scientific community – was released for all to see. Although these specific numbers focus on the situation in the UK, the literature gathered for the 2017 Royal Society and Wellcome Trust review considers a broad data source, including North America, Asia, and Australasia as well as the UK. The review set out to find what (if any) "specific mental health needs" there were among researchers.

It's worth taking a moment to understand why the 2017 mental health review was commissioned at all. If you look at the statistics for the population of England alone, there are reportedly six million people suffering from a mental health condition at any one time. Six million! That's enough people to fill a premier league soccer stadium a hundred times over. Six million is about one-tenth of England's population, and 2% of the total number of Twitter users back in 2017. More people in England suffer a mental health issue than there are people in all of Denmark. Six million is a huge number and it's horrifying.

In monetary terms, the reported levels of mental health illness are enough to cost £26 billion to the UK, and over £1,000 per employee across the working nation. If you can't quite wrap your head around how much £26 billion actually is, imagine each pound was a second in time. Twenty-six billion seconds is close to fifty thousand *years*.

In 2020, a related report from Wellcome painted no prettier picture, sharing the dire statistic that over half of researchers in the UK and globally have sought support for anxiety or depression.[9] On Twitter, I personally scraped 15,000 tweets on the subject of academic mental health posted between 2017 and 2021. 99% of those tweets fell within the last two years.

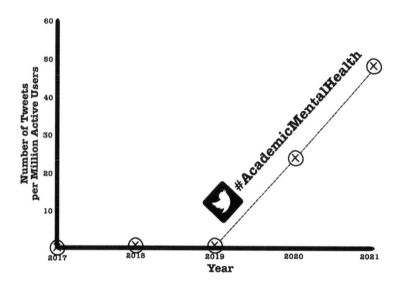

Increasing instances of tweets containing "#AcademicMentalHealth", corrected for the number of active Twitter subscribers per year.

Even when correcting for the growing Twitter user base over time, it is still the case that the use of the term 'mental health advocate' has increased more than 700% since 2013.

The academic mental health crisis is extensive.

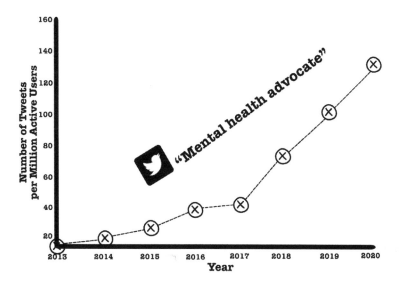

Increasing instances of the phrase "mental health advocate" appearing on Twitter, corrected for the number of active Twitter subscribers per year.

So, what makes the higher education environment so damn stressful? Why is this sector the seat of such potent concern? Remember, the growing number of reports on mental health problems relates to both students and staff. For students, one reason for the increase is that the number of graduating students – undergraduate and postgraduate – is increasing annually. For instance, the number of PhD graduates has doubled in the last twenty years up to the time of me writing this book.[10] Despite there being more graduates, the jobs available in the sector have not increased by the same amount.[11]

For staff in academia, limited funding sources have plateaued in some research areas and decreased in others, but the competition for grants remains as fierce as it ever was. It's tougher for young academics starting out now than a generation ago.

Work-life balance, pressure to publish, competition for jobs, short-term contracts, inconsistent managerial support, and increasing competition in the education sector all contribute to a community on the edge. Higher education is approaching a collective mental breakdown.[12] The anxiety-inducing hell of uncertain employment has even led to sociologist Vik Loveday coining the term the *neurotic academic*.[13] The social media phenomenon exaggerates the temptation to perpetually compare oneself to others with exhaustingly little context.

At the time of writing, it has been over a decade since I came through the UK higher education system and started my scientific career. So it's been a while since I first walked through the university doors, hopeful, inspired, and with a lot more hair on my head than I have now. Over those ten plus years in higher education, and for my whole life, I have genuinely loved science. But in the last few years, I started to notice a worrying change in my behaviour that was in no way a reflection of my best self.

The reflections and realisations you will read in this book started at a fork in the road of my academic career. For me, a series of career-progressing shifts revealed to me a particular kind of stress...a stress I never thought possible. So, don't read my story in isolation. Rather, take it as a nudge to more deeply analyse your own points of professional pressure.

Having trained as a scientist, the fork on the road that gave me cold sweats took the form of a career question:

Industry or academia?

Where should my career go? What jobs should I apply for? What sort of scientist will this choice make of me? Is there a correct decision? Will I love the choice? Will I regret it forever?

And after speaking with many others, I realised I was not alone. Many of us feel this way. Regardless, more and more questions filled my mind with unnecessary worry and dread. It was like a crashing ring of dominos falling one after the other in regimented chaos. On and on, questions would tumble around in my mind, gathering into a shapeless grey mass of anxiety; swirling, darkening, growing, and groaning. These dark thoughts had a hunger that could not be satisfied. Monstrous career stress was taking hold, and it would do so in a very particular way.

Modesty hat off, I have accomplished a lot in my academic life to date. I managed to complete high school with nothing lower than an A grade. I graduated at the top of my university Chemistry class, completed an award-winning PhD, and earned a decorated postdoctoral research post. When I started writing this book, I was beginning my independent academic research career: running my own lab, mentoring my own team, building collaborations, and working with companies.

Along the way, I've earned various prizes, awards, scholarships, grants, and honours. I've written and published peer-reviewed articles in prestigious journals and lectured in more countries around the world than I've got fingers and toes. If you can excuse my cringeworthy big headedness here, understand that I am a classic overachiever.

I probably sound like that one insufferable guy at the party who talks only about himself, but please trust me, there's a good reason for telling you all of this stuff about my own career.

Towards the later stages of what could safely be classed as a successful career in science so far, I noticed that I was becoming increasingly tired. Shattered, even. My thoughts started telling me a new story, telling me that I was not at all successful. In that decade-plus career progression leading to my first academic job, my mind was slowly but surely turning against me.

As I learned more and more about life in academia, a new monster emerged from the career questions swirling around in my head:

Am I good enough?

Was I ready for this path? Did I really qualify? Did I know enough? Should I even bother? Could I ever be as good as all the other people walking the same path?

I was doubting my abilities and habitually making damned comparisons between myself and my peers. The excitement for creatively carving out my own academic career after a life-long love of science was in danger. My career was being overshadowed by one of the many monsters behind mental health issues in higher education:

The so-called* *Imposter Syndrome*: the feeling that you are a fraud, that you are not good enough for your job, and that you are always in danger of being 'found out'.

As you progress through this book, you will learn about the journaling exercise I used to help me record my own thoughts about feeling like an imposter. Together, we will look at what imposter experiences mean to the 800+ participants from the survey research that grew out of my journaling and now underpins this book. We look closer at the unfounded thoughts and feelings of inferiority that many students and staff in higher education face. Feeling like an imposter almost drowned me. I share the discoveries that stopped me from digging a mental hole from which I might never have recovered.

Feeling like an imposter is not a syndrome.

Journaling and studying the problem has helped me to no end. It still helps me. By treating my neurotic thoughts like any other scientific problem, I felt an incredible ease come over me when I began to understand this so-called Imposter Syndrome in more detail. I have learned from other people who have waded through self-doubt and emerged enlightened out the other side.

In the process, I discovered masterful works of literature that were almost lost in a fireplace. I've come to appreciate the power of persistence for writers, actors, researchers, and politicians in enduring what we might call the Imposter Syndrome. Through my story and the stories of others, I wanted to dissect and anatomise the experience of feeling like a fraud in order to make it easier to manage.

---

*We will be having a whole discussion on why *Imposter Syndrome* is not a syndrome.

I thought very deeply about whether or not to release any of this to anyone other than myself. It began, after all, as an exercise to help me cope with the thoughts that were threatening to crush my career before it began. But there was a moment I knew I had to share it.

When I spoke at a chemistry careers conference for young students and researchers, I took the opportunity to road test some of this book's emerging content. I spoke about the ubiquitous term 'Imposter Syndrome' and found myself quivering close to tears as I shared my experiences for students who might be suffering in similar ways. Rather than being ridiculed, I was embraced. And when one student, timid and curious, approached me after my talk and said, "It really helped", I was overwhelmed. From that moment on, I took the view that, if my story helps one other person, it'll all have been worth it.

Before you read on, allow me to be clear. I am not a trained psychologist. Nor, in fact, am I a sociologist, psychiatrist, counsellor, or social scientist. I am simply someone – as a student and mentor – who has felt, and still feels the serrated dagger of imposter experiences! (My draft book was originally titled *Pull Out the Dagger* before it was finalised.) I have been in the eye of the mental storm and whirled round its violent perimeter. I have studied this particular mental struggle in intimate detail. I know it well. Although I am not a clinician or psychologist, I am a scientist. And, as an academic who has worked in a university, my life has been spent in one of the most notoriously neurotic and competitive environments we know of. It is a breeding ground for all dimensions of the imposter experience and more. I have seen, heard, experienced, and taught students in many scenarios in which the feeling of being a phoney has reared its ugly head.

You Are (Not) a Fraud is all about how I learned to manage my imposter experiences and keep moving on. I wanted to share the low points and the stories and the data that have helped me to recognise imposter experiences and to best understand how to deal with them.

Notice, I did not say "to cure" Imposter Syndrome. I did not say "crush", or "solve", or "quash" Imposter Syndrome.

It is not something to cure but something for you to recognise and manage.

It sounds easy, doesn't it? I've rhymed off the self-help rattle as if I am some sort of millennial messiah. The truth is that my own struggles to move forever forward in my career have taken a genuine mental toll. This book shares that story, and offers the liberating knowledge I have picked up along the way. You'll learn about the history of the Imposter Phenomenon, who it affects, and why. You'll think about real imposters, and what we really mean when we define success as just being 'lucky'. Going further, you'll dance with failure, rejections, and social comparisons in new ways. Productive ways! And you, the would-be imposter, will learn a little about what these thoughts in your head really are (and are not).

If you have made it this far, I'm willing to bet that you're dancing with ambition. You have something you want to achieve and you're here trying to find at least some of the answers to the hurdles that you've raised against yourself. Whether it's the book, a chapter, or a sentence, I genuinely hope something here makes you look at your own story in a different light.

Alas, for whatever ambition you carry, and the questions you have for yourself, only you can answer the specifics. That's not the scariest part. There is something more than this self-reliance that is just as important to keep in mind. Whether it is now, soon, or inconceivably far off in your future, you will have someone else in your care other than yourself.

We can all understand what true imposters are.

We can all understand how to be mindful of useless comparisons we make between ourselves and other people.

We can all understand how the Imposter Phenomenon might always be there...but it should never stop you from achieving the goals you set out in your life and career.

Marc Reid (June 8, 2022)

Read and Journal

For each of the **Your Chapter Challenges** closing chapter sections, consider completing the accompanying *Your Are Not a Fraud: Journal Resources* as you go.

The resource contains ready-made templates for each of the 18 challenges presented to you throughout the book.

Available from wherever you purchased your copy of the book.

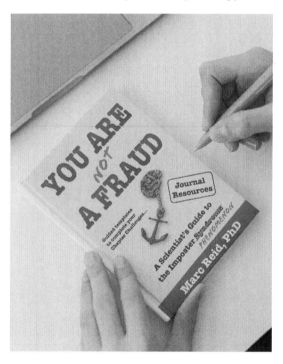

Chapter 1: An Innocent Fraud is Born

I don't know happiness. But overachievement and an overwhelming dread? With them, I'm intimate. If you're here, that resonates, and you don't have a damn clue what to do about it. I didn't either.

Before we get to my career woes or yours, allow me to tell you a story.

Part 1 – The Intimidated Actor

A young African American actor was preparing to make the treacherous leap from small-time TV to the Big Screen. Full of hope and adventure, the year 2000 brought the actor a rare chance to make it in the cutthroat business of cinema. Through the sludge of cheesy game shows, charmless work as a bodyguard, small commercials, forgettable independent movies, and cancelled shows, this was it. One chance to escape the small time.

The aspiring actor was tailor-made for the hitman role he was playing in his inaugural movie. Before TV, the actor had survived a hard-hitting career in sport. This new movie, his first movie, was a singular moment in which to start a new and bold adventure. He knew that such a chance might never present itself again.

Eventually, the day finally came when our young ambitious actor dressed himself for the part. His lines were rehearsed and he was good to go. The star of the show, the lead actor, was also on set that day. The director called "ACTION!", and it was time to shine. Now enveloped in his role as a serpentine assassin, our young actor said his first line to the star of the movie. The lead actor turned to respond to the lines just whispered into the air of the suburban sci-fi set. When their eyes met, the young actor froze.

There was a problem.

A sharp intake of breath from the cold night caught in his throat. The unseen icy droplets cut like microscopic daggers. The young actor's mind flooded with horrible thoughts, like bone-chilling water consuming the hull of a sinking ship. As if from nowhere, looking into the eyes of the lead actor gave voice to terrible whispers in the young actor's mind:

"You don't deserve to be here."

"You're just a dumb football player!"

"You are a farce! These people are going to figure you out."

More thoughts kept rushing into his mind, one after the other, like an emotionless swarm of locusts digesting and degrading everything in their path:

"These people are going to figure you out."

"You're a fake. You're a phoney!"

"You fooled everybody. It's a wrap. They're going to find out and they are going to KICK YOU OUT OF HERE!"

The passionate young performer felt like he had frozen stiff in front of the other actor for hours. In reality, he had merely blinked. That one glance into the eyes of a more established colleague made him think his own efforts were somehow useless. His shredded ego was nothing more than the cooling ash flicked from a filthy cigarette, falling through the air and disintegrating underfoot. All his crippling thoughts came at once, all before his watch had the chance to tick.

By chance, in the same moment, there was an issue with the movie set. The lighting was wrong and they had to do another take. A sigh of relief trembled gently from the actor's lungs. He had frozen. It was obvious. A shot at a movie career was so nearly wasted.

In that short serendipitous break between takes, the young actor had another series of thoughts.

Instead of repeating the cycle and declaring himself a fake, he challenged himself to question what might happen if he listened to the initial onslaught of abusive thoughts that told him to give up.

Would he really want to go back to his old sporting career? Would he really want to go back to doing security jobs and sweeping floors? Not a chance. On the second take, he said his lines and committed to doing the best job he possibly could. Since then, he has only looked back to recount this story to people suffering the same neurotic thought process.

That actor was former American football player Terry Crews. Almost two decades after that testing experience as a young actor, Crews became a celebrated actor in TV and film. He also grew to become a successful artist, businessman, and live entertainer. The lead actor he was so deeply intimidated by in that early movie shoot was Arnold Schwarzenegger (who, by the way, was another sportsman turned movie star). The movie was *The Sixth Day*, a box office success that earned nominations for best and worst movie alike.[14]

During that fateful movie shoot back in 2000, Crews had mustered up the courage to rebrand himself. He had initially trained for one job – pro football – and then tried to escape that mould. Through it all, he was conscious of judgement from those who thought he was wasting his time and that he couldn't make the transition. More than that, he was almost crippled by the internal doubts about his ability to change career.

The other key point to this story is that Terry had been starstruck by Arnold Schwarzenegger, a bodybuilder turned actor who had earned his break by struggling through terrible B-movies and persisting in the face of constant criticism. Crews was so awe-inspired by Schwarzenegger's present glittering movie career that he wasn't seeing how the comparisons he made between himself and Arnie were unjustified. Terry was nothing, a 'nobody' in the movie business. But here was Arnold Schwarzenegger, a man who had moved country as well as career to get to where he was when Terry met him. Arnie was *The Terminator*, for crying out loud! The fact that Arnie had a twenty-year head start didn't seem to matter to Crews when he had his flash of despair. That instant comparison was still enough for Terry Crews' mind to scream out, convincing him that he was some sort of fraud.

There is something remarkable about the Terry Crews story that I haven't yet called out. And it's the part of the story that most resonated with me and my own struggles of feeling like a fraud. Somehow, through the panic and the pain, Crews was able to call himself out on those dark, debilitating thoughts that almost ruined his new acting career. In the momentary calm between takes, he was able to mindfully separate the reality of his situation from the unfounded thoughts that could so easily have roadblocked the whole movie and his part in it.

The career of a millionaire movie star may seem like a world away from our lifestyles but I'm willing to bet that you probably noticed similarities between Terry's self-destructive thought process and a memorable moment in your own life. I'm betting that there has been a time when you questioned your own value and position despite your abundance of tangible hard work and well-documented progress.

This is what happened to me when I heard Terry Crews' talk about his story for the first time. I was sitting on the bus on my way to my university office, headphones lodged in my ears, listening to Crews being interviewed for the renowned business podcast, *The Tim Ferriss Show*.[15] Crews recalled his story with such passion and heart that I listened intently, cocooned from the outside world, grasping his every syllable. I was utterly transfixed. I heard Terry's story and

I was truly listening to it. With every second that passed, Terry's story resonated with mine, ticking all the same boxes of feeling like a fraud. If the Terry Crews story truly isn't for you, you'll read similar accounts from Kate Winslet (Oscar-winning actress),[16] Leo Tolstoy (famous writer of greats such as War and Peace), Gloria Vanderbilt (famed 20th century artist and businesswoman),[17] Mike Cannon-Brookes (tech billionaire, co-CEO of Atlassian),[18] Denis Diderot (18th century French polymath),[19] Emma Watson (Harry Potter and celebrated stage actress),[20] and Neil Gaiman (graphic novelist).[21] This list goes on, and if you look for more stories of self-doubters from within your own interests, you will find at least one.

I am not an actor and have never been a sportsman (at least, not one of note). I have, however, aspired to a career working in a competitive environment, and I've thought deeply about whether or not I've ever been worthy of working where I am. And I'm willing to bet you're still here because you've got your own imposter story to tell. So, allow me to share with you a little more on how these imposter feelings first arose in me.

Part 2 – Phoney in the Family

Growing up in a working-class family, I was always playfully labelled 'the smart kid'. At home, my childhood love of dinosaurs and my inexplicable desire to be a palaeontologist sparked seemingly harmless jokes from family about someone having picked up the 'wrong kid' from the maternity ward.* There was never any malice in being pigeon-holed like this at home. School was a little more difficult.

---

*This joke would inevitably tie into me becoming the first generation in my immediate family to go to university straight from school. By the way, in case you're wondering, the whole dinosaur thing made Ross Geller my favourite character from Friends. A choice that has somehow horrified 95% of people I've ever met.

In primary school (or grade school depending on where you're from), I was dubbed 'The Professor', a nickname signalling that I tended to do well on assignments and class tests. At that time, being curious and academically inclined was seen as somewhat out-of-the-ordinary. It was worthy of some regular (albeit good-humoured) ridicule. Apathy was to fit in at school, aptitude was not.

My teachers, with their bird's eye view above a class full of three-foot-tall kids, could see this most clearly. They could see a student's place among the crowd and saw that a kid who projected any academic interest would likely be seen as a threat by the others. Innocent but sometimes exiled. I had friends but I also had enemies. On my very last day of school, one young teacher, Mrs Lockhart, inscribed a notebook of mine saying:

"Good luck for the future. Let me know when you discover the fountain of youth."

At the time, I felt deeply encouraged. I still have that notebook.

Looking back, being seen as 'the clever one' at home and in school seeded expectations in my mind for years to come. It's not like I was a 'boy genius' in my youth. I couldn't tie my own shoelaces till I was about eight years old. I was twenty-one before I could use a washing machine unsupervised, and I have never been able to drive a car.

Curious about everything, I worked hard and performed well in exams. I was voted *Most Likely to Succeed* in my high school yearbook. In truth, I played right into those early 'smart kid' labels I acquired at home and in grade school. From then on, the expectation to be the best, to be the smartest person in the room, has stayed with me. Whenever this position has been challenged, I've panicked. Quietly, regularly, painfully. I panicked.

Like many people of my generation (technically a Millennial, having been born in the late 1980s), I benefited enormously from opportunities created by my working-class parents and grandparents.

I was the first in my family to go to university straight from school. Only my maternal grandfather had been to university before me, but not until he was in his forties, having amassed a lifetime of labour-intensive jobs.

Professionally, I dedicated the first third of my life to science and to building a career in academia. It's a bit like climbing an oily ladder to reach the window of a tall house. Some rungs on the ladder are just waiting to sink splinters into your gripping hands. This troubled climb up the ladder towards an academic career amounts to about 3–7 years for a first degree, 3+ years for a PhD, and several postdoctoral jobs over an ill-defined number of years, all before eventually landing a trial job as a walking, talking, lecturing, researching, exam-marking, paper-writing, grant-bidding academic. Even then, you still haven't climbed in the high window of the tall house. That job isn't yet permanent. It might never be permanent. There are some rungs left on the ladder, maybe some splinters, and maybe a complete collapse that sends you cascading back to the bottom. You can never know how many steps are left. Author, speaker, and business coach Simon Sinek calls this never-ending career gauntlet the Infinite Game. And it was the very practice of trying to step up to the next rung on my career ladder that led to more threatening problems.[22]

Part 3 – Convinced of Being a Fraud

When I started my job as a postdoctoral researcher, after my PhD and before independent research, it marked the first extensive period in my career that I had taken on research outside the comfort of my PhD group. The people I had known, the surroundings I had become familiar with, the PhD research I was doing, it had all become comfortable and safe. Those PhD days had certainly been peppered with anxious and exciting times spent in other countries, at conferences large and small. The job move from PhD to postdoc was altogether different.

As well as moving to a new city for my postdoc, I was also entering a brand-new laboratory with new equipment and new people to learn from. I had a scholarship on my CV and money in my pocket. What wasn't to like? In many ways, I was living the scientist's dream. I was climbing the ladder and I could now see the window I was aiming for. But that all changed after the first day in the new job. In an instant, I started comparing myself to the other postdocs in the group, looking at their track records, their publications, their experiences. The rapid conclusion drawn in my head was:

I am not as good as these people. How the hell did I get into this group?

This worrying thought was made worse by the fact that I planted the seeds of doubt by Googling my new colleagues' professional biographies before I ever met them in person.

During my earlier PhD days, before the postdoc, I would happily bury my head in a research project, read papers, expand my scientific horizons, and exercise my creativity. In the postdoc job, my mind was telling me that I could no longer do that. From that first day on the new job, I felt a crushing pressure to be the best.

The weighty comparisons I was making between myself and others were crippling my productivity. They were almost powerful enough to physically crush my spine, exposing my marrow as well as my spirit. I somehow found that I couldn't enjoy my work the way I used to. As with the young Terry Crews starting out in the world of film, an immediate and intimate alarm in my head was now consuming my every waking moment. I was rapidly convincing myself that I was going to be stripped of my degree and humiliated, paraded through town like a medieval heretic. A professional pariah. A fraud exposed!

You would be forgiven for thinking I hated my new job, but I didn't. The two years in that postdoctoral position were brilliant in many ways. What persisted beneath the surface, however, was

my neurotic self-doubt. It was always there. With the rhythm of daylight, those thoughts would come and go. Come and go. Come and go. And with the regularity of the days came a regimented draining of my confidence. In secret, in desperation, it was only by opening an empty word document and typing out these thoughts in a journal that I ever made it to the end of that postdoc contract.

Even when I climbed the ladder again and started my first independent academic post (two years after the postdoc job), I went through the same thought cycle all over again. In the first few days of my independent research fellowship, I went to visit some of the more experienced academics and see what their take on life in academia was like. In my eyes, these colleagues had made it. They had climbed the ladder, avoided the slips, and pulled out the splinters. They were free and clear and had climbed through the window atop the ladder. They were in.

With a sickening feeling of déjà vu, all I could focus on were the successes those other academics had, the grants they had won, the number of students they had. I felt so deeply shaken and panicked after talking with one colleague in particular that, after the meeting, I paced through the corridors into a toilet cubicle, sat on the seat, and held my head in my hands. I was enveloped by the sensation that I was in the WRONG place. The WRONG job. How had I managed to fool everyone into thinking I was able to make a difference here? Was I not wasting their time as well as my own?

I was being silly. Knowing what I know now, it is plain to see that I was wrapped up in a small, egotistical view of a situation that was, in fact, completely under my control. I was needlessly engulfed by the deep-set concept that, through a flash comparison, I was instantly worthless in the shadow of my colleagues. It was all absolute bullshit.

When speaking to academic colleagues, I never once stopped to acknowledge that they were years ahead of me, with different experiences, different training, different paths to the same career crossroads. I didn't stop to think that they might also be comparing themselves to me.

In my enduring self-doubt, not one millisecond had been reserved for me to realise that my colleagues saw that I had a different and valuable perspective to bring to the team. Such feelings have haunted my career. I know now, through stories like that of Terry Crews, and others that I'll share with you in this book, that I am far from being the only one who struggles with the feelings of not knowing enough.

Feeling like a fake, a fraud, a phoney, someone waiting to be 'found out', is widely known by the common term *Imposter Syndrome.** It's something that has taken me an embarrassing number of years to identify internally, and even longer to find some means of managing it. It's this story of discovering and coming to terms with the so-called *Imposter Syndrome* that I want to tell you more about. It's a story that begins, appropriately enough, by having discovered that the word 'Syndrome' itself is something to be questioned with more care. Is that really what we should be calling this thing?

---

*Past literature is peppered with 'imposter' spelled as written, with an 'er', but also as 'impostor', with an 'or'. For consistency, we'll be sticking to 'er' throughout.

Your Chapter Challenges

The bottom of every chapter includes actions for you to try before continuing with the book. Challenge yourself to consider the following points right now before moving on:

1. Anyone can feel like a fraud. Find the others! References 2–8 in the Notes section for Chapter 1 give you a taste, but now it's your turn to discover this fact for yourself.

Find three more stories of people who have reported feeling like a fraud.

Find one famous person, one friend, and one colleague or family member.

Who are they? What was the scenario in which they felt like a fraud?

2. Build some awareness of your internal and external pressures to succeed.

What are the places around you that influence your view of success?

Who are the people in your life who shape your definition of success?

What drives you to succeed, even when no one is looking?

Chapter 2: It's Not a Syndrome

If you know what something is called, it doesn't mean you know anything about it. I learned that along my way to building a career in academia. Jargon is the easiest mask to hide behind. In this chapter, I want you to lean into the value of knowing something versus knowing the name of it. And let's frame that through this horrendous experience we so often call Imposter 'Syndrome'.

Part 1 – Learning to Love the Puzzle

As a kid, I remember being curious about everything. I would annoy my tired and patient parents with endless questions about why things are the way they are. My appetite for answers was never satisfied. First, it was dinosaurs, then planets, then all the cool gadgets that comic book anti-hero Batman had at his disposal. I can only assume that I must have been a harmlessly irritating little shit. Thankfully, my childlike fascination with the world persisted as I grew up, surviving the mild ridicule on the playground.

From the regimented complexity in a grain of sand to the celestial catastrophe of starlight, it is all awesome and all connected. It is, as Richard Dawkins describes it, the *Magic of Reality*.[23] A little corny, yes, but nonetheless true. My wonder for how stuff works slowly but surely became a pursuit of all things Science. Especially chemistry.

One of the things I always loved about chemistry was the creative puzzle of its infinite combinations. Like a box of Lego, discrete blocks come together, through ingenuity and imagination, to give innumerable structures and functions and materials. The creative game of Lego is the science of chemistry. What's even more alluring is that it's not always clear how the Lego blocks are actually put together, step-by-step.

You might leave someone with a box of Lego and return to find a magnificent castle has somehow been assembled in your absence. You can have an educated guess on how that castle was built, while the exact order of steps is hidden from view. Only through close examination of the bricks in the walls can the builder's methods be uncovered. Without that knowledge, the castle's structure can't ever be reproduced faithfully. It can't be miniaturised or expanded without serious threat of collapse. Without knowing specifically how the bricks are each united to form the macroscopic fortitude of the castle, another one can never be built. In the end, knowing that the Lego structure is called a 'castle' tells you nothing about where the castle came from or how it was built.

Beyond chemistry and Lego and castles, knowing how something works, how it came to be, puts you in the best position to improve that particular something. I've found this to be the case with feelings of being an imposter, too. One significant time in my life was when I was halfway through my postdoctoral position and well on the way to working in academia. That feeling of not belonging among my peers, not being good enough, took a brain-draining toll on me. There was the compulsion to work myself into the ground. But, as with the mysterious mechanisms behind building with chemistry and Lego, I realised that if I was ever going to manage my self-doubt and climb the career ladder, I simply had to recognise what was happening to me. Knowing how to deal with the recurrent feelings of being nothing but a phoney was now vital. I needed to understand the action of the cogs that were turning and crunching uncontrollably in my mind. A Lego brick monument to the feeling of being a fraud stood without a maker. Now, I had to learn how to deconstruct it in order to build something new. Knowing its name wasn't enough. I had to learn more about this ethereal thing that I kept hearing being called the *Imposter Syndrome.*

Part 2 – The Rose in my Thorn

When I started researching Imposter Syndrome, I did what everybody in the Internet age does best. I Googled it. I Googled hard. When I opened the web browser to start my search, I typed out the letters of "I-m-p-o-s-t-e-r [space] S-y-n-d-r-o-m-e", slowly, deliberately, and secretly. The subtle shame of my web browsing made it seem like I was a naughty teenager searching for something altogether more illicit.

After searching for the term 'Imposter Syndrome' and reading the obligatory Wikipedia page, dictionary.com, and some other forgettable pages, I scrolled deep into the Google page hits and found an hour-long lecture from the National Institutes of Health (NIH, a major government research funding body in the United States).[24] It was the 12th Annual NIH Graduate Symposium, and a crowd of hopeful young graduates were settling into silence as one of their peers took to the stage.

A crisply dressed young man stood up to introduce the keynote speaker for the ceremony. Slightly hunched, he stood behind a varnished wooden podium, leaning into a goose-necked microphone. His nerves shone only through widened eyes as he welcomed the speaker: clinical psychotherapist, Dr Pauline Rose Clance.

With a relieved smile, the student left the stage. As the crowd's applause rang out, the top of someone's head could be seen just above the podium but they didn't stop to take to the same microphone as the announcer. Instead, a petite elderly lady emerged from the left side of the podium as she walked towards a smaller table at the centre of the stage. It was Dr Clance. Clance was small in stature but a giant among the respectfully silent student audience. She wore a pristinely well-ironed suit, shiny and mauve, almost brown against the warm conference hall light. A weightless floral scarf and neatly trimmed hair completed her sophisticated look. From behind gold-rimmed glasses, she looked for a small stack of A4 paper. She wasn't nervous in holding her speech in physical form, it was more like she had an important message to deliver and didn't want to miss a beat. Clance greeted the graduates with a smile and began to read them her story; the story of her life investigating the *Impostor Phenomenon*.

"Wait a minute", I thought, intrigued with what my Google search had produced.

"Impostor...with an 'o'?". My confusion deepened.

"Phenomenon?! What happened to 'Syndrome'?", I gasped.

Pauline Rose Clance was one of the first practicing psychologists to formally study the experience of high achieving people feeling like an imposter. Together with her colleague Suzanne Imes, they coined the term *"Impostor Phenomenon"* in the late 1970s.

As a kid, Clance grew up near the Appalachian Mountains in the US state of Virginia. Having persevered through her poorly resourced grade school, she then made it to high school and thrived. She did so well in her studies that she was competitively elected senior class president, beating the captain of the football team to the post. It's worth pausing here. Clance, attending school as a woman in the 1950s and 60s, beat a man (the football team captain no less) to class president. And she didn't just get the job, she was voted in. It was a big deal.

Despite all this promise, Clance's high school didn't cover as many grades as other schools. Her teachers, therefore, warned that she might expect to do worse than other students when she eventually went to college. The teachers were wrong. Clance earned a PhD in Clinical Psychology from the University of Kentucky, one of only four in a class of fifteen to do so. During the process, she became routinely anxious before exams but kept the fears internalised to avoid irritating her study group. In the end, she made it, and then started her academic career in Oberlin College in Ohio.

At Oberlin, and later at Georgia State University, Clance started to notice a strange and consistent behaviour among the female students she was speaking to. Young women with high grades were expressing serious doubts about how smart they were. Regardless of the hard, objective data in their shining records, despite praise and support from their professors, these women wholeheartedly believed they were on the verge of being caught out. They felt like they did not deserve their positions in academia. They felt like imposters.

Part 3 – The First Paper on Imposters

As the video of Clance's speech to NIH graduates rolled on, I was transfixed by the familiarity of the stories she was telling. The experiences she described sounded excruciatingly familiar. It was like staring dead ahead into my hopeless reflection and finally beginning to recognise what I was looking at. Following my Google search and Clance's keynote speech, I dug deeper to source the original research papers and understand more about what was happening to me. I started reading.

At Georgia State University, Clance's fellow psychotherapist, Suzanne Imes, was observing oddly repetitive instances of women feeling like they did not belong in academic circles. Imes was one of those women. This was similar to what Clance had first noticed in discussions with female students at Oberlin.

And so, in the late 1970s, Clance and Imes worked together to get to the bottom of what was going on. In 1978, they submitted their work in a manuscript called *The Impostor Phenomenon in High Achieving Women*.[25] The experience of feeling like a fraud had finally been named. It was the beginning of formal studies on high-achieving self-doubters.

Reading Clance and Imes' seminal paper, my eyes glided over the words as if they were golden coins from long-lost treasure. Everything they wrote triggered memories of my own experience. I read on and on, highlighting passages that read to me like they had been raised from the page:

"...these [people] find innumerable means of negating any external evidence that contradicts their belief that they are, in reality, unintelligent".

Clance and Imes' research found that, no matter what hard evidence was available to show the women that their successes were earned, they could always twist that success into a hideous lie. Successes could always be explained away by luck or, if not luck, something equally unfounded.

The original research on the Imposter Phenomenon was specific to the experiences of women because that's where the phenomenon was most immediately evident at the time. It was reported to show up as a feeling of believing they could not be as good as a man in a similar professional position. Women had their apparent societal roles as second-class citizens ingrained within them, likely from a young age. By going to college, earning advanced degrees, and taking high-powered positions, these conflicted women were, in their minds, breaking the rules. They had it in their heads that they were supposed to be the baby-makers and housewives of the world, not pioneering professionals. Many simply could not accept that their success was earned, despite the fact that their hard work and scholarship had placed them exactly where they deserved to be.

Clance and Imes' interviews with the women from the 1978 paper contained the increasingly familiar phrases associated with someone – man or woman[26] – displaying tell-tale signs of the Imposter Phenomenon:

"I'm not good enough to be on the faculty here...Some mistake was made...".

"...my abilities have been overestimated".

"I was convinced that I would be discovered as a phoney".

How strongly do these phrases resonate with you? It was only in later reading I realised that broader studies of the Imposter Phenomenon showed that the experience was not unique to women.[27] Some studies suggest men perceive and report their imposter experiences differently to women.[28] Others acknowledge that there is a danger of conflating the fact of more women than men coming forward for such studies with the interpretation that women suffer from imposter experiences more than men.[29] It's not a definitively gendered experience. Even before I realised this, the context of Clance's original work didn't seem to matter. The words read as if the study had been written about me.[30]

Early work on the Imposter Phenomenon also shared theories on the root causes of the experience. Why exactly were these academically brilliant women so authoritatively convinced that they were imposters? Two of the causal ideas presented by Clance focused on a person's immediate family. Deliberately or not, a family moulds and nurtures their daughter on how to see the world. In one scenario, childhood labels matter. The girl has a sibling or close family member who is labelled 'the intelligent one'. She, on the other hand, is somehow 'the sensitive one'. This label, endowed by her parents, is different from what she has actually grown up to be. She works hard and earns a job meant for an 'intelligent' person. The family has labelled and treated and talked to her like she is the 'sensitive' one, not the 'intelligent' one.

The unfortunate effect, as suggested by Clance and Imes, was that the grown-up woman, successful and progressive, feels like her position isn't deserved because it wasn't part of her label growing up. She was supposed to be 'sensitive', not 'smart'. What's more, she thinks that her family is secretly disappointed or angry that she has acted out against the role set for her in her youthful label. The worst part about it is that, whether it's me writing it or you reading it, we both know it's a ridiculous notion. She doesn't need to feel this way. Nonetheless, it's not ridiculous to those at the centre of such experiences.

In the second scenario proposed as an origin of the Imposter Phenomenon, the family tells their daughter she can do no wrong. She is so able and so intelligent that there is nothing she cannot do. Her intellect carries her on a flying carpet to success with ease and grace. Inadvertently, the family has set a rusty and serrated bear trap in the young woman's mind. Whilst she walks through life with tremendous parenting and heaps of praise, she is stopped in her path by the sharp snap...the experience of finding out that some things in life are difficult.

Such is the family reinforcement of their daughter's perfectionism and ability to gather skills without hardship that, when something comes along that the daughter finds difficult, it's a shock to her. She's been raised to sprint down the 100-metre running track and win every time. No problem. But when she finds out that she has to run an extra 10-metres and jump hurdles, things change. Now, the daughter comes across something she isn't able to conquer right away. The thought of revealing this to her parents rains shame upon her. If she fails, she will feel like a lifelong fake. Growing up with the feeling of being indestructible has inadvertently planted a crippling fear of failure in the woman's mind.

Bringing the imposter origin ideas together, Clance and Imes had suggested that socially acquired expectations could lead to doubt in someone's position later in life. Think about it. If your success isn't in keeping with the role set out for you by the environment you grew up in, then you are predisposed to believing that your success is ill-gained. You become more likely to suffer from the symptoms leading to Clance and Imes' Imposter Phenomenon.

Both origin stories – one of being labelled in a particular way, and the other of believing success would always be easy – made me once again recoil in reflection. As I read the articles, I nodded in recognition and shook my head in disbelief. I let out quiet bursts of "hmm" and "huh", aghast at just how familiar these imposter theories appeared to me. There was a deep unease in how this research predictively told the story of my own experiences. I was, after all, the first kid in my family to go to university straight from school. Without knowing, and being innocent of any crime, my family labelled me as the 'smart' kid, and I was supported as such. Growing up, I made myself a rank overachiever and crafted a mirage of expectations that I pressured myself to meet. My behaviour became characteristic of someone suffering imposter experiences, which brings us to how you can spot your own tell-tale behaviours.

Part 4 – Behaviour and the Imposter Phenomenon

There are (at minimum) three habits that ripen the cocktail of ingredients necessary to experience the Imposter Phenomenon:

(1) **The Workaholic Imposter**: If you work hard, you work yourself to the bone for fear of being caught out. That hard work creates the second habit.[31]

(2) **The Agreeable Imposter**: You wear a veil under which you hide the fullness of your thoughts. You say what you think people want to hear, not what you actually think. In your head, if you were to become disagreeable, you increase your chances of being caught out.

(3) **The Charismatic Imposter**: And thirdly, you think your charm and charisma have served up sleight of hand, fooling your peers into thinking that you are one of them.

In each of the three cases, there is success. There is also a mechanism to downplay that success. You avoid appearing head and shoulders above the crowd. Through this work and later contributions, the media took the idea to the world, giving Clance the opportunity to define the Imposter Phenomenon for a bigger audience. In one newspaper interview, Clance noted:

"...people from many different professions experienced a haunting fear that they could not continue repeating their successes and that they were not as bright and as capable as they needed or wanted to be, even though there was strong objective evidence that they were truly intelligent."

As I read on and on, research papers on the imposter experience rang true to my ears with deafening clarity. Gradually, it was slowly becoming easier for me to see that this imposter experience was not a singular entity. It is the chilling and chronic result of several behaviours colluding to convince you that you are a fake. In fact, it originates from one or a combination of several sources and can take one of several forms. This is where the confusion of using the term 'syndrome' rather than 'phenomenon' originates. Clance herself reserved *syndrome* for symptoms leading to an "official clinical diagnosis".

Her coining of Imposter Phenomenon (rather than Imposter Syndrome) reflected a concerted effort to signal that imposter experiences are not technically a syndrome of any sort.*

Let's take a moment to look a little deeper at this issue of 'Impostor Syndrome' versus 'Impostor Phenomenon'.

It began in 1982. Dr Carol Tavris wrote a piece about the Impostor Phenomenon for Vogue magazine. In her article, Tavris made the first recorded reference to 'Imposter Syndrome'.[32] This unconsciously seeded the term 'Impostor Syndrome' to become part of the zeitgeist, and 'Impostor Phenomenon' to remain comparatively hidden.

---

*In her speech to NIH graduates, Clance went further, making the more subtle point that those suffering from individual imposter experiences may develop clinically diagnosable conditions like anxiety or depression.

In the academic literature, article titles containing both terms – Phenomenon and Syndrome – have trickled along since the 1980s, increasing more rapidly after 2015. In 2018, the Oxford English Dictionary created draft additions for both terms.[33] Yet, in Google search trends, it's not even close. Impostor Syndrome is far more prominent than Impostor Phenomenon. So, why should we take issue? Why is it worth your time reclaiming such experiences as being a *phenomenon* rather than a *syndrome*?

The first alarm bell that rings with the use of the word 'syndrome' is its multiple definitions. In the Oxford English Dictionary, the first of three definitions of 'syndrome' places it in the realms of a pathology:

"A concurrence of several symptoms in a disease."

Government, scientific, and other official literature is full of inconsistent uses of words like 'syndrome' and 'disease'. In 2003, a team of medical professionals called it out.[34] To draw some necessary distinctions, a 'syndrome' was defined as:

"...a recognisable complex of symptoms and physical findings which indicate a specific condition for which a direct cause is not necessarily understood."

When the unknown cause becomes more clearly diagnostic and treatable, it becomes a 'disease'.

All in all, reference to the imposter experience as a 'syndrome' is misguided. While the experience does involve a collection of symptoms, they are not the same for everyone, and there are no "physical findings" as such. Marrying the imposter experience to a dictionary term linked to pathology reinforces the notion that feeling like an imposter is a diagnosable illness rather than simply being a pervasive part of our collective human condition.

Terminology aside, no matter what variation of the imposter mask you wear, there's a cycle of rotten behaviour that goes with it. For your current project, for anything you ever try, you'll doubt yourself, you'll procrastinate, you'll overwork, and yeah, you'll eventually get the job done. But that's where things get really interesting because you won't stop long to celebrate. Those suffering imposter experiences never stop. There is always more work to do.

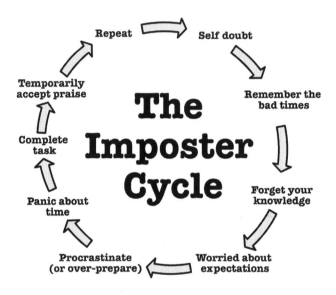

The Imposter Cycle. Collected behaviours experienced by people suffering imposter experiences.

Bringing all this seminal research together, Clance developed an Impostor Test to help people determine whether or not they were predisposed to imposter feelings. The test helped quantify just how often someone falls into feeling like an imposter. All parts of the test are answered on a scale from 1 (not true at all) to 5 (very true), according to how much the participant agrees with a particular statement. The twenty statements included:

(1) I have often succeeded in a test/task when I thought beforehand that I would fail.
(2) I can give the impression that I'm more competent than I really am.
(3) I avoid evaluations where possible and dread being evaluated.

(4) When I receive praise, I'm afraid I won't live up to future expectations.

(5) I often put success down to right-place-right-time or knowing the right people.

(6) I'm afraid of being found out that I'm not that capable.

(7) I tend to remember my failures more than my successes.

(8) I rarely complete a task as well as I'd like.

(9) I sometimes feel that my success is down to some sort of mistake in the system.

(10) It's hard for me to accept compliments.

(11) I sometimes feel my success is down to luck.

(12) I'm sometimes disappointed in what I've achieved and feel like I could've done more.

(13) I'm sometimes afraid others will discover the knowledge I lack.

(14) I'm often afraid I'll fail when generally I do well.

(15) When I've received praise for an accomplishment, I'm afraid I won't be able to repeat it.

(16) When I receive praise, I tend to discount the importance of what I've done.

(17) I often compare my abilities to those around me, and think they might be better than I am.

(18) I often worry about project failure, even when others around me have confidence in me.

(19) If I'm going for a promotion or prize, I don't tell others until it's an accomplished fact.

(20) I feel bad or discouraged if I'm not 'the best' or 'very special'.

Out of a maximum score of 100, low scores less than 40 indicated someone who rarely feels like an imposter. Higher numbers, 50 or above, indicate increasingly frequent bouts with imposter experiences. I scored 70. For this test, I knew I was beginning to understand the thoughts that were burning me out. I knew, in hard numerical terms, that I thought I was an imposter. And I had such thoughts often.[35] This *Clance Imposter Phenomenon Scale (CIPS)* is what I later used as part of a larger survey of over 800 participants.

You can see the overall result in the figure below, and more on that in the next chapter.

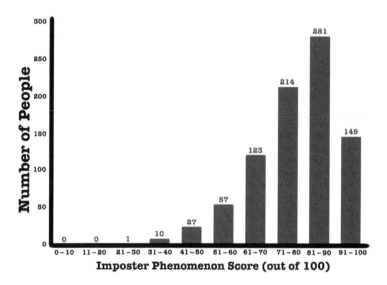

Clance Imposter Phenomenon Scores for 862 participants. Higher scores indicate more severe imposter experiences.

As well as recognising imposter experiences in ourselves, it's equally important to acknowledge and identify those external sources that can exacerbate the situation. Consider starting at the beginning – with family and upbringing. What you hear when you are young tends to stay with you, and more than you'd like to imagine. What you hear provides a kind of frame with which to reference your personality. How a family treats you when you grow up has a big impact on the adjectives you choose to describe yourself.

There are four common elements of the imposter experience originating from family life. In each case below, I have cited an exemplar comment made by participants in my own research who reflected on why they felt like imposters:

(1) **Differences in your family's image of you and the world's image of you** - discrepancies between these two impressions of who you are can lead to confusion.

> **Participant reflection:** *"I was always misunderstood by my parents, who were/are not smart, and ignored or brushed off or told I think too much or I don't know how the world works. That's probably very much at the heart of why these situations are hard..."*

(2) **Placing high importance on 'making something' of oneself by being 'smart'** - you might feel like you always want to be seen as the smartest person in the room.

> **Participant reflection:** *"My parents have always pushed my brother and I to be the bests in whatever we decide to do, so maybe that generated a pressure difficult to handle when I wasn't clearly the best."*

(3) **Square peg in a round hole** - you feel different from other family members and their career paths, particularly if you're the first in your family to be educated beyond school.

> **Participant reflection:** *"I think I just never saw myself as someone who could/would achieve this level of success in my chosen field - I've no family/friends in this line of work (my parents didn't work and my aunts/uncles/-cousins worked in factories) and so I never really had anyone to 'model' myself on, either from my own circles, or in wider media/society."*

(4) **Lack of praise** – your parents might tell of their friends about your success and neglect (consciously or not) ever encouraging you.

Participant reflection: *"I was always brought up to do my best and my parents are not very forgiving of failure. Hard to get over that feeling of letting people down."*

Some parents expect so much from their kids that they dilute any praise for successes. Others are hypercritical, always questioning, always looking for holes, never sharing any pride. Being among siblings can further trap families into labelling each child with a given characteristic. If you achieved something academically but hadn't been labelled the 'smart one', then praise for your accomplishments might have been downplayed. However, if you were labelled 'smart', there began the pressure you now feel to always be the cleverest person in the room.

The parental influences on the Imposter Phenomenon don't stop there. My own research also showed how many of those participants reflecting on why they felt like imposters made explicit causal links to their family. Despite such why-type questions being dominated by work, jobs, and careers (collectively mentioned over 400 times), parents and family (mentioned 80 times) nonetheless provided a telling signal. Over 30 people (about 4% of all participants) went deep. They cited their attempts to please parents, or the pressure of being the first in their family to go to university as drivers for feeling like a fraud.

You can get the collection of insightful and anonymised quotes from the participant stories as part of the book's bonus material. For now, let me share with you the one that resonated most with me:

"I feel enormous pressure to do well. I am the person in the family that everyone thinks is 'super smart' and that would never fail at anything. Therefore, I feel like failing is not an option, as I don't want to embarrass myself, or let anyone down. I don't really have much confidence in myself or my work. I always think that someone is going to repeat my work and prove me wrong; even though I have done everything right...".

How did that reflection parental influence sit with you? I wonder...

Part 5 – Summary

From my first nervous Google search for "Imposter Syndrome" to finding Dr Clance's speech to graduates about the Imposter Phenomenon, I had started to scratch the surface of understanding how I was feeling about my own life and career. What was once a private, undefinable experience, singular to me, was now made plain and common.

But following my discovery of how Imposter Phenomenon (not Syndrome) came to be defined and studied, I began to voraciously read the follow-up research. I found stories of artists,[36] scientists,[37] philosophers,[38] librarians,[39] prisoners turned scholars,[40] and medical students.[41] Stories of men and women, people coming from different backgrounds and walks of life, all experiencing the sinking sensation of being a fake. All of them had clear evidence supporting their earned success. It didn't matter. All of them believed that they were lucky. All of them were sure that if they tried for more success, they would surely fail. All of them believed they were imposters.

Suddenly, I wasn't alone. I had never been alone. But it would take a rather horrible conference experience to fully come to terms with the fact that I wasn't as isolated as I originally thought. None of us are...

Your Chapter Challenges

1. Managing your imposter experiences begins with breaking them down. You can categorise your imposter experiences by their origin and how they manifest in you.

Look again at the exemplar imposter 'types' listed in Part 4 of this chapter: workaholic, agreeable, and charismatic. If you want to go further, use the available journaling template to write out the reasons you believe you belong to one or more of these categories.

Which of these imposter types most closely aligns with your own imposter experiences? Write it down before moving on to the next challenge.

2. Recognise the trap of the Imposter Cycle as the mechanism that drives your procrastination and overwork.

Use the blank Imposter Cycle template to write out a specific instance of how your bout with the Imposter Phenomenon played out. If applicable, you can do this for more than one instance or story of when you have felt like a fraud.

Don't hold back. Go diary-level deep on this. And repeat it if you have to. The electronic version of the available journal resource will serve you best for repeating the challenge.

3. Feeling like an imposter is not a syndrome.

Dare to help others by respectfully calling it out when you hear 'Imposter Syndrome' being used instead of 'Imposter Phenomenon'.

Encourage the use of the latter term. Use what you've learned from this chapter to explain why 'Imposter Phenomenon' (or even 'Imposter Experience') is more accurate and more helpful than 'Imposter Syndrome'.

Don't worry, you're right to think this third challenge will be the toughest. You can be a conversation starter without being a callous know-it-all. As a first step, consider using the book's hashtag (#YouAreNotAFraud) to share the message with your network.

*To tag me and spread the word further, use my appropriate social handle (listed in the **Contact the Author** section). A list is provided on the contact page at the end of the book.*

Take a photo of the passage in Part 4 of this chapter that discusses 'syndrome' versus 'phenomenon' and share it.

Chapter 3: No Longer Alone

Conference travel is a big part of life in academia. It's a great way to find new collaborators and take bite-sized chunks out of worldwide travel, one meeting at a time. I travelled to many conferences in many countries in the early stages of my career: UK, Germany, Japan, Brazil, the US, and many other places. It's a true privilege and perk of the job...but it's a privilege with a dark side. A dark side that exemplifies a crippling loneliness that can accompany your imposter experiences.

Part 1 – The Lonely Conference Road

Long before the university road to academia, during the perpetual awkwardness of my teenage years, I loved the 2001 film *Donnie Darko*.[42] It's the haunting story of a brilliant but troubled teenage boy struggling to come to terms with a near-death experience. A haunting hallucination of a giant rabbit called Frank leads Donnie out of his bedroom in the middle of the night, moments before a mysteriously traceless jet engine comes crashing through his bedroom. Had Donnie not followed Frank, he would have been crushed under a hunk of metal.

Donnie's mental health issues compounded the hormonal roller-coaster of teenage life, and he needed professional help. During a session with his therapist, he recounts a chilling message whispered to him by a senile old lady in his neighbourhood:

"Every living creature on Earth dies alone."

It was as if the old lady's message was meant to send Donnie deeper into crisis. Disturbed by the message, Donnie remembers watching his old pet dog crawl under the porch of the family home before it died. He realised that his dog went there to be alone. And when his therapist asked if that scared him, Donnie answered through whimpering and broken tones of absolute certainty:

"I don't wanna be alone."

Few things in life are scarier or more silently damaging to your health than the feeling of being alone.[43] Isolated. Rejected. Outcast. Unnoticed. Loneliness can make us feel like we have been tied to driftwood and left floating on a deadly tide. Adrift without sight of land, loneliness carries an expansive and harrowing sense of utter abandonment. My memories of feeling like an imposter are all, in part, memories of feeling alone. Every single one of them.

On a conference trip, not long after starting my independent academic post, I travelled to London to join fellow early career academics in Chemistry to talk about opportunities for collaboration. Excited and keen, I travelled down from Glasgow on the train the night before the meeting was due to start. From the serenity of the cross-country train line to the organised pandemonium of the London Underground, I eventually made it to my hotel room late in the evening. I performed a quick-change act from jeans into slacks, grabbed a cold drink, and lay on the bed in my hotel room to watch TV.

The noise of people talking to me through the screen did well to simulate a sense of company for a lonely traveller. I lay on the bed and scrolled through my phone. My attention was spread everywhere and concentrated nowhere. I skipped from social platform to social platform and then, as if inevitably, to my emails. Once there, I took the opportunity to remind myself why I was in London. I read over the conference welcome email and downloaded the schedule telling conference attendees all about who was presenting and on what areas of research. As soon as I started scanning over that document, my once calm and periodic breaths became ever shallower. Erratic.

When I put my phone down, I sat up from the bed, swung my feet onto the thin, abrasive carpet, and hunched my palpitating torso over my knees. My hands became a shaky cradle for my heavy head. The quiet company of the TV was drowned out by an isolating ringfence of panicked thoughts:

"What am I doing here?"

"I'm not ready to be here."

"I'm not a true part of this group."

"Maybe I should just fake an illness."

"I should just go home and stop wasting everyone's time."

Looking through the conference booklet at my colleagues' research somehow ignited the dark emotional muscle memory of the imposter experience in my head. My synapses fired off down a well-trodden path, destined to arrive at the same old conclusion. I was a fake among the genuine. An imposter among superstars.

Locked in my hotel room, I couldn't console myself. A horizontal slumber had become an upright terror. I couldn't pick up the phone to call my wife. In that moment, I could not make any sense of what I was thinking. I could only see the unchallenged assumption that I was, without any doubt, a phoney. No one could've told me otherwise. Collapsing and curling up in the unfamiliar bed, I stared hopelessly at the hotel room ceiling as my internal screams telekinetically muted the TV. I was lost. I was tired. I was scared and alone.

On the other side of loneliness, there is an involuntary sigh of relief that comes with finding out that you are not alone, that you're not the only person feeling what you feel, or suffering what you suffer.[44] So strong is this sensation that the pain of loneliness has been linked to physical pain mechanisms in the body.

It was only later, after the conference in question, that my reading of the Imposter Phenomenon began. And it has only been through my efforts to build self-awareness that I have been able to stop every subsequent conference trip turning into the torturous solitude of my trip to London.

When I started researching the Imposter Phenomenon, I immediately started to feel a small but hopeful sense of belonging. The reading wasn't just helping me materialise the poisonous thoughts in my mind. Rather, once I recognised the sense of feeling like an imposter, I started seeing it in other people. Reading similar experiences to mine from other people around the world was sort of liberating. Loneliness was becoming community. Confusion was becoming clarity. I had to know more about these other people who suffered as I did.

Part 2 – Who Feels Like an Imposter?

Over time, my frantic internet searches on the Imposter Phenomenon (and 'Syndrome') amassed significant presence on my laptop. My amassed notes, links, PDFs, articles, and blog posts* began to exert their own gravitational pull; a tangible collection of reminders that I was no longer alone in feeling like an imposter.

It soon became clear to me that pretty much anyone from any background could suffer from the unfounded feelings of being a fraud. Although the Imposter Phenomenon was first formalised with studies of high-achieving women, its reach was (and remains) much, much broader.

Indeed, later research has shown that men, too, suffer the imposter experience, and just as often as women, in some cases more so.[45] Men typically find the Imposter Phenomenon harder to talk about openly. All in, across sex or gender, colour, culture, creed, or country, it doesn't seem to matter. Despite exhaustively going through statistical A versus B comparisons in my own research findings, it

---

*A collection of all my notes and sources for this book can be found at: www.dr-marc-reid.com/book.

was all hair-splitting. Men and women, public and private sector workers, those starting out and those seeking retirement.

All the differences recorded between groups, significant or not, all fell in the region of average Imposter Phenomenon scores (introduced in **Chapter 2**) over 70, and often over 80. In other words, both sides of most demographic splits lay in the realms of frequent and even chronic imposter experiences.

Imposter experiences can hit anyone who is aiming to improve.

That can mean improvement (most commonly) in your career, in your social standing, or with your relationship to your kids. For me, I was primarily concerned with my academic career and its uncertain trajectory.

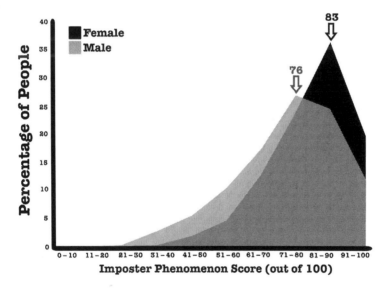

Imposter Phenomenon Scores split by gender. Number of male participants = 283; Number of females = 571. Median score in males = 76; Median score in females = 83.

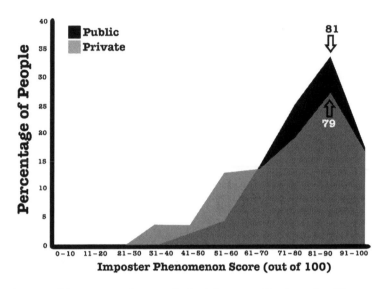

Imposter Phenomenon Score (out of 100)

Imposter Phenomenon Scores split by job sector. Number of public sector participants = 690; Number of private sector participants = 142. Median score in public sector = 81; Median score in private sector = 79.

As I discovered more about the community of imposter experience sufferers, some numbers started to emerge from the literature that helped lift me out of my feeling of loneliness. Beyond the pioneering work of Pauline Clance, one particular Imposter Phenomenon statistic kept resurfacing as if to beat my loneliness into submission:

70%.

I have found this magical '70%' to be one of the most quoted statistics about the Imposter Phenomenon. It comes from a study by Dr Gail Matthews (Old Dominion College, San Rafael, CA). From her US study in the 1980s, it was shown that about 70% of professionally successful people suffer from feelings of being an imposter.[46]

The same study by Dr Matthews also suggested that 40% of everyone in any career feels like an imposter in at least one instance in their life.[47] Matthews showed that young and successful people were most likely to accelerate towards the imposter experience and see themselves as frauds. It echoed Clance's point that students, as aspiring professionals, were among the worst sufferers of the Imposter Phenomenon. They'd cite luck or chance as the key to their success. They'd forget that luck plays side by side with mindful hard work. They'd feel the lonely impending sense of being discovered as a fake. They'd forget the work they'd accomplished. Once again, the words I was reading smoothed out into a reflective surface to show me staring back at myself. I thought:

So just who were all these other people feeling like an imposter?

I had to wonder.

Searching online for all the different variations on 'Imposter' versus 'Impostor', and 'Syndrome' versus 'Phenomenon', I found over half a million videos on the topic.* Similar searches for 'funny cat video' returned close to 80 million hits. Nonetheless, finding so many videos about imposter feelings was reassuring to me. And among all the YouTube content I found, one video, in particular, stood out.

From a short series of videos from graduate students at Stanford University, MBA student Chika Okoro described her experience of grad school, having previously been an undergraduate at Harvard. She had also worked at Google and delivered a powerful TEDx talk on racism and colourism.[48] I remember, when I first came across her work back in 2016, thinking that she was a seriously impressive individual. And that's before mentioning that she is also a gifted public speaker with a sharp wit. She was hard-working, driven, informed, and persuasive. Despite all of that, I watched Okoro's Stanford interview as she timidly admitted the way she saw herself:

"...99% of me knows I deserve to be here, I'm smart, I work hard...but there's that 1% that'll be like, 'You're not that smart...you just got

---

*To give you more of an idea of just how much the term 'Imposter Syndrome' has overshadowed the technically correct and originally intended term 'Imposter Phenomenon', consider the following. My searches for videos on "Imposte(o)r Syndrome" returned 550,000 videos. Comparable searches for 'Imposte(o)r Phenomenon' returned just 3,150.

to be here because you check two boxes (being black and being a female)...you don't really know anything'."

I saw then that even someone as accomplished and ascendant as Chika Okoro suffered from imposter feelings. She constantly had to tell herself that she was *'enough'.*

High achievers think they are just the opposite. Lifelong sufferer of imposter experiences, Joyce Roché was the first black and female vice president of cosmetic giant Avon, and CEO of female empowerment charity Girls, Inc. In her book, *The Empress Has No Clothes,*[49] Roché eloquently recounts her struggles to overcome her poor upbringing and ethnicity to get to a place of amazing success:

"In over 25 years of singular achievements in corporate America, I had risen to unprecedented heights for an African American woman...just about every new accomplishment, however, came with the stultifying doubt that I did not deserve the success, and that sooner or later I would be discovered as an imposter."

Even Hollywood's own evergreen nice guy Tom Hanks has fought with self-doubt, saying in a 2016 NPR interview:[50]

"...there comes a point where you think, 'How did I get here? When are they going to discover that I am, in fact, a fraud and take everything away from me?'"

But enough of the quotes now, here's the deal.

Anyone, anywhere can feel like an imposter at some time in their life.

And now it's time for you to see that conclusion dressed in data. The people documenting the loneliness of their imposter experiences can speak to our imposter struggles in numbers. Finding more and more imposter stories in the media urged me to take the chance to put one of my relatively new research skills to work. Around the same time I started to truly suffer from repeated bouts of the Imposter Phenomenon, I was learning how to code. More specifically, I was learning how to scrape data from social media, and describe the beautiful soup of words on imposter experiences in numbers.

In my quest to learn more from the online communities who felt as fraudulent as I did, I used some of my programming skills to gain a sense of how we, as a social collective and group of web-browsing agonizers, felt about the Imposter Phenomenon. Whether it's a crisp and concise tweet of less than 280 characters on Twitter, or dramatic purple prose in a lengthy blog post on Facebook, a cry for help on a Reddit thread, or a hack for success through LinkedIn, the ability to gain a collective understanding of how people define and respond to the Imposter Phenomenon is at our fingertips. An unimaginable ocean of textually digitised human expressions can be distilled down to its educational essence. It was this data mine that I wanted to tap into.

Part 3 – The Data Show We Are Not Alone

As a data-driven, analytical scientist (a pedantic pain in the ass to some), I wanted to check my new sense that I wasn't alone in feeling like an imposter; that, in fact, more and more people were talking about their imposter experiences. This went beyond the 800 survey participants. Using a web-scraping computer program written by me and my team, we collected tweeted instances of the terms 'Imposter Syndrome', 'Imposter Phenomenon' (with both 'er' and 'or' spellings), and the hashtag versions of each term.

We did this for every year that Twitter has been active, from 2007 to 2021. When I looked at the tweets, year by year, I found that the number of instances of tweets linked with the various 'imposter' terms was creeping up. But what really stunned me was that, even when I accounted for the increasing number of Twitter users year on year, the number of people tweeting about 'Imposter Syndrome' or 'Imposter Phenomenon' maintained an upward trend. It didn't level off. Compare that result to something like a search for tweets containing 'Haiti'. Haiti suffered a devastating earthquake in 2010. Consistent with that awful event, the tweets peaked in 2010 and tailed off thereafter. Those tweets didn't continue to rise year on year, not like the 'imposter' terms.

The number of people talking about their imposter experiences is on the rise.

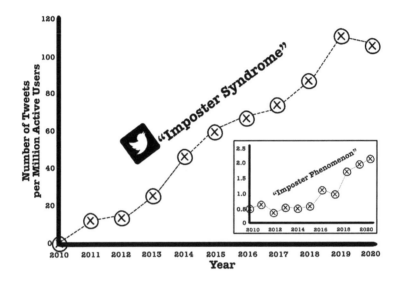

Increasing number of tweets including the term "Imposter Syndrome" (top) and "Imposter Phenomenon" (bottom) per year.

A single tweet is often a window to a world of information behind it. Looking more closely at the scattered tweets I had collected, it became clear that a lot of people were not necessarily sharing direct thoughts on imposter experiences but instead sharing links to blogs and articles on the subject. People were sharing information on how others in their community could identify the imposter experience and become acquainted with it.

In addition to the tweets, I collected and read a lot of articles and blogs, adding more mass to the data I had already gathered. I had a sense of the increase in the number of people talking about the Imposter Phenomenon over time. I now wanted to gain some numerical sense of the tone with which other people were writing about their imposter experiences.

The hidden value of a forest of text strings lies in the specific arrangements and word choices. The specific construction of a sentence provides intriguing clues to how people, en masse, feel about certain discussion topics. How will an election go? How are people responding to the latest hurricane in North America? How do people feel about a celebrity scandal? From the thoughts in our minds to the clicks of our fingers on the keyboard, we electronically leak out the way we feel through the words we type. Text analysis, sentiment analysis, linguistic programming, and even simple word counting (like in the case of the Twitter exercise), allow us to materialise insights from the ether of typed text.

The Linguistic Inquiry and Word Count (LIWC, pronounced 'Luke') tool is a text analysis computer program that counts percentages of words in a text to infer different thinking styles and emotions.[51] The LIWC is a tool used mainly by psychologists. It takes in a written text and compares each and every word against a store of internal reference words. In this way, it answers simple queries like:

- *What's the word count?*
- *How many words are there per sentence?*
- *How many words in the text match the words in the reference list?*
- *What sort of pronouns are used ('I', 'me', 'you', 'he', 'she', 'they')?*

And questions like:

- *Does the text contain positive emotion ('love', 'nice', 'sweet', etc.)?*
- *Does the text contain negative emotion ('hurt', 'ugly', 'nasty', etc.)?*

- *Does the text contain anxiety ('worried', 'fearful', etc.)?
- *Are there words associated with social processes ('talk', 'friend', 'they',etc.)?*
- *What words present are associated with cognition ('know', 'think', 'because', 'maybe', etc.)?*

The program does this for 90 numerical output variables, all reported as percentages. These numbers act like breadcrumbs on a path to the underlying truth. Each number comes together like pieces of the textual puzzle, and together give us a picture of what all the text is conveying, functionally and emotionally.

I put LIWC into action on 50 articles and blogs on the Imposter 'Syndrome' (there's that word again). I combined 115,000 words and utterances on the topic, all from people either sharing their experience, or acting to educate an audience on the basics. In my loneliness, I expected to churn through the numbers and find that the combined texts reflected the negative, woeful way that I was feeling about my own imposter experiences...but that's not what I found, at all.

Upfront, and perhaps obviously, my analysis found that words used to describe personal concerns were mostly work-related. This made sense given that most of the articles and blogs I had read mentioned words like 'career' or 'job'. The unexpected result came later.

By looking at all the words associated with psychological affect – words reflecting positive emotion, negative emotion, anxiety, anger, sadness – I found that the highest proportion of such words was not negative, or anxious, or sad. They were positive in tone. There were 4.1% of words linked with positive emotion but only 2.6% were bound to negative feelings. Why? This was a significant and, to me, surprising find. And being forced to think about it more, it started to make sense.

If you Google articles on 'Imposter Syndrome', you'll find that most people writing articles on the subject are giving advice on how to handle the experience. Authors of these articles are trying to be positive. In the comments to these blogs and articles, readers often report their own experiences and elation with having read something that helps them. As obvious as that sounds, the positivity in Imposter Phenomenon articles simply wasn't apparent to me when I was feeling alone. It wasn't obvious in that hotel room before the conference in London. But there's more.

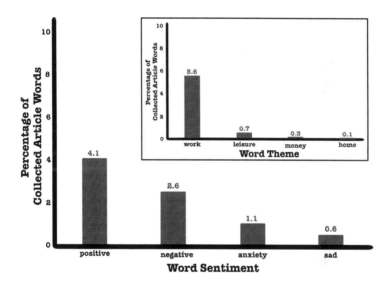

Breakdown of sentiment captured in collected text from 50 magazine articles themed around "Imposter Syndrome". Inset: breakdown of themes discussed in collected text from the same 50 magazine articles on the "Imposter Syndrome".

From my research, the survey respondents did more than evaluate their imposter experiences in the hard numerical terms of Clance's scale. They answered open questions that enabled them to share the fullness of their individual story. By processing over 380,000 words, the top ten distilled utterances of Imposter Phenomenon sufferers emerged.

(1) *"I don't know enough"*
(2) *"I'm not good enough"*
(3) *"I'm underqualified"*
(4) *"I don't deserve it"*
(5) *"I don't belong"*
(6) *"I'm not smart enough"*
(7) *"I'm out of place"*
(8) *"I don't understand"*
(9) *"I lack confidence"*
(10) *"I'm not able"*

The same text was analysed to see where responses lay on a scale of *subjective* (personal, opinionated) responses through to objective (cold, fact-based) responses. A text score between 0 and 1 denotes more subjective language. Anything below 0, in the negative region of text scores, suggests something more even-handed. Similarly, the text can be analysed on another scale: *polarity*. That is whether the text carries a mostly negative sentiment (scores below 0), neutral sentiment (scores around 0), or positive sentiment (scores above 0).

What did we find? While the *polarity* of responses centred around 0 (neither positive or negative, on average), every single response from over 800 lay in the opinionated rather than the fact-based region (all scores of *subjectivity* above 0).

The numbers more robustly decorate what you might have suspected. For me, the research brought a warmth, a relief, and a confidence to say what I say to you now, where I would never have dared before.

There is no set unfeeling, unflinching, immovably moulded single experience that is said to be the Imposter Phenomenon.

Some stories might overlap, yes, but all are unique. And so is yours.

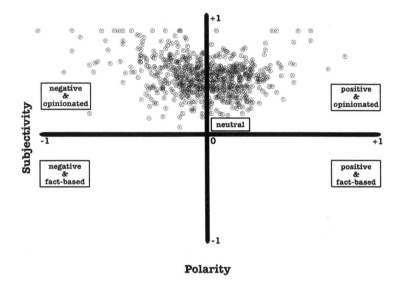

Polarity

Using natural language processing, responses from 800+ survey participants were mapped onto scales of Polarity and Subjectivity. Mean (average) polarity = -0.03; Mean (average) subjectivity = 0.53. Overall: stories of imposter experiences are individual and opinionated rather than general and fact-based.

Part 4 – Summary

From all the articles quoting the magical *70%* figure as the number of people suffering from imposter experiences, to the new research that I've shared with you here, there comes the same distilled message for you in your own struggles with the Imposter Phenomenon:

You are not alone.

It was only after looking to the wider world for stories of the Imposter Phenomenon that I felt comfortable enough to do what I should have done from the very beginning of my lonely struggles. I spoke to someone – my wife. From then on, every time I was preparing for those conference trips, I told my wife I was worried about fucking up, worried about being 'found out'. Verbalising the thoughts crystallised their absurdity, and my wife was quick to point this out on each occasion.

Like the participants in the research, my own imposter experiences were more opinionated than factual. More assumption than assertion. The relief of being able to say how you feel like a fraud is made even more satisfying by the listener showing you that your conclusions are nonsense.* Perhaps counterintuitively, resilience is also bred from those able to seek help from others and face the anxious awkwardness of the constructive criticism they receive. The height of your ambition, and the depths of your imposter experiences, need not be traversed in loneliness.

In an interview for the New York Times in 1984, Dr Joan Harvey, a psychologist and one of the leading researchers in the Imposter Phenomenon, noted that, by its very nature, feeling like an imposter is a secret.[52] Those who suffer such feelings rarely share them. Flashing forward to our time, this simple statement may seem somewhat diluted given the fact that the internet grants a voice to everyone, but it remains true.

People who feel like an imposter might never admit it openly. Yet, speaking about your imposter experience can provide immeasurable relief.

When I asked our research participants who they had told about their own imposter experiences, one in five admitted to never having told anyone at all.

Realising that I wasn't alone was a leap. Our Imposter Phenomenon experiences are individual but they are not isolated. Rather, yours, for all its specificity and enlightening individuality, is one story in a collection. A contribution to a community. There were many other people needlessly hijacking their careers with radical conclusions about being unworthy of success.

---

*Questioning your imposter thoughts is something we'll revisit in much more detail in Chapter 8.

Finding out that I wasn't alone was more than reassuring. It lit a rocket under my ass and propelled me to go further. This is no longer just about learning what the Imposter Phenomenon is...it's now about how we challenge these thoughts that live in our heads. To do that, we have to properly define one word that has been hiding in plain sight. I wonder if it's a word you've thought much about.

What do we really mean by the term *'Imposter'*?

Your Chapter Challenges

1. Increasing numbers of people – famous and not – experience imposter feelings. Let everyone know it.

Tap into the vein that is the social media trends shared in this chapter.

Use #YouAreNotAFraud, take a photo of a page in this chapter, and share your own message for those in your network who need to know they do not suffer alone.

2. Be aware of imposter feelings leading to loneliness. Never suffer alone.

Talk to people that will help show you that you are not an imposter. You can use the available template to write out the reasons for thinking you are a fraud, and the hard evidence against you being an imposter.

The latter should be drawn out in conversation.

Chapter 4: Genuine Imposters

My necessary adventures to understand the Imposter Phenomenon began to seed an altogether more challenging question in my mind. Was I such a fraud? Was I walking the path of a genuine imposter? And so now I turn that thorny question to you. Are you really an imposter? If so, prove it. Show your evidence! And while you wonder whether I'm trying to help you or harass you (spoiler alert, it's the former), allow me to tell you about the stories and the parts of my research that brought these tougher questions into being.

Part 1 – Asking the Obvious Question

For the imposter stories gathered in my own research, each was categorised into a theme and subtheme. This pigeon-hole exercise was done to help pick out all the different emotions, environments, and other triggers that participants reported as being at the heart of their individual brushes with the Imposter Phenomenon. In 96 cases (around 12% total), participants openly admitted to feeling like a fraud. Here are some examples of what they said:

- *"I meet other PhD students, and I always feel that they are much better than me and that if we have a conversation, they will see that I'm a fraud."*
- *"I have 20 years of experience across multiple fields, and still wake up terrified someone's going to figure out I don't actually have the right qualifications or that most of my knowledge and skills have been picked up along the way."*
- *"I quickly realised that several more junior employees have greater expertise in several specific areas of the field, and*

sometimes feel the people who hired me didn't appreciate the people they have. So, I sometimes feel that I will be 'found out' – despite being at this company for over a year."

Granted, 96 stories out of over 800 possible stories in my study doesn't sound like a lot. That is until you look at some of the questions making up the total Clance Imposter Phenomenon Scores (CIPS). From **Chapter 2**, recall that the overall CIPS test that I employed in my study is composed of 20 questions, each scored out of 5, with a total maximum overall imposter score of 100. In questions 2, 6, and 13, covering competence, knowledge, and being 'found out', the vast majority of *all* participants in my research scored their experience 4 or 5 out of 5. Most people had genuine struggles with thinking that they were frauds.

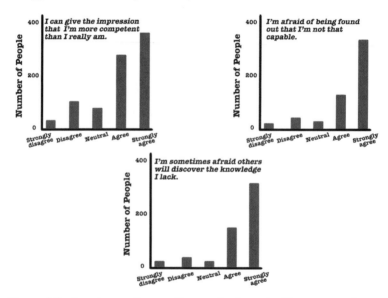

Three of the twenty questions making up the Imposter Phenomenon Scores where the questions had a connection to feeling like a fraud.

My time spent travelling to work has always been immersed in audiobooks; the dread of being found out is temporarily silenced by the sage wisdom of authors who seem to have it all figured out.

I've always been a non-fiction junkie. For as long as I've been an academic, I've hopped from self-help fix to self-help fix on how to do this, and when to do that, how to think small, and when to dream big. An 'hours listened' chart on my audiobook phone app was always on the scholarly rise. Every book 'marked as read' was an attempt to free myself from unending self-doubt. Whilst I had started to realise that talking to people could help me question my nonsense imposter thoughts, I hadn't yet figured out how to question *myself*. I still wondered how I could possibly debunk my own neurosis and ask an obvious question:

What does it actually mean to be an 'imposter'?

It wasn't until my 26th audiobook that I found a story which prompted me to dig deeper on the 'imposter' part of the mis-named 'Imposter Syndrome'. Scrolling the online bookshelves for intellectual salvation, I came across a book whose cover was set against a coal-black background. Bold letters in an angry red hue emphatically stamped the words 'Bad Blood' onto the screen. I downloaded the book and researched its background. I was about to discover a story that I really needed to hear. A story that changed my relationship with the imposter experience by making me ask what an imposter is. And this is what I'll show you.

Part 2 – A Bloody Tale of Fraud

In September 2014, a young businesswoman called Elizabeth Holmes gave a speech at a high-status healthcare conference.[53] She walked onto the stage with silent steps. She was tall and slender. Her pale skin was set in glowing contrast against her black turtleneck sweater.

With a ripple of welcoming applause, Elizabeth took to the red circular carpet in the centre of the conference stage. She raised her hands to chest height, palms forward, and trained her eyes on the audience as she started to speak. Her soft features and petite frame made the deep voice that bellowed from her throat surprising yet utterly captivating. She spoke in short, measured bursts of a few words, with lingering pauses to stretch sentences beyond seconds into minutes. Her message was like a love potion, and the audience drank it up. Slowly, deliberately, the staccato of Elizabeth's cadence should have been annoying but it just...mesmerised.

This improbably young business titan made the stage her own as she spoke of problems in US healthcare. The audience heard emotive stories of family, friends, and clients whose illnesses had been diagnosed too late, loved ones stolen from life before their time. Elizabeth's audience remained still and attentive. A spell had been cast. In the wake of her tragic revelations, the question, *"What if...?"* became the hopeful thought on the tip of everyone's tongue. What if our loved ones could be diagnosed before their illnesses cut their lives tragically short?

Elizabeth then revealed the wondrous developments in science that were beginning to make positive changes to the *status quo* in healthcare. She spoke of her company's technology that enabled patients to escape painful and repeated blood draws needed to diagnose disease. Passionately and forcefully, the crowd was told of a solution to the problem of disease diagnosis that was no longer imaginary. With Elizabeth's new technology, several test tubes of blood needed for a standard blood test could be reduced to a single pinprick of the patient's finger and a blood container the size of a peanut. Patients could now, according to Elizabeth, test themselves for various diseases, at home. Now, patients could take test results to their doctor rather than waiting on results *from* their doctor. With her revolutionary technology, disease could be diagnosed and treated with time to spare. No more loved ones dying too soon.

Elizabeth's words commanded silence. She wasn't giving a speech; she was delivering a sermon. This wasn't just some new gizmo or party trick. This was a new norm in healthcare. Her message was the promise of an ability to diagnose disease much faster, cheaper, and more accurately than ever before. This was something never possible with standard voluminous blood draws. She ended her baritone speech with a powerful vision for how her company's blood-testing technology was creating an amazing future:

"We will change our lives, and the lives of those we love will change, and we'll begin to change our healthcare system...and our world."

At that moment, with that affirmation, it was as if the stars and planets aligned to bring Elizabeth's life story full circle. This wealthy and ambitious young woman was once a dreamy-eyed little girl who wrote a letter to her father saying:

"What I really want out of life is to discover something new, something that mankind didn't know was possible to do."

It was exciting. It was revolutionary. **And it was all a lie.**

Four years after her conference speech, Elizabeth and her company, Theranos, were served a civil lawsuit. A few months after that, Elizabeth was arrested on federal charges of wire fraud. Quotes from her prosecutors read like nails being hammered into her coffin:

"[Elizabeth] not only defrauded investors" but also *"...misled doctors and patients about the reliability of medical tests that endangered health and lives."*

Later the same year, the company Theranos was in the process of being dissolved, and the last drips of its cash were paid out to frustrated investors. Elizabeth Holmes had sold a dream and delivered a nightmare. Theranos promised a new device capable of using minuscule samples of blood to tell a patient the story of their current health. Chemical engineering wizardry was the claim. In truth, Theranos scrambled for years, succeeding only to produce a forever-failing device that worked only on the occasion when investors needed to be impressed and when more money was needed to keep the research going. Outside of Elizabeth's inner circle, Theranos employees saw the warning signs of the company blinded by the hype for its leader. Alas, Elizabeth forced her people and the technology onward, ready or not.

In the end, Elizabeth's company had to void the results of over a million blood tests. Over a million patients had to learn that they had been the victim of mass fraud. What Theranos achieved in healthcare was like saying they had invented a new, mind-blowing *Coca-Cola*, when they had actually sold the same old Coke with a more variable taste than the original.

Three years before the ultimate collapse of Elizabeth's empire, *The Wall Street Journal* published articles that lifted the lid on what Theranos was up to. John Carreyrou, the investigative journalist who spearheaded the revelation, published ten damning articles that sparked the beginning of the end for Elizabeth's misled mission. The same journalist would later become the author of *Bad Blood*,[54] that book cast in abysmal black and angry red ink, the 26th audiobook on my playlist. *Bad Blood* told the warts-and-all story of the rise and fall of Elizabeth Holmes and Theranos.

The story of Elizabeth Holmes became the biggest case of fraud in the history of the tech world.* Holmes was a bona fide fake and the embodiment of one class of true imposter. She was found out. Exposed. Cast out. The story shook my bones and rattled them to dust. What I wanted to know, what I had to know, and what all the business world wanted to learn, was *why*. Why did a promising young business owner with such a worthy mission descend into fraud?

We can spend so much of our school and professional lives labelling ourselves as imposters that we rarely stop to look at the genuine cases of fraud. The Elizabeth Holmes story is what made that penny drop for me. To help manage imposter experiences, it helps to truly understand the true imposters in whose company you think you sit. And if you want to understand the fraud of a visionary tech

---

*On 3 January, 2022, while I was finalising this book, Holmes was found guilty of three counts of wire fraud and one count of conspiracy to commit wire fraud. She could serve up to 65 years in prison.

tycoon like Elizabeth Holmes, you need to understand a rebel cop searching for a serial killer...

Part 3 – Dirty Harry and Noble Cause Corruption

In the 1970s and 80s, a Criminal Justice professor named Carl B. Klockars was studying dilemmas in police work. He wanted to know how and why good cops became bad cops. Why did cops ever take the law into their own hands? In 1980, Klockars wrote a paper called "The Dirty Harry Problem",[55] named after the classic 1971 movie, *Dirty Harry*, starring Clint Eastwood as Harry Callaghan.[56]

Hard. Gritty. Unshakable. Harry is a no-frills sort of guy. He's a rogue cop for whom the law is a barrier to real justice. He bends the rules and doesn't break a sweat doing so. Harry doesn't arrest rapists and robbers on the run, he shoots them. The bad guys get what's coming to them, through the smoky end of Harry's Colt 44 magnum pistol. When a young girl is kidnapped by a psychopathic serial killer called Scorpio, Harry's journey to find the girl before she is killed reveals a counterintuitive path to someone becoming a genuine imposter.

Inspired by the *Dirty Harry* plot, Professor Klockars was investigating why real cops were ever driven to break the law. But more than that, Klockars was interested in how these dirty cops were able to convince themselves that they had done the *wrong* thing for all the *right* reasons. Klockars wanted to understand why cops would willingly turn themselves into frauds of the police force and become vigilantes masking their actions as police work in pursuit of justice.

In the movie, when Clint Eastwood's *Dirty Harry* finally confronts the serial killer (who, spoiler alert, had already killed the girl), Harry fires his last bullet into the killer's chest before the killer can fire at him. The killer falls from a riverside dock into the water, floating away in still and bloody silence. Harry stares at the killer's body then down at his police badge. Through gritted teeth, Harry hurls his golden star-shaped badge into the water. Satisfied with his own brand of justice, Harry walks away from the scene, knowing that to have remained a cop would be to live as an imposter. Harry had been wearing the mask of a policeman. In doing what he saw as the right thing, he'd become a fraud in the police force.

Any cop can become a Dirty Harry. The Klockars' paper referred to the unusual situation in which cops, more than most other groups of people, are routinely placed in situations where seemingly *good* outcomes can be achieved through *bad* means. In his paper, Klockars formalised four situations – pairings of means and ends – that a cop might face. The first combination of means and ends is using morally dirty means to reach morally dirty ends. That's like stealing a car to run over someone: one morally dirty act facilitates another. This *bad-means-for-bad-ends* pairing isn't police work, it's standard criminal behaviour.

In the second of Klockars' means–ends pairings, morally good means reach morally dirty ends. Collecting money for a charity only to pocket the cash for yourself is an example of good means leading to dirty ends. The third of the four pairings is perhaps the easiest to understand. That is the use of morally good means to reach morally good ends.

Giving that same charity collection (good means) to the needy people you are collecting the money for (good ends) fits this situation. However, it's the fourth and final means-ends pairing that Klockars used to describe the unusually common dilemma for cops: using morally *dirty* means to reach morally *good* ends. In Harry's case, this is ignoring a killer's civil right to a trial by shooting them dead and watching their body drift away in a watery grave. Sound familiar?

Klockars described the dirty means for good ends pairing like so:

"...the good to be achieved is so unquestionably good and so passionately felt that even a small possibility of its achievement demands that it be tried."

In other words, the ends justify the means. This is how a good cop becomes an imposter to his badge. It's the same as using investors' money to release a revolutionary blood-testing device before it's ready to be used on sick patients. Be it gun-slinging cops or healthcare billionaires, this is the *Dirty Harry Problem.*

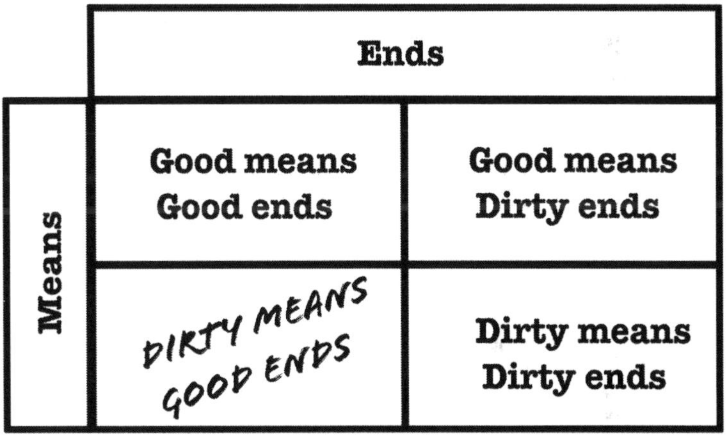
Ends
Means
Good means
Good ends
Good means
Dirty ends
DIRTY MEANS
GOOD ENDS
Dirty means
Dirty ends

Combinations of means that achieve particular ends. The Dirty Harry Problem focuses on those cases where dirty means are employed to achieve morally good outcomes.

Part 4 – Elizabeth Holmes and Dirty Harry

For the young Elizabeth Holmes, 'growing up' was held in the same breath as 'moving around.'[57] But a dynamic, nomadic home life didn't stop Elizabeth from dreaming big and showing a competitive streak. When she was seven, she drew out schematics for her design of a time machine. That was two years before writing her amazingly ambitious letter to her father.

When she set off to college, her parents gave her a copy of the book *Meditations* by Marcus Aurelius. From Ancient Rome, Holmes was gifted a collection of inspirations for living a life with purpose. Elizabeth's parents made the morally good ends clear, but what about the means?

Elizabeth dropped out of her Chemical Engineering course at Stanford to follow her desire to form a company. She founded Real-Time Cures one month later. With ferocious ambition, she wanted her company to revolutionise blood-testing and diagnostics. To fit the mission, the newly minted Real-Time Cures was renamed to the purposefully god-like Theranos (an amalgam of 'Therapy' and 'Diagnosis'). By the end of the same year that she dropped out of college, Elizabeth had raised over $6 million from investors. Theranos was alive, and Elizabeth was on her way to the morally good ends of changing the world through a life of purpose.

During the peak of the company's blood test development, Theranos' board members actually voted Elizabeth out as CEO to get an older, more experienced hand to run things. For Elizabeth, she simply could not allow this to happen. She was so unshakably determined to lead the company in its purpose that a two-hour meeting was all she needed to convince the board to make a U-turn and keep her in place as CEO.

In the year leading up to Elizabeth's powerful speech at the medical conference, the stratospheric rise in funding for Theranos gripped the attention of the tech world. Elizabeth was the darling of *Forbes* and *Fortune* magazines. She was on top of the world. At her peak, she was the world's youngest self-made billionaire, worth over $4.5 billion. She had plenty of means to work towards her lofty ends of revolutionising healthcare. A glowing Holmes profile article from that time makes for cringe-worthy reading today. In the interview,

Elizabeth affirms:

*""I have done something, and we have done something, that has changed people's lives...I would much rather live a **life of purpose** than one in which I might have other things but not that.""**58

Read that again. *"I have done something, and we have done something."* When Elizabeth is defining the means to her company's ends, which did she think was more important, "I" or "we"?

Over the course of ten arduous years invested in developing her blood-testing technology, Elizabeth's most fateful dirty-means decision was made in the fall of 2013. Despite concerns from lab scientists, despite last-minute failures before product demos, Elizabeth Holmes' company started selling their pin prick tests to the American public. At that time, the company was running out of money, and it was thought that the apparent success of using these prematurely publicised commercial blood tests might help solicit more money from investors.

Rather than being a revolutionary new blood-testing device, Theranos' technology used hacked third-party liquid analysers, retrofitted to handle the small samples that made Theranos famous and Elizabeth so alluring. In reality, patient blood samples had to be diluted to work in the instrument, making any diagnosis completely untrustworthy. Elizabeth was trying to deliver a new form of healthcare without the scientific rigour to back it up. She had strong and purposeful ends, but highly questionable means with which to achieve them.

After the damning revelations that her company was not all that it seemed, Elizabeth was interviewed over a satellite link to be given the chance to answer the scathing charges raised against Theranos in the press. In opening the interview, she answered:

*"This is what happens when you work to change things...First they think you're crazy, then they fight you, then all of a sudden you change the world..."*59

At a similar time, Holmes tweeted a quote and a picture of Winston Churchill. The words and picture were framed in the mint green colour of Theranos branding, reading:

"We make a living by what we get, but we make a life by what we give."[60]

The tweet was posted with the hashtag #lifeofpurpose.

Elizabeth's Twitter account has been derelict ever since.

Her childhood ambition has been crystallised in the handwritten note to her dad that said she wanted to *"...do something that mankind didn't know was possible to do"*. Elizabeth's parents wanted her to live a *life with purpose*. Her pursuit of that noble purpose became a lesson to us all. Just not the lesson she planned for. The diseases that were robbing people of full and healthy lives were like Scorpio the serial killer. Elizabeth was hell-bent on eradicating these diseases by developing her Theranos blood-testing technology by any means necessary. Elizabeth became *Dirty Harry*. Gunning for good ends by dirty means. Her noble cause led to corruption and fraud.

What once seemed like an unusual line of questioning was now an inevitable question in my mind. So, let me ask you again as I did at the beginning of this chapter.

Are *you* such a fraud?

Are *you* trying to use dirty means for good ends?

Are *you* walking the path of a genuine imposter?

No! But going through the imposter experience, we never stop to consider the true stories of the 'real deal'. The phonies incarnate.

We rarely try to define what an imposter is...we instead jump straight to branding ourselves as one.

Finding the book *Bad Blood* introduced me to the story of Elizabeth Holmes and one way in which someone could become a real imposter. But Elizabeth Holmes and *Dirty Harry* were just the beginning. There were other stories of real-life imposters that began to show me that, by calling myself an imposter, I truly was being unfair to myself. One such story takes us away from entrepreneurial indignities and back inside the walls of the academy.

Part 5 – The Desperation for Academic Success

Academia is famous for its tenure system.* Young-blooded wannabe professors entering a university position come in through what is known as a pre-tenured or tenure-track position. They have up to five years to set up their lab, publish papers, and prove their scholarly worth. When it comes time to have the pre-tenure record reviewed, a lengthy document and a committee come together to decide one thing: *does this young academic deserve an open-ended position?* Essentially, with few exceptions, it's a decision on whether that person has earned a job for life. Short of teaching students using X-rated movies or stealing money (both of which have actually happened, by the way), it's extraordinarily difficult to get fired if you have tenure. It's the golden ticket in academia. No more pressure to find a job. No worrying about where the money is coming from to pay the bills.

Dr Brian McNaughton was one such pre-tenure academic working towards the golden ticket of a longer-term position. In the beginning, it all looked great for Brian. His lab soared to a flying start at Colorado State University, earning a big research grant worth over $300,000. But as pressure mounted towards tenure review, McNaughton grew resentful of apparent favouritism in his department. To make matters worse, his lab was running out of money. He was denied breaks from teaching to focus on bringing

---

*The term "tenure" is itself largely a North American phenomenon. That said, there are academic systems the world over that have tenure-track systems of employment in all but name.

in more research grants. All of this was happening whilst he was trying to provide for his wife and young family.

During Brian's rocky road to academic job security, the stress crippled the relationship with his wife. One evening, as their marriage descended into failure, arguments between the couple reached near-violent levels, at least to those people in their neighbourhood who called the cops.

Brian needed tenure, and it wasn't looking good. If he was just able to achieve tenure, he'd have no job worries, a lot less stress, and a steady cash flow for his family and their middle-class suburban lifestyle. Tenure, therefore, represented good ends for Brian. However, the *means* of achieving tenure rested on being picked for promotion by the tenure committee at Colorado State. Brian didn't wait to be picked. He decided on his own means. He found a different kind of opportunity and picked himself.

When a star academic is offered a competing post at another institution, this can act as a wake-up call for the current host university to make their own counter offer, to keep that same academic star. The competing offer might be a promotion for the academic, more student support, more equipment. After all, universities want to avoid the loss of staff who are making significant contributions to the institutional rankings. In this mechanism of one university pitching against another for the services of an academic, Brian McNaughton would find the means to choose himself without being picked.

Brian took the opportunity to present an offer letter to his senior colleagues at Colorado State. The letter cited a new position for Brian at a rival university. The new offer came with a tenured position for Brian, a higher salary, and more research support. He had his golden ticket in sight. All he had to do was switch sides and move to another university. The only problem was that there was, in fact, *no* offer from another university. Brian faked the letter. He wrote the ideal offer himself. A lucrative academic job and a clear path to supporting his family was the end goal, but Brian used the stress of his current role to justify fraudulent means.

Behind the fake letter, Brian's plan was to pressurise his superiors at Colorado State into meeting his demands for a raise and more lab support...and he got it. In that moment, Brian McNaughton sealed the deal on using dirty means to reach his desired ends. Just like the closing scenes of *Dirty Harry*, here was another case of a cop watching a killer float down the river before throwing his badge away. As Harry's police badge sank into the sediment, so, too, did Brian McNaughton's academic career.

McNaughton was convicted of fraud in 2018. In a five-page confessional he released prior to his charge, Brian wrote:

"I gave in to enormous pressures, frustration, and my own ego..."[61]

With an image to uphold, mouths to feed, crumbling professional and personal relationships, Brian saw a tenured academic job as a way to relieve all his stress. Striving for tenure seemed so valuable that it was worth pursuing by any means necessary, even those means that would risk him being exposed as a genuine fraud. In the end, Brian paid back over $90,000 that he swindled from Colorado State. But no amount of money could buy back his reputation. At the time of writing this chapter, Brian McNaughton is no longer an academic scientist. He works in sales.

Brian's story, like Elizabeth Holmes' before him, was another story of true scientific fraud that I found to be a revelation. It was another story that brought about the question of why I had ever been seeing myself as an imposter. But yet, another penny was still to drop. Here were two cases of otherwise impressive and inspirational minds using dirty means to reach genuinely worthy ends. Furthermore, I've told you two stories here that really stuck with me. There are, alas, even more cases like this. Scientists inflating results and faking data, the stress of achieving a competitive edge reaches far and wide. But looking back at the Klockars study on all the means–ends combinations, I realised that the pairing that would help me really start to poke major holes in calling myself an imposter was perhaps the most obvious pairing of all. What about the darker side of fraud? What about imposters who have used dirty means for dirty ends?

Part 6 – The Two Johns and Their Different Kinds of Art Fraud

Once I became aware of Klockars' *Dirty Harry* formalism and thought more about genuine imposters, I started collecting all sorts of stories of imposters from all walks of life. One particularly curious story led me to find what appeared to be two types of imposter in one place. One of them revealed to me the other type of imposter who would help continue the deconstruction of my own imposter experiences. One fraudster was using dirty ends for dirty means.

Two very different Johns

When I was collecting stories of imposters, I found two newspaper articles that I'd like you to consider now. Two articles attending two very different types of people, both of whom were part of the same case of major art fraud. One article interviewed a man by the name of John Myatt, a talented and humble artist who was particularly skilled in recreating works of art's best-known masters.[62] From the journalists who met Myatt, he was said to be unassuming. Polite. His prison cellmates endearingly nicknamed him Picasso, and those who jailed him later hired him to create legal paintings.

A sister article from another newspaper spoke of another John, John Drewe.[63] This second article read with far darker connotations. In a report of this master criminal, policemen were quoted as saying that *"the world will be a much safer place with Drewe in jail"*.

Why were the two Johns, Myatt and Drewe, who were both working at the same time to defraud the art world, written about so differently? Why was Myatt reported to be more or less the perfect gentleman with misplaced motives, whilst Drewe was defiled as a hardcore crook? Dirty Harry's gun comes back out the holster.

John Myatt

During the 1980s, John Myatt worked as a substitute teacher and lived in the picturesque English countryside with his wife and two young children. However, Myatt later found himself in financial trouble when his wife walked out. Quite suddenly, frighteningly, Myatt was a single parent. He had mouths to feed and precious few means with which to do so. The threat of social workers taking his children away loomed. So, in order to spend more time with his children, Myatt decided to quit his teaching job and work from home employing an altogether more creative pursuit – recreating classic artworks.

Myatt was now an impoverished artist, down on his luck and, a little like Brian McNaughton, was a proud working parent with a family to care for. You, like me, might be tempted to think that because John Myatt needed more money to look after his kids (altogether good ends) that his serviceable talent for art recreation provided the dirty means through which to solve his troubles. In fact, John Myatt's art reproductions were sold for what they were. Fakes! He painted and sold reproductions as house decorations; as innocent as gift shop postcards. Myatt, in his new-found struggle, was employing good means to meet good ends. He advertised his services in a magazine:

GENUINE FAKES
19th and 20th century artworks
from £150".

The customers came, and Myatt's second ad comfortably read the same as the first, except prices were now *"from £250"*. A full £100 more expensive than before. His good means started achieving good ends for his kids. But while Myatt was gaining one-time or at best two-time customers for his works, he had one customer who kept coming back again and again: John Drewe.

John Drewe

The other John, John Drewe, was originally born John Cockett. He changed his name after dropping out of school at age 17. He had a reported IQ of 165 (higher than Albert Einstein and 99.99% of the general population). Unlike Myatt, Drewe emanated all the tell-tale signs of a person who wasn't quite as they appeared to be. Together, the two very different Johns would soon become a pair of very different imposters.

The inception of the scandal

Drewe was inspired to concoct a scheme to defraud the art world, after seeing Myatt's almost hidden magazine adverts selling *Genuine Fakes*. Steadily, repeatedly, Drewe came back, buying repainted classic works from Myatt's expert hand. The two Johns met at train stations and coffee shops, conducting honest business between artist and repeat customer. Later, Drewe invited Myatt to his home, in turn meeting his wife and kids. As Myatt and Drewe built up their relationship, Drewe's wife knew nothing about what moonlighting schemes her husband was formulating in his mind.

Drewe inevitably ran out of requests for paintings to buy from Myatt. Instead, he asked what Myatt would like to paint and sell. Myatt chose the work of a little-known German artist called Albert Gleizes, the self-professed inventor of the abstract style known as Cubism. It was a style that intrigued Myatt, and so that's what he produced for Drewe. This is when everything started to change.

Once Myatt had produced the cubist painting for Drewe, Drewe took it to art auctioneers Christies in London and convinced them that Myatt's innocent reproduction of a Gleizes piece was by Gleizes himself. Only once Drewe had convinced the auctioneers to buy Myatt's work did Drewe then phone Myatt with a surprising offer. Drewe had sold the Albert Gleizes reproduction to Christies for a cool £25,000. Drewe's enticing question to his friend John Myatt was then very simple:

Would he rather be paid £250 as advertised, or would he instead like £12,500?

Alas, to Myatt, the cash-strapped father-of-two, Drewe's offer was too tempting, too exciting to refuse. Good ends by dirty means. After all, Myatt was stunned by the fact that his simple homages were somehow being accepted as original works by the art world's seemingly most revered experts. In accepting Drewe's offer, Myatt became complicit in a scandal that would eventually shake the art scene to its core. The two Johns, Myatt and Drewe, were now partners in crime.

Fakes and Forgeries

To more fully understand the differences between John Myatt and John Drewe, you need to understand the difference between a *fake* and a *forgery*. John Myatt was creating *fakes*, honest recreations of classic artworks. That's how he advertised them. That's what customers knew they were getting. In some cases, customers even requested Myatt to paint their own faces in place of classic portraits. Myatt painted his so-called *Genuine Fakes* and sold them at a modest price to the sorts of people who get a kick out of having a family pet's face painted onto a famous royal body.

Drewe, on the other hand, was consciously scheming to sell *forgeries*. Drewe, a master con man by all expert accounts, went to mind-blowing lengths to re-write art history and provide documentary proof that what he was selling was actually the real thing. He knew that, beyond any doubt the art dealers had about the quality of the paintings themselves, the paper trail, more commonly known as *provenance*, was sacrosanct in confirming whether or not a piece of art was genuine. Provenance allowed buyers and dealers to read the life story of the artwork and track it, through sales and exhibitions, all the way back through time to the original artist. It was in creating intricately forged provenance that John Drewe drove his dirty means to dirty ends.

In Myatt's view, he couldn't believe that the scam he became caught up in could run undetected for years. He was painting fakes using nothing more than house paint, jelly, coffee stains, and vacuum dust.

At the height of the scandal, Drewe managed to sell Myatt's recreation from 20th century artist Alberto Giacometti for $300,000 at an auction house in New York. Myatt, well and truly sucked into Drewe's fraud, was earning much-needed cash from work that took him just five hours to complete.

As the scam grew in size, Drewe was forced to recruit a small team of middlemen to sell the works so he could avoid suspicion. But despite Drewe's complex lies to evade detection, the scheme didn't last forever.

The entire plot unravelled when an English art dealer called Peter Nahum became suspicious of having been sold a second painting by the same artist. In interviews recounting the story,[64] Nahum exudes the image of an art dealer. He's a tall man, thin but robust, and dressed in a combination of tweed threads, big spectacles, wispy white hair, and the occasional bow tie.

At a similar time, Mary Lisa Palmer, director of the Giacometti Association in Paris started to raise suspicions about certain supposed works by the artist after whom her institute was named, Alberto Giacometti. Palmer's straight and aquiline face matched the sharpness of her analytical intellect and the directness of her words. And it wasn't until Palmer conducted detailed detective work to prove that Drewe's Giacometti provenance had been expertly forged, that she could start to convince dealers in London that they had been the victims of a meticulously planned fraud.

While John Drewe remained comfortable spinning a web of lies to maintain the con, John Myatt grew increasingly uneasy with the scam. After eight years, Myatt stepped back and stopped working with Drewe. Myatt likened the relief to having swum through choppy seas and making it onto the serene sands of a quiet beach. The final nail in the coffin for this case of art fraud came from John Drewe's now ex-wife. When their common-law marriage fell apart, Drewe left home but, disastrously for him, left behind a mass of paperwork pointing to his immense scheme. It was then only a matter of time before his estranged and angered ex-wife dumped Drewe's incriminating papers into a bin bag and gifted them to the police who were investigating the suspected fraud.

The Fallout

Drewe was the mastermind behind the fraud. He created an incredibly detailed plan full of dirty means to achieve his dirty ends of making a lot of money, and intellectually humiliating those he felt were not as smart as he was. He found Myatt, assessed his skill, built a relationship as a repeat customer, and exploited the weakness of Myatt's family circumstance.

Before the art forgery, Drewe had been such a masterful fraud that he convinced the UK government's Atomic Energy Authority that he had a PhD in Physics. He got fired from that job after two years when he was found out. But he didn't stop there. Before the art fraud, long before he met Myatt, Drewe continued to wear the mask of a physicist and faked his way to becoming the Head of Physics at a grammar school in the south of England. John Drewe was a genuine imposter who was completely comfortable with employing dirty means to reach dirty and self-preserving ends. John Myatt's attempts to employ good means for good ends placed him in the wrong place at the wrong time.

Even when the game was up, John Drewe proclaimed that all Myatt's recreations were genuine, original artworks. During prosecution, Drewe, ever the imposter, faked two heart attacks to suspend the hearing. On the third occasion, he had his day in court. And reminiscent of sophisticated serial killer Ted Bundy, Drewe sacked his legal representation during the trial in order to defend himself through his own craftsmanship and enticing charm. Myatt, conversely, happily pleaded guilty.

Ironically, Myatt estimated that he probably made the same money creating art for John Drewe as he would have made if he had remained a teacher rather than turning to crime. When he openly confessed to his crimes and worked with the police, John Myatt became a legitimate artist, selling his now infamous recreations under the signed title of his first magazine advert from the 1980s: *Genuine Fakes.* His first customer was the man who arrested him.

The story of John Drewe and John Myatt has been called the greatest contemporary art fraud of the 20th century. Drewe's insidious scheme to make money from forged (not faked) copies of modern artworks tells a very different story to those of Elizabeth Holmes and Brian McNaughton, and even of co-conspirator John Myatt. Drewe duped several prestigious galleries into purchasing and reselling his forgeries as original artworks.

Christies, the Victoria & Albert Museum, and the Tate Modern were among those fooled into working with Drewe and selling the forgeries he'd commissioned from the talented and unassuming Myatt. The case against Drewe and Myatt cost £4 million and lasted six months. The damage to the reputations and archives of modern artists like Ben Nicholson, Graham Sutherland, Alberto Giacometti, Jean Dubuffet, Roger Bissière, Marc Chagall, Nicolas de Staël, and Henri Matisse, on account of their collections being laced with forgeries, is far more difficult to quantify.

Elizabeth Holmes, Brian McNaughton, the Two Johns: their stories help a lot when it comes to genuine imposters who fit neatly into Klockars' Dirty Harry model. The one itch left to scratch was in that person we know is overconfident...but they don't know it themselves.

Part 7 – The Opposite of the Imposter Phenomenon

On April 19th, 1995, McArthur Wheeler stood aghast at the front door of his home. He wasn't expecting to be greeted by arresting policemen. In a story that has now attained an arguable level of infamy, the reprimanded Wheeler didn't plead innocence when the police took him away. Instead, he exclaimed, with genuine surprise, the words:

"But I wore the juice. I wore the juice."

The detectives who arrested McArthur Wheeler were led to his address by tip-offs from the public who saw stills of Wheeler, captured on bank CCTV footage, reported on the 11 o'clock news. By 12:10am, Wheeler was in handcuffs.[65] The bank robber's arrest wasn't eye-wateringly fast on the account of any particularly sophisticated investigative work. McArthur Wheeler robbed Fidelity Savings Bank and Mellon Bank wearing no mask, no disguise. He did, however, wear lemon juice over his face. Before robbing the banks, Wheeler learned about the use of lemon juice as invisible ink (which only becomes visible on heating). He deduced that smearing the citrus spy ink on his face would render his face unidentifiable to video cameras. To Wheeler's credit, he actually tried to test his invisible face theory before robbing the banks. Unfortunately, a poorly aimed selfie blurred the photo but served to convince Wheeler of the obscuring magic of lemon juice.

When you first learn something new, your confidence grows fast. You knew nothing before you started, now you're so much more aware. What you are not aware of at this point is that you're staring out over the world from atop Mount Stupid. Once that penny drops, so does your confidence, straight into the Valley of Despair. You thought you knew it all, but you don't. And now begins the real grunt work to grow your confidence, legitimately, up to genuine skill mastery. But there are those who stay on Mount Stupid. Those who thrive there. They are confident, incompetent, and completely unaware of their true lack of skill.

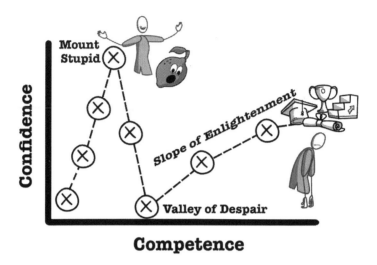

The conceptual balance of confidence and competence.

They are terrible at karaoke but swagger off the stage after dropping the mic, convinced that they nailed the song. They are the competent employees, striving for the managerial jobs they have no leadership skills to fill. These poor unfortunate souls are the entrepreneurs who think they'll be setting themselves up for early retirement, shielded from failure by the pure brilliance of their business idea. They, alas, are you and me. All of us. No one is spared from the reach of the opposite of imposter experiences. Because all of us, whether we like it or not, whether we're rich or poor, simple or supremely sentient, are not very good at evaluating our ability.*

Inspired by the McArthur Wheeler robberies, Cornell Professor of Social Psychology David Dunning and graduate student Justin Kruger designed a series of experiments to understand how it is

---

*We'll come back to evaluating ability by the mechanism of social comparison in a later chapter.

that someone can be so utterly convinced by their own stupidity. By setting undergraduate students to answer questionnaires on logic, humour, and grammar, Dunning and Kruger measured a person's assessment of their performance versus the actual questionnaire grade.[66] The easy part was plotting a graph of grades versus rank in the class (as measured by the grades). As you move from the bottom left of the plot to the top right, you move to higher ranks in the class, which is beautifully tracked by a concurrent move to higher questionnaire grades. The plot is of a line. The higher the person's rank in the class, the higher the grade on Dunning and Kruger's questionnaires. What was utterly bewildering was how this straight-line plot of the actual scores compared to the scores that the study volunteers guessed they had scored. Those in the bottom of the class, with the worst test scores, tended to drastically overestimate their score. In the logic questionnaire, for example, those students scoring in the bottom quarter of the class recorded actual scores of around 10%.

When asked to guess how well they'd performed, those same students from the bottom ranks said they'd scored around 60%. That's not all. What about the students in the top quarter of the class? They, alas, underestimated their performance. The top students felt they'd scored around 70% on the logic questionnaire when, in fact, they'd scored closer to 90%.

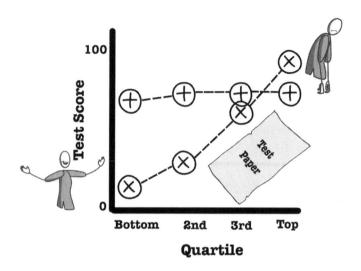

Example outcome from Dunning and Kruger's seminal work. Those scoring lowest in several tests reported the highest perception of their ability or performance. Conversely, those scoring highest reported the lowest perceived ability or performance.

What the researchers found earned them infamy in what is now known as the Dunning–Kruger effect.[67] Those of us who suffer from a lack of ability in a given area suffer a "dual burden", so-termed by the researchers. The lack of ability comes hand in hand with no ability to self-assess that lack of ability and therefore no way to improve. The Imposter Phenomenon occurs in people like us who are hyper-aware of their hard work. The Dunning–Kruger effect, the closest thing we have to an opposite of imposter experiences, occurs in true imposters who have no idea that they are imposters.

McArthur Wheeler wasn't smart enough to realise the flaws in his lemon juice disguise. At the same time, he was stunned when police showed him the footage that identified him as the two-time bank robber because he did not have the ability to reassess his seemingly fool-proof plan.

Part 8 – Summary

You can spend so much time thinking about the Imposter Phenomenon that you lose sight of the word 'Imposter'. Diving deeper into the *Dirty Harry Problem* (the means and ends that can make some of us become genuine imposters) and the *Dunning–Kruger effect* (being unskilled and unaware of it) helps frame the word 'imposter' with more structure.

Finding the Elizabeth Holmes story in Bad Blood, my 26th audiobook, was the first time I had ever stopped to reflect on what an imposter was. Before then, I was burying myself in the shame of thinking I simply wasn't good enough to be a scientist. I had lost all awareness of the fact I was cursing myself under the same breath as the real fraudsters.

I immersed myself in the fraudulent behaviour of scientists and scholars because that was the world I was living in. Those were the stories of real fraud that helped me see that I wasn't one. I thought myself an imposter because I was assuming other academics were better than I was; their work mattered more than mine. In researching cases of genuine imposters, I soon realised – as simple as it sounds – that real fraud ran much deeper and darker than scientific or academic misconduct. Then came the key question:

Did I really see myself in the same light as someone who faked blood test results? Would I fake a letter to get a better job? Would I defraud art dealers with substandard forgeries?

Of course, I wouldn't. Yet, for some reason, my mind was okay with telling me I was some sort of phoney. Your influences will be different to mine, so I challenge you to find the stories of fraud that are closest to the experiences that are prompting you to call yourself a fraud.

Famed statistician Hans Rosling wrote in his book *Factfulness*[68] that meaning in measurement comes from comparing one to another.

A number without a reference point is meaningless. And so it is with language and our collective illusion under the Imposter Phenomenon. To call yourself an imposter without any real evidence, without comparison to genuine imposters, is a complete waste of your time. Understanding true cases of people being 'found out', people who knowingly deceive others (with good intentions or not), shows us the imposter reference that each of us really needs to see our judge imposter experiences more compassionately. Calling yourself a fraud or an imposter is, thankfully, kind of ridiculous. We can provoke an even deeper question here. Darker, even. Ask yourself this:

Are you really prepared to call yourself an imposter? Are you the same as Bernie Madoff, the Wall Street banker who, in the 2008 financial crash, bankrupted helpless pensioners whose money he'd invested?[69] Darker still, do your imposter experiences really liken you to the priests pretending to be guardians only to abuse the trust of innocent children in order to satisfy a sordid fantasy?[70] Are you pretending to be someone you're not during an online date to then reveal your unexpected identity in real life?[71] Probably not.

Whatever the motives (good means or bad), the examples of fraud I've shared with you all serve to set a reality check against your feelings of being a fraud. I was tarring myself with the same brush as the cheating scientists, the murderers, the paedophiles, the greedy bankers, and the social predators who all wore the true mask of an imposter.

Defining stories of true fraud, of real imposters, was what it took for me to realise I could call bullshit on the damaging thoughts I was having. That's not to say I was getting rid of those thoughts completely, but I was starting to see a way of effectively acknowledging them. Not all thoughts have meaning. And a lot of nonsense thoughts, like believing I was an imposter, could be managed and recognised by comparing myself to the real imposters.

I was just a guy bending myself out of shape over a poor assumption that my work and my abilities were inferior to others'. I had no evidence, no reason, just an unconscious feeling that I didn't belong. And it was an unconscious feeling that had painted me with the same brush as John Drewe and all the other genuine fraudsters. How did I not see it before?

My audiobook habit has led me to understand the value of comparing myself to real imposters. However, I was still struggling with debilitating comparisons, not with imposters, but my colleagues. My imposter experiences were still fuelled by a fear of failure. And dealing with these challenges would require an altogether different approach, and an altogether different perspective...

Your Chapter Challenges

1. Imposters and real frauds are everywhere in many forms.

Read about cases of genuine fraud that interest you.

Use the template provided in the book's journal resource to capture the person, the situation, and the fallout from their particular case of fraud.

2. Learning to question your unfounded conclusions of being a fraud is helped by trying to present the case in favour of your questionable conclusion.

List all the reasons why you think you are an imposter.

Compare those reasons to the seriousness of the true stories of fraud that you find in Challenge 1.

Still think you're an imposter?

Chapter 5: Finding Perspective

Being told to 'live in the moment' is, in many ways, sound advice. It's safe phrasing for an inspiring social post...or ten. To be present is a skill but it's increasingly easy to live solely in the present. The excitement, the anxiousness for tomorrow's mystery can endanger your individual sense of history. And yet, there's a particular way to value your yesterdays to better manage the Imposter Phenomenon in every one of your tomorrows. Before writing this for you, I first had to articulate that same message for someone very close to my heart.

Part 1 – A Letter to my Daughter

"Our Dearest Adaline,

When you were a tiny baby, you loved the bath. You would look up to us with those amazing blue eyes, smile as wide as your ears, and splash, splash, splash!

You, our cute and curious little girl, also loved to play with a little toy turtle at bath time. When you weren't splashing with your handies, you would reach for the little green turtle, slowly pick it up with your little fingers and thumbs, only to chew it like you chewed on everything else back then!

Your little turtle toy was about the size of a golf ball. Imagine that it wasn't the size of a golf ball but the size of a peanut. If we threw the little peanut-sized turtle toy in the bath, you – our brilliant love – would still find it. It would be a bit more difficult finding a toy in the bath the size of a peanut rather than one the size of a golf ball, sure...but we know you would find it!

Imagine, instead of throwing your wee peanut-sized turtle toy into the bath, that it was thrown into the deep blue sea. A very big bath! You would find it much harder to pick up your toy because you probably wouldn't know where in the deep blue sea it went. You could splash, splash, splash for all the days and all the nights and it would still be hard to find that toy again. You might even say it was impossible!

We tell you this silly story, our gorgeous angel, because, to us, finding you was like finding a tiny bath toy in the big blue sea! It was almost impossible...but we found you. And to us, you are the most special person in the whole wide world.

Yours, with all the biggest kisses and cuddles,

Mummy and Daddy"

That was a letter I wrote to my infant daughter. I wrote that message to her (to be read for family and friends on her Naming Day celebration),* inspired by some things I had desperately needed to learn for myself in striving to manage my imposter experiences. The story that I told for my daughter is the one I want to tell you in much more detail now. Each of us, each in our own singular way, is like finding that turtle toy in the bath.

When asked a series of questions about luck-related markers of success, the majority of our Imposter Phenomenon study participants strongly agreed that their success was down to luck. They felt like frauds because they could not accept their success as being a result of hard work or making their place in time work to their utmost advantage.

---

*If you're reading this chapter fewer than 10 years after I first published the book in 2022, it's very likely that my daughter hasn't even read that letter yet. The plan was to give her the sealed envelope with the handwritten original on her 10th birthday. Since the letter and this book were both written, we've also had the joy of welcoming a little boy into the world. (Don't worry, we love you, too, Lachlan!).

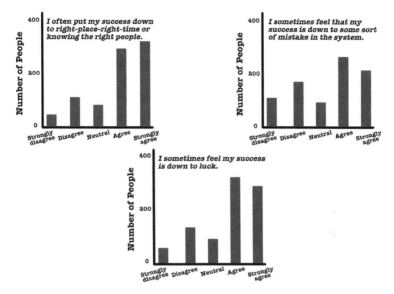

Imposter Phenomenon Score questions attending 'luck' or 'chance' as the perceived cause of success.

You may well be one of those people who cites luck as the arbiter of your success. Your very being is, however, more impossible than it is imposter.

The story of you being born hides a wonderful tool to manage your imposter experiences.

Before we get to that, I have to share with you the story of the horrible low point that eventually led me to the high of writing that letter to my daughter.

Part 2 – A Somber Business Trip

I remember an oddly inseparable blend of panic, relief, and guilt.

Ignoring everything, I stared out my train window. Beyond. Shallow breaths dried out the hours-old caffeine on my tongue. The view outside somehow switched from green hills to grey suburbs without my noticing. I was a mess, and about to wake up on multiple levels. There's an emotional exposure that comes with being far from home.

It was still very early in my career, at a similar time to the lonely conference trips and shy Google researches on the Imposter Phenomenon. Yet here I was, on the road again, alone, and still haunted by thoughts of being a fraud among more genuine colleagues. Despite all I was learning about imposter experiences – the seminal research, my own research, imposter stories from famous people, looking at real imposters – I still didn't have it all figured out. I didn't think I belonged in my job. So, don't worry if the stories and tools we've covered so far haven't scratched all your imposter itches.

I had won a small grant to work in another city with a friend and colleague for a few months. On the train, the more I drifted from my imposter-stricken office back home, the more my shoulders relaxed. I was being ripped in half; blinking made my cheeks wet with the thought of moving away from my wife of less than two years. The panic, the relief, and the guilt; the oil and water and gravel that blended as one. The eyes of my fellow passengers burned their pity into my back. Thankfully, it's not all I remember from the trip...

At the station, I was embraced by the stereotypical buzz of a commuter hotspot. I allowed myself a brief smile in the direction of the unique buck-toothed flair of a bronze statue dedicated to the city's comedy hero. According to my travel instructions, I was supposed to be looking for the mysterious grandeur of a tall black wooden storm door. My temporary home from home. My spritely landlord's welcoming nature, warm regional accent, and energetic conversation made me forget, just for a few seconds every day, why my mind was at perpetual unease.

Dim-lights inside the storm door hinted at the brick walls and theatrical posters decorating a metal stairwell. Inside my apartment, an oriental theme dressed what was now my private world away from the thespian staircase. My head was full of imposter-driven thoughts and now I had ample space in which to pour them out. Through the walls, I could hear the hushed waves of travelling troupers warming up their voices for another night on the boards.

I remember, one evening, my ears tilted to the soft singing voice of a woman in the apartment above mine. All the while, I stared at the ceiling and imagined that she was rehearsing in front of a bright ring of lights around a perfectly chaotic dressing table. The same neighbouring apartment would later host a Star Wars-loving flautist who was no stranger to the thundering sobriety of the Imperial Death March. How apt...

During this academic business trip, the unfamiliar city kept me conveniently distracted. I was rarely far from opulence. The town hall stood on Olympian pillars like centuries-old tree trunks. On-lookers leant back to see where the building ended and the sky began. On the nearby theatre, a billboard proudly announced a show starring an actress who was native to the city. Further on down the road, the riverside promenade made for an analgesic stroll. Clouds drifted with the hush of the waves and the engines of the ferries. The dance of fiddling buskers and shanty singers put a spring in the step of even the most reserved of tourists. Along the river's railings, sealed padlocks declared the unbreakable bond of countless unnamed lovers and placed a familiar, longing lump in my throat.

Part 3 – The Bookshop

An old bookshop sat one street down from my apartment. It was an unassuming location, to say the least. The smell of fresh paint had long since drifted off. The road naturally led down to the main hub of the city, to the town hall, the theatre, on to the musical riverside, and the university I was working in during the trip.

It was on one such walk that I eventually stopped to visit the bookshop itself. It had an overhanging wine-red exterior. Gold lettering announced its name. The main entrance was flanked by two trolleys of neatly piled books from famous authors whose work would have commanded a healthy price, once upon a time. A large clock above the entrance, frozen at thirty-eight minutes past three, was a teaser for the singularly timeless scene hidden behind the shop's front door.*

When I heard the creak of the door and the ringing of the entrance bell, I quietly gasped. I had stumbled upon a portal and fallen into another dimension. As if by magic, I stood in a world of forgotten tomes and silent diaries. As my eyes scanned three stories of open space, the warm glow of the tungsten lights caramelised countless bookshelves. A single U-shaped path made way for visitors to squeeze by one another on their way to more literary links to the past.

The enrapturing smell of ageing books filled my lungs with curiosity. In the middle of the paper jungle, a hunched and bespectacled man, dressed in denim, was hidden beneath a pile of books and an analogue cash register. Only his white hair and infrequent twitches flagged his position. From his whispers of polite conversation, he revealed that he had checked out of the daily working grind forty years previous and had looked after the bookshop, in peace and autonomy, ever since. No endless career ladder to worry about, no stressful comparisons with ambitious colleagues. Anyone who asked him the price of a particular book heard, in his response, a price that was laughably lower than any customer expected. Money was a courtesy here. On a tired old street, a mere stone's throw from my apartment, I had found my refuge.

If the draw to escape my imposter experiences wasn't enough, this antiquated hideout on an unkept street was the gift that kept on giving. One gift, however, would come to stand out from the rest.

---

*If you're ever in Liverpool, UK, consider stopping by Henry Bohn Books on London Road, if it's still around. You can thank me later...if I'm still around!

A two-volume set bound in deep red leather earned a therapeutic place in my long-term memory; a memory so pivotally helpful to me in managing my inner dialogue, that I will, in this chapter, turn it into a challenge for you.

For less than the cost of a coffee, I bought a pair of books that told the comprehensive family history of one Sir Francis Drake.[72] Who was he? Francis Drake was a famous 16th century naval commander, who, in service to Queen Elizabeth I of England, stopped the British from being invaded by the Spanish. In the 1500s, Sir Francis Drake was the first person to complete a seafaring circumnavigation of the globe. In the annals of English history, Francis Drake is a big deal. I, on the other hand, knew little of him. Admittedly, Google reminded me. You'd be forgiven, by the way, for not yet having any clue how this all links to managing the Imposter Phenomenon. Stay with me. Keep reading.

After buying the Sir Francis Drake family history book set, I returned to my apartment and melted into a chair. I cracked open the first of the two book volumes with care. Intrigue. On the first few pages, I discovered that the author (obscured on the fading cover) was Lady Elizabeth Beatrice Fuller-Elliot-Drake. Writing in 1911, she was a descendant chronicling her family four centuries after the famous Sir Francis Drake sailed uncharted seas.

Scarcely could I imagine, however, that this random family's story would later help me reflect on my imposter experiences. Climb through the Drake family tree with me and you'll see why such an exercise – with you at the centre of the story – can be so deeply useful in repositioning any imposter nonsense that might be circling around your head.

Part 4 – What's in a (Drake) Name?

Imagine for a moment that the name Francis Drake is not just a person but a sort of baton to be passed on through time. Like between runners in a relay race, the baton is passed from person to person. Each member of the relay team is the next generation of the family. You might also think of the Francis Drake name as a kind of family heirloom (perhaps jewellery, a painting, or a patchwork quilt). It can be passed on to symbolise an ever-growing thread tying new generations to those long gone. But let's stick to this idea of passing on a name. I, by the way, am named after my father save for a subtle swap of the 'k' for a 'c' in 'Marc', and he (with the middle name Archibald) carried the name of his father before him. In reading Lady Elliot-Drake's account of her ancestral family tree, the 'Francis Drake' name was passed from ancestor to descendant for *hundreds* of years.* Or so I thought.

The name started with the famous sea captain Sir Francis Drake from the 1500s, and ended (in a way) with another Sir Francis Drake in the 1700s. So, how was the name passed down through the ages? The answer seemed clear. From my own family experience, and maybe like in parts of your own, I assumed that the original Sir Francis Drake would name his own child Francis, then, when Francis the younger grew up and had his or her own kids, they would name a child Francis, too. And so, down the ages, Francis the elder would pass their name, like an untouchable family heirloom, to Francis the younger. Right? If only keeping a name alive for two hundred years could be so simple. And it's in this weirdness, with these curious genealogy books, that I found a way to view the Imposter Phenomenon – and its association with luck – in a whole new way.

I'm about to guide you through exactly how the Francis Drake

---

*In fact, if you look at portraits of Sir Francis Drake (painted in 1500s) and Lady Eliott-Drake (born in the 1800s), you will see that they are each wearing the same family jewel. It had passed down the generations, surviving to be painted in two portraits 300 years apart.

name passed through the branches of an intricate family tree, so let's cover the core assumption one more time. It might seem relatively safe to assume that Francis senior would pass his name to Francis junior. Easy. But passing the 'Francis Drake' name down through the ages was far more onerous than we might first assume. Here's how it *actually* happened.

Born in 1542, the famed naval admiral Sir Francis Drake, first to hold that name, had a brother named Thomas. In 1588, Sir Thomas Drake and his wife Elizabeth welcomed their firstborn son, baby Francis, into the world. He was Sir Francis Drake's nephew. When baby Francis was born, Thomas Drake was working at the most southerly coast of the British Isles, about 10 miles from their opulent family home of Buckland Abbey,* assisting in his brother's naval conquests around the globe. But in naming their son Francis, Thomas and Elizabeth Drake were doing more than honouring the name of Thomas' seafaring brother. Thomas and Elizabeth were starting the trend of passing the 'Francis Drake' name down the ages. Baby Francis now held the baton of the 'Francis Drake' name. So, it was the *nephew* of the man who sailed around the planet, who became the second Sir Francis Drake.

For all of this to eventually be of any use to you, the important question to ask is why the baton was passed to the nephew and not the son of the original Sir Francis Drake. Why couldn't the first Francis simply pass the baton himself and name his own son or daughter after himself? Because, alas, the famous Francis Drake died on a voyage far from home, twice married but childless, in the delirium of fluid-draining dysentery. He had no direct heir to his name. If the naval hero had been without his brother Thomas, there would have been no baby Francis to speak of. No one to whom the baton could be passed. The unbroken line of the 'Francis Drake' name would have stopped dead in its tracks. Yet, it persisted.

---

*Buckland Abbey was another heirloom of the Drakes. It was the same manor house in which Lady Eliott-Drake would later write the two-volume Drake family history I found in the old bookshop during my business trip.

At this point in the story of the Francis Drake name, I'm sharing a picture of the smallest, most zoomed-in part of the family tree that we need to understand from Lady Elliot-Drake's account. Think of it as a visual summary of everything we need to understand to this point. The baton started with Sir Francis Drake, and almost died with him because he had no kids. But the name lived on through his brother Thomas, whose son was named Francis Drake. In this way, Francis 1 passed the baton to Francis 2.

For another four generations, the baton of the 'Francis Drake' name would be passed down to a Francis: 3, 4, 5, and 6. Baby Francis (Francis 2) grew up to hold the lofty title of 1st Baronet (a British hereditary title like a knighthood) of Buckland Abbey. Each successive Francis Drake had his own life and story to tell. Each Francis in turn became the 2nd, 3rd, 4th, and 5th Baronets of Buckland Abbey. Each Francis Drake edged ever closer in time toward Lady Elizabeth Beatrice Fuller-Elliot-Drake, whose writings I found in the wonderful bookshop during my imposter embattled secondment. So, we've seen how Francis 1 passed the name to Francis 2. How do we get from Francis 2 to Francis 3?

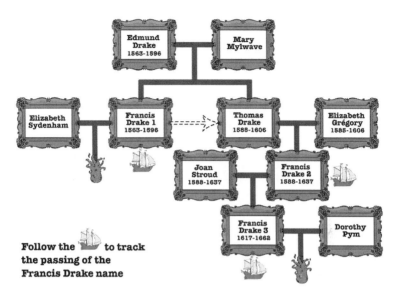

Follow the ⛵ to track
the passing of the
Francis Drake name

Partial Drake family tree, showing the parental origin of the famous 'Francis Drake' and how his name was carried on for the first two generations after him.

Back in the sunken comfort of my apartment chair, when I was reading the books for the first time, I began to sense deep transcendent thoughts brewing in my head. The magnitude of what I was reading about the Francis Drake family tree whispered in my ear but I couldn't yet hear what it was saying. I peeled my eyes off the book and drew a deep breath. I stared up to the ceiling from where music once came, before allowing my eyes to glance back down to the page. I read on.

Part 5 – The View from Above

Our baby Francis in this story (Francis 2), nephew of the first and most famous Sir Francis Drake, was baptised into his parents' Christian faith on the day of his birth, 16th September, 1588. The rush to baptise baby Francis was apparently for fear that he was too frail to live beyond securing an anointed place in the Heaven his parents believed in. The passing of the Francis Drake baton was almost compromised, not just because the eldest Francis died without a son, but also because his nephew, a desperately delicate newborn, almost died before he could carry the name of Francis Drake for even a single day.

Having somehow escaped the clutches of death and grown into adulthood, life wasn't all sweetness and light for the second Francis Drake. The same baby Francis suffered the loss of his first wife, Jane. As if that wasn't bad enough, Francis 2 also suffered the loss of their only child, Dorothy, who died an infant. Dorothy was not as fortunate a baby as her father had been. It was only with baby Francis' second wife, Joan, that the *third* of six successive Francis Drakes was brought into existence.

Equal measures of chance and tragedy were playing their respective parts in making this family tree a lot more complicated than you or I might ever assume.

Three Francis Drakes down. There were still three more Francis Drakes to come. Further down the branches of the family tree, the fourth Francis Drake was *not* the son of the third Francis. Number 3 (like his great-uncle the naval hero, Francis 1) died without children. But yet again, the baton was passed and the Francis Drake name persisted.

The fourth Francis, born almost a hundred years after the death of the first, was the nephew of Francis 3. What's even more incredible is that fourth Francis was not even the firstborn Francis among his siblings in the same generation. Another Francis, like so many unknown Drakes before him, died young. It was only with the final two of six successive Francis Drakes that the more obvious route played out. Francis 5 was the son of Francis 4. Francis 6 was the son of Francis 5. The fuller picture of the Drake family tree shared with you below should start to make one point particularly clear and it is this:

When you add up all the 'what if?' moments, the tragic losses,

and triumphant forks in the road, you see that passing on the name of 'Francis Drake' was ridiculously improbable.

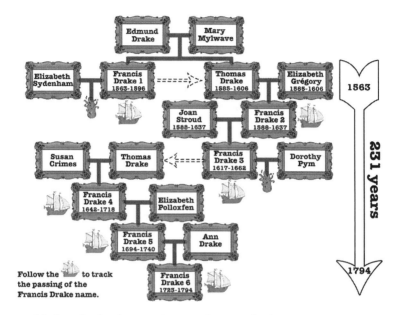

Simplified Drake family tree, showing the name 'Francis Drake' descending over nearly two hundred years. Follow the ship symbol. The slightest variation in events would make the same family tree unrecognisable.

Part 6 – The Man That Might Never Have Been

This whole exercise was no longer just about the curiosity of how a name like Francis Drake can be passed on for so many generations, this was now about how any one of those Francis Drakes, especially the first, ever came into existence at all.

A question for you:

What comes to mind when you read about the following three events in the early life of our famous ship commander?

(1) In part because his father Edmund sent him to work on a ship during his younger years, Francis 1 had a ship bequeathed to him in a family will.

(2) When Francis 1 later needed money to fund a rare chance of sailing full time under the command of his older, business-savvy cousins, he had that ship in his possession to sell.

You might, for example, ask yourself: *what if Francis' dad had sent him to work somewhere else?* Or: *what if Francis never sold the ship that he was gifted in a family will?* Or: *what if Francis had no cousins to speak of?* You might even be wondering: *what does any of this have to do with the Imposter Phenomenon?* What should become clear to you is that, if those events (and many others) never happened, if everything didn't all line up just so, there would likely never have been a Sir Francis Drake to speak of in the history books. At all. Francis' life could have been far less extravagant. And because his life, in this hypothetical 'what if?' case, is different, his brother Thomas' life would probably be wildly different, too. Imagine, then, all the ripples in your life that could have been tsunamis of something so very different than what you know.

Remember, Thomas Drake was the faithful brother who followed Francis on many of his seafaring quests. So, who's to say Sir Francis Drake's nephew, baby Francis (or Francis 2) would ever have been born through Thomas and his wife Elizabeth? Their distant descendant Lady Elliot-Drake might never have lived, never mind written a two-volume family history for anyone to later discover in an old bookshop.*

The early Drakes settled at the southwest coast of Britain around the mid-1300s, two hundred years before the Elizabethan admiral, the first Sir Francis Drake in this story, was born. Those earliest Drakes before the first Francis all had their own lives and loves and misfortunes to bear, all but forgotten, and all, it seemed, in just the right order to grow the branches of the tree towards Edmund and Mary Drake, mum and dad to Sir Francis Drake. It was only after reading all of this historic lore that a note made by Lady Elliot-Drake at the start of her book made any sense:

"...if the biography of any person could be written perfectly truthfully, if all could be told, there are few, even of the most ordinary beings, whose story would be without a deep human interest."

The once inaudible whisper in my head grew louder the more I devoured those little red leather books. Back in my apartment, I closed Lady Elliot-Drake's book and leaned back in smiling silence, waiting for my musical neighbours to return.

A family tree is amazingly insightful.

If you just take the time to look beyond a name, the stories will talk to you through a stunningly intricate collection of earth-shattering forks in the road. A perfectly truthful tale, from even the seemingly most unremarkable of people, took this story out of history and back into my own life.†

---

*Flash forward to Sir Francis Drake's slow death by dysentery, and even this undignified death becomes stunningly improbable when the details of Drake's life story are revealed. The fact that it was a fluid-draining illness that eventually claimed Francis was made surprising to me when I read of the many grave battle injuries he endured on several occasions before his delirious demise. It turned out, as I discovered while flicking through the Drake genealogy, that Francis could so easily have been one of his unfortunate brothers, Joseph or John, who both died during shared battles at sea.

†The amazing case of the Drakes is by no means the only famous family tree known. The longest known family tree is derived from the Chinese thinker Confucius (551-479 BC, who popularised the practice of paying respect to one's ancestors). For more than 2,000 years, his family tree has stretched through time, sprouting over 80 generations. Around the time of writing this book, Confucius had more than 1.3 million descendants alive in modern times.

Part 7 – Turning Inward

When I look back on finding the bookshop and reading about the Drake family tree, I think of all the other famous lineages I wanted to write about for you in this book. But as I was scrawling away, scraping through draft after draft, I was dealt a thunderous uppercut of perspective. The grand fortunes of family trees would later come alive on a far more personal level. Whilst all this reading of famous family trees was helping me escape from the ever-beckoning call to the Imposter Phenomenon, the same reading was soon to help me answer a deeper question; a question you should ask yourself:

"How likely is it that any of us emerge from our own family tree?"

A few years later, long after reading about family trees, I created a new family branch of my own. When my daughter was born, my wife and I took her to visit my grandparents. She, in her innocent ignorance, got to meet her great-grandparents. As my daughter lay smiling in my paternal grandfather's lap, with my grandmother smiling on, I scrambled for my phone and snapped a photograph.

My camera captured the shared gaze and collective joy of three people born three generations apart. Little did I know that it would be the first and last time my daughter would ever see the man who held her that day. A short time later, I received the phone call and news that no one ever wants to hear.

My grandfather (Archibald Reid), and grandmother (Margaret) met their great-granddaughter, Adaline, a few weeks after her birth and a few weeks before Archie's death.

With the hindsight of the Drake books, my grandfather's death moved me to understand how the baton had been passed down through my family tree to my daughter. I didn't have to look far.In their youth, my grandparents' hometown was bitterly segregated between Catholic and Protestant Christian upbringings.

Archie was raised Catholic, and Margaret was Protestant. Despite the often violent clashes between people on either side of this religious divide, there was one philosophy that Archie's and Margaret's parents shared: Catholics and Protestants should not mix. When Archie sent Margaret letters home from his army station in Germany, they both knew what their parents would think. So, when Archie and Margaret announced their intention to marry, Archie's father all but disowned him. Neither of their parents attended the wedding. But marry they did. And here I am.

The unlikeliness of my life was made even clearer during a conversation with my maternal grandfather. In 1960, nearly thirty years before I was born, our hometown suffered one of the world's worst-ever peacetime fires. A whisky warehouse on Glasgow's Cheapside Street set ablaze, killing nineteen fire servicemen.[73] Had my grandfather Joseph been working that night, the death toll would most likely have been twenty.

What if you turned this same lens on yourself? What if you considered how the baton of life was handed to you? What stories would you find? What twists in the tale would be revealed to show how you might never have been born? What if your grandparents had never hit it off? What if your great-grandmother's eyes had never met those of the man who would become your great-grandfather? Where would you be if any of these people were externally influenced to walk another way?

If you knew the true odds of being alive, how much would you really care about your fleeting and repeating imposter experiences? Here's how we put numbers against the enlightening unlikeliness of either you or me ever being here.

Part 8 – The Absolute Improbability of You

I originally left home for my academic secondment as a sunken mess. Ravaged by guilt and panic, I was one with the train floor. When I eventually returned home, I had a newfound boldness. By discovering a fascination with family trees and interrogating my own past, I was leading myself to another valuable hand in pulling myself up from the depths of the Imposter Phenomenon. So, what I'm ultimately getting at this:

The odds of you, me, any of us being born...are almost zero.

The truth is even more bizarre, because it's not merely the fact of being born you want to think about here. What about the likelihood of growing up in a place where your primary concern isn't survival, or war, or hunger? And what about the privilege of being so highly educated that the Imposter Phenomenon or experience (or whatever the hell we want to call it) is even on your radar? The improbability of all of those stars aligning in your favour is more than any divine miracle. It's statistically significant magic. I found out long after my business trip and reading about famous families that some people have actually worked out the numbers behind the stupidly low odds of being alive......

Author and clinical hypnotherapist, Dr Ali Binazir built the online dating platform, *Tao of Dating*[74] with the aim to improve success rates for those seeking love and companionship. His fourth book, by the way, subtitled *The Smart Woman's Guide to Being Absolutely Irresistible*, spent four years atop the Amazon chart for dating books. To understand the likelihood of finding a companion, Binazir wrote a blog on the chances of ever being born. He valiantly stuck a wet finger in the air and calculated sensible odds of you becoming you. In other words, Binazir wondered just how likely it was that a family tree, like the Francis Drake case or any other, could ever grow over time.

It starts with a simple question. How likely is it that your father ever met your mother? In the TV show *How I Met Your Mother*,[75] it took nine years and 208 episodes for the intricacies of a chance event like boy meets girl to play out; the numbers Ali Binazir calculated made it clear why. If your father met one new person every single day between ages 15 and 40, that would add up to 10,000 people.

You could then ask how many people he *could* have possibly met. If you loosely assume he worked, lived, and travelled across 10% of the globe, that would be a possible 400 million people (assuming the world's population 20 years before the time of Binazir publishing his blog in 2011). Half of those 400 million possible interactions would be female, meaning your dad had a 10,000 divided by 200 million or a 1 in 20,000 chance of meeting your mum. That's a 0.005% chance of you having the parents that you know. But this doesn't even scratch the surface of how stupendously unlikely it is that you are sitting here now, alive and breathing and reading this book.

Consider now that, even if your parents were lucky enough to have bumped into each other, beating the odds of 1 in 20,000, there was also an additional, say, 1 in 10 chance that they ever spoke to one another. On top of that, there's a 1 in 10 chance that they went on a first date, a 1 in 10 chance that they went on a second date, and a 1 in 10 chance that they went on more serious dates over the longer term. For good measure, there's also a coin flip of a chance, a 50:50 shot, that they stayed together long enough to consider conceiving a child (who may or may not have become you, but more on that later).

By the time you multiply all those additional odds together, the chance of your parents' union resulting in a kid is about 1 in 2,000 overall. But wait. That 1 in 2,000 is multiplied by the tiny 1 in 20,000 chance of your mum and dad ever meeting in the first place. At this stage, the overall calculated odds of your parents meeting, having a relationship, and having a kid (who may not even be you) is a staggering 1 in 40 *million.*

Around the same odds as picking 6 lotto jackpot-winning num-

bers from a choice of numbers 1 through 59.

If this *still* doesn't convince you that your life is riding the same unlikely path as the Francis Drake name, here's where Binazir's back-of-the-envelope odds of existing get seriously mind-blowing.

Nothing in this hypothetical meeting of your parents has cared to mention the probability of the most obvious event that had to happen for you to be here. (Cue the soft saxophone music). Eventually, after all the successful dates, and the relationship becoming more serious, there was conception. The right sperm had to meet the right egg at the right time. Those odds alone, forgetting all the other stuff about dad meeting mum, are around 1 in 400 trillion (that's 400 with *15 zeros after it*). And that's just for the generation of your family (your parents) that directly resulted in you. What, then, about the odds of your grandparents each producing your mother and father, or your great-grandparents producing your grandparents, and so on, for 150,000 generations back to the start of human existence? I suspect you're now getting the point.

If you took anything from the story about passing on the Francis Drake name five times over 200 years, imagine what it means to have passed the baton not five times...but 150,000 times, in order to get to you. To put a number on it, that's a 1 in 10^{45000} chance of all your ancestors surviving to produce you. And by the time you multiply all the odds of all these crazy events that had to align, the chance that you are here now, worrying about imposter syndrome is about 1 in $10^{2685000000}$. There are only 1080 atoms in the known Universe. In truth, I don't know how best to distil these odds, but I can safely tell you this:

The odds of your existence are practically zero.

You, me, Francis Drake, his honourably-named descendants, everyone you have ever known, loved, laughed with, and cried for, are all insanely improbable flashes of consciousness. The survival of your ancestors and the passing of their baton down the ages to you is genuinely more valuable than any lotto win, and less likely than rolling the same number on a pair of trillion-sided dice. Evolutionary biologist Professor Richard Dawkins puts this point of ancestry eloquently:

"No doubt some of your cousins and great-uncles died in childhood, but not a single one of your ancestors did. Ancestors just don't die young!"[76]

It's not just lofty university professors who have helped make us aware of the minuscule odds of being alive. Gary Vaynerchuk, wine selling entrepreneur turned social media marketing motivator, pulls no punches in his interpretation:

"Your mum and dad could have had sex three minutes later and you wouldn't even exist."[77]

For all those Francis Drakes that emerged as the name was passed from one to the next, each one of them was winning the lotto jackpot and then some. When my paternal grandparents decided to ignore their religious parents and marry regardless, when my maternal grandfather unconsciously avoided a fatal nightshift with the fire service, I was unknowingly winning the game of rolling two trillion-sided dice and getting the same number on both. If my wife's Austrian grandmother was of another religion, she, as a child, would never have come to Scotland, but rather perished under Hitler's spine-chilling persecution.

In the words of Imposter Phenomenon pioneer Pauline Clance:

"In truth, they may indeed have had a certain amount of luck. Yet what they forget is that they had the capacity and intelligence to utilise the good fortune that came their way and to make the most of it."[78]

Part 9 – Summary

There is an almost taboo side to the Imposter Phenomenon and why it occurs. Far from a simple self-loathing or veil of unworthiness, we can link imposter experiences to self-centredness. Thinking about the decorated randomness of a family tree is one example of a gratitude exercise. Gratitude exercises help us take the time to be mindful of what we have, rather than fretting about what we don't.

If you consider your family tree, whether you can trace it back two generations, 20, or 200, it doesn't matter. Your family tree is as long as that of Confucius or the Drakes, because you're here, now. Your ancestors, from cave dwellers to city slickers, have brought you into the world, and given you a shot.

An articulate view on being thankful for who you are comes from legendary Hollywood talent manager Shep Gordon (who counted Alice Cooper and Pink Floyd among his clients). As a fortunate Jewish American looking back on an illustrious career, Shep said:

"...just where you drop out of the womb, you won the game...You have a chance. You can get clean water. You get food. Hopefully you get some love. There's not a bomb dropping on your head every second. That alone is something to meditate on every day..." [79]

From the business trip that led to the discovery of the Francis Drake story, to the revelations from my grandparents, I tried to apply some of this big picture thinking to my never-ending bouts of feeling like an imposter at work. Whenever I'd been wading through the sludge of imposter experiences, I was too immersed to ever consider that this curse was actually a blessing. Being able to sit here, write this book, call myself a scientist struggling with imposter experiences...is a privilege.

Ancestry is a way to help us remain truly grateful to have been born somewhere in the world where our baseless imposter experiences – not a lack of food or water or love or shelter – are of central concern.

Websites like Ancestry.com exist because we all have that eternal itch to scratch. Subconsciously, we want to know where we came from because we all know where we will end up, and we don't want to talk about that.

So, look at your experiences as a fraud, those times you thought you weren't qualified to be in the room, and remind yourself of a simple question:

What are you grateful for?

Sometimes, it takes a serious wake-up call to remember that we make mountains out of molehills. After all, I moved two hundred miles away and locked myself in academic solitude to learn this lesson through books I might never have chanced upon!

Yet, beyond this super useful revelation, you and I both know we can't always rely on the Big Picture perspective to stop us worrying about the same old same old. That's what I want to explore with you in the next chapter. Far from the grandeur of family trees, we're going down to the gritty base unit of fear that feeds the Imposter Phenomenon.

Nothing kicks you in the ass harder than rejection. And the story behind this one, is a story I am ashamed to tell...

Your Chapter Challenges

1. The branches of your family tree can reveal the chance occurrences that led to you. Remember, none of your direct ancestors died before having children.

Map a few generations of your family. You can use the template in the accompanying journal toolkit to prompt you.

For each person you add to the tree, write down one event from their life that had to happen to eventually lead to you.

2. Worrying about imposter experiences is a privilege, not a burden. Be mindful that you fell out into the world in a place where you have a shot to do something other than worry about food.

Identify and list the elements of your imposter experiences that could be reframed as things to be grateful for.

The chance of meeting those around you is even more unlikely than either one of you being born.

3. The odds of you being alive are practically zero.

For those who need to hear it, share the ridiculous estimated odds of being alive.

For the conversation, or email, or tweet (however you want to share your challenge), that statistic again is 1 in $10^{2685000000}$. Take a picture of the graphic below to start sharing these empowering odds!

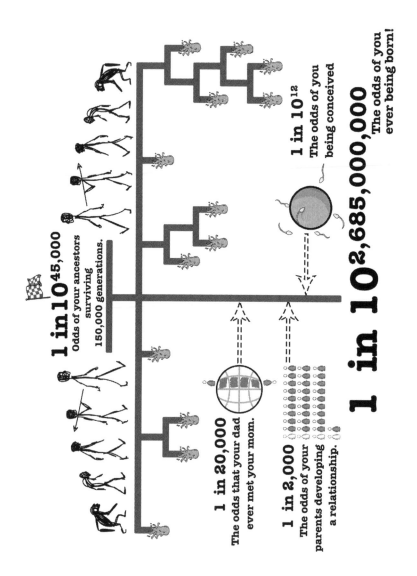

1 in 10^45,000
Odds of your ancestors surviving 150,000 generations.

1 in 20,000
The odds that your dad ever met your mom.

1 in 2,000
The odds of your parents developing a relationship.

1 in 10^12
The odds of you being conceived

1 in 10^2,685,000,000
The odds of you ever being born!

Chapter 6: Failing Better

There is no doubt that you will have people you admire and look up to. Despite what your imposter thoughts would make you assume about these people, no one is ever perfectly produced. Not from any place, or from any time. And yet, there remains the temptation to assume the success of those in your sphere has somehow been endowed.

While your efforts toward a goal feel like drudgery, their achievements look divinely inspired. Why is that? What do we often forget to place in context? Even if you think you are too young, too old, too specialised, too niche, or too novice to apply yourself to an opportunity, you are none of these things. They are, on the other hand, exquisite excuses to avoid ever trying, or ever failing. Whether you're on an academic track like me or part of another profession entirely, failure is part of your footpath. Fear of that failure plays right into the hands of the Imposter Phenomenon.

Part 1 – Failing to Handle Failure

When you think of someone who has (for lack of a better term) 'made it', how do you think they got there? Is that person a genius or cleverer than everyone else? Do they take risks with ease? Are they riding solely on the luck of their demographic lottery win?

The temptation is to answer 'yes' to all of the above, to think that the successful person is smarter than you, braver than you, and better equipped for professional success than you will ever be.

This is certainly how most instances of my imposter panic were initiated in my postdoctoral research days. I kept on assuming that all my colleagues — whom I judged as better than me — had just somehow been 'successful' for all of time. I had the unwavering assumption that these people had never known hardship, or stress, or failure. Only by digging deeper, by finding the hidden histories in the stories of success did I come to grow a healthier set of assumptions on how a successful person ever came to be.

A huge part of any imposter experience is rooted in a fear of rejection. As we first discussed in Chapter 2, the Imposter Cycle can keep you on a loop of an unsustainable workload, never stopping to accept praise for fear of never being able to repeat a particular win. Repeated rejection is the fuel that keeps the Imposter Cycle spinning. Repeat rejection is everywhere inside academia and everywhere beyond.[80]

Among the participants I surveyed as part of my own Imposter Phenomenon research, the vast majority strongly agreed with three telling statements on failure. Contrary to any evidence or support for their eminent competence, most people reported a tendency to remember their failures over their successes. People suffering from imposter experiences are bound by a collective fear of professional failure.

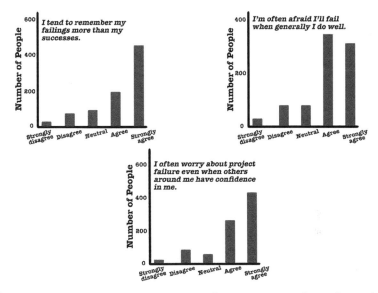

Imposter Phenomenon Score questions probing participant relationship with failure.

In academia, the fear could be related to rejection of your manuscript from a journal, rejection from an awards process, rejection of a grant proposal, rejection of a job application, rejection from a special society membership, or perhaps rejection in the form of countless failed experiments in the lab. Outside higher education, this freezing fear might be manifest in a career pivot, a bid for promotion, or performing for an unfamiliar audience. The scenarios and environments may differ between each of us. Nonetheless, the fear of failure overlaps with a fundamental fear of all things unknown.

A tempting and easy thing to do when you are rejected is to find an external excuse for it. You might exhibit what psychologists refer to as an *external locus of control*.[81] Coupled with the imposter experience telling you that you're not good enough, you might put rejection down to the biassed system that is out to get you.

You could blame your failure on a bias against, say, your naive youth, where you come from, your previous place of work, or countless other possible injustices in the world.

It is partly true that certain external forces in play can work against you.* Yet, while a long list of external factors can predispose any of us to failure, it is far from the whole story.

External factors do not reflect what is in *your* own control.

There is an uncomfortable amount you can understand about rejection and failure that can help place powerful responsibility back on one pair of shoulders. Your own.

I was only a year into a career path that typically demands 3–4 years' experience after training, so my exploration of more senior positions seemed risky, at best. Some people I spoke to thought I was wasting my time. I was inclined to agree. Nevertheless, having set a direction for what I wanted my broader life to be, I listed all the possible routes forward to an academic post that I could find or imagine: lectureships, junior research fellowships, part-sponsored fellowships, group leadership opportunities, adjunct professorships, all of them! After filtering out those adverts that strictly demanded more experienced applicants, I settled on a list of four jobs that I wanted to go for.

There's nothing quite like reminding yourself of an application deadline date to instil some creative urgency. See above, procrastination and the Imposter Cycle (**Chapter 2**)! This was probably the single greatest benefit to taking an early and arguably futile start to applying for positions beyond my reach.

If you think you are not good enough, not the right fit, not the right gender, the wrong age, wrong shape, not the right colour or creed to even start applying for your next role, question those assumptions. Rather than worrying about failure before you have ever tasted it,

---

*For just one scary data driven example, check out the website *WTF Happened in 1971*, where you will see statistics on arrested growth on all sorts of dimensions since 1971 that make any individual progress now much harder than it was one or two generations ago. Find the wide-ranging time series at: https://bit.ly/3JF3NOV.

have you ever thought about what you would gain if you *allowed* yourself to fail? Targeting an opportunity before you think you're ready will focus your mind on a key question:

What do you actually want for your future?

When I put that question in my head for the four academic research positions I was considering, my eyes widened and my peripheral vision blurred. I had direction. I thought deeply and obsessively about current problems in my discipline, and the sorts of chemical solutions I was equipped to create. I read various literatures voraciously, bounced ideas off colleagues, took notes, scrapped notes, and crafted summary schemes on a never-ending drip feed of loose paper sheets.

Despite my focus, I never stopped narrating to myself that this was all pointless, that I had no chance of competing for the jobs I was applying for. But what I could do with my inane insecure internal nattering was to acknowledge it, and then focus, focus, focus on the task at hand...these bloody job applications and their submission deadlines!

After eventually hitting 'send' on all the job applications, those familiar thoughts of being a phoney eventually came flooding back when rejection letters started oozing into my email account. I didn't handle the news at all well.

I wasn't fully prepared for when I received my first rejection letter. My shoulders sank, and I sighed, but something bubbled beyond plain disappointment. I was overcome by a strong and disturbing sensation of downright *mediocrity*.

The words "We regret to inform you..." stared back at me from an unfeeling font, and my eyes absorbed the size 11 text as if it towered above me at point size 80. By the time I had staggered onto the second paragraph of the rejection letter, I could have struck a match on my tongue. The phrase "high volume of well-qualified applicants" haunted my every thought in the minutes and hours and days that followed. *Was I not good enough? Were my ideas not worthy of exploration? Who had been judged more suitable than me?* I let my ego get the best of me. I thought I deserved to be on the interview shortlist, and I wasn't.

Rather than focusing on how to up my game and improve my chances for the next such application, I turned off my computer screen (not bothering to shut the thing down), stormed home from the lab, bounded upstairs to my shitty little rented room, and punched the tired pillow on my bed. Many times. A breathlessness consumed me. Tears wet my lashes. A fly on the wall would've seen a big kid set ablaze by a tantrum.

At the time of that first rejection letter, I didn't have the mental resources to take the failure for what it was worth. I wasn't able to use it to build some actionable responsibility for how to improve the future me over the present me. And little did I know, in those enraged moments, that my first rejection would later sit in a collection with a second, and a third, and a fourth.

We all want to be accepted, and losing out on a job can feel like having a knife plunged into your side, and the handle slowly twisted. Rejection, compounded by observing the achievements of our peers,[82] laid bare on social media,[83] can fuel a perplexingly jealous panic, and an unanswered scream:

Why am I not able to achieve what these other people have achieved?

In such times, all your efforts might seem hopeless.

Beware that imposter experiences can strike hardest during times of rejection.

Rejection can act like the first domino to fall in a cascade of thoughts that lead you to conclude that you are not good enough to ever succeed. For those in academia, it is understandably tempting to view it as the singular institutional framework in which repeated rejection is at its most fierce, but this is only partly true.

While academia does well to foster enduring rejection as some sort of initiation, it is by no means an experience particular to that one environment, and treating it as such isn't helping anyone. Not you. Not me. No one.

From the all-consuming depths of a tear-soaked pillow, during those rejection-filled postdoc years, I had to find a way to deal with the painful fact that I was going to have the door shut on my face again and again. I have found some therapeutic gems in the lore of failure that I want to share with you. Reading some of the stories I will share with you now helped me bring more discipline and maturity to how I handled failure. More surprisingly, among those to help me reframe what, previously, I could only see as a horrible embarrassment, was an old lady from London.

Part 2 – We Regret to Inform You

The Bulldog in Old Lace

London, in the 1950s, was amidst a rebirth after the troubles of the war. A new Queen was crowned. The clatter of horses had all but been replaced by metallic beetles on wheels. This was the time before tablets and swiping, when Technicolor TV and telephones in red boxes were all the rage. And, while the nation's wartime leader Winston Churchill was now fighting a battle against old age, a cello could be heard playing in the city's West End.

An elderly woman, with long toughened fingers, wearing a berry hat, firm old lace dress, and long overcoat, sat gliding her bow across the four strings of her lonely orchestral instrument. Alongside her sheet music, and a collection box, stood a tall sign at about half her height. The sign was covered top to bottom in immaculate horizontal hand-painted words, displayed with linearity, regularity, and strict discipline as if produced on a keyboard. Passers-by walking slow enough to look over the woman's busking pitch, or the park rangers who stopped to move her on, would read the words on her sign:

"Dear People,

Do not think I profess to be a musician, but despair makes me play to you to obtain your attention. I have been trying 20 years to get a novel published and have come to the painful conclusion that, without influence, acceptance in these difficult times would be a miracle.

While I do not want your charity I appeal to you – is there anyone here who could help me to get one of my six novels published? Human stories which if well produced would make amusing films or radio serials likely to appeal to a wide public.

Yours sincerely,

Zora Raeburn"[84]

It's time for you to meet Zora Raeburn.

The description I just gave you of our old lady playing music in the streets of London comes from a collection of photographs taken by Ken Russell (who would later go on to become a famous film director). Zora never knew such fame, but she was familiar with the cheers of a thankful audience. This elderly solo street cellist had once sat with an orchestra inside the building whose crumbling remains she later busked outside. The only cheers she heard later in life were the sporadic clattering of coins each time one would fall into her collection box from the hand of a passing stranger.

If, at this point, in learning any of this story, you are feeling sorry for Zora, don't. This curious character, who played alone, dwarfed by the towering pillars outside the National Gallery on Trafalgar Square, has a rather inspiring story to tell. We are not merely addressing old Zora Raeburn here. No, no. We are playing back the memory of the title of Ken Russell's photo collection. Our lady on the street was *"Zora, the unvanquished"*.[85]

If you were to search online for Zora Raeburn right now, you would more than likely find a handful of blogs and social media posts, all telling more or less the same paragraph's worth of story behind the same single image of Zora. The most well-known image of our sweet and mysterious cellist shows her standing on the second-highest rung of a step ladder. She's next to the brick wall of a building that is taller than the frame of the image. With her right hand gripping the top of the ladder, her left wielded an old pointing stick; the kind you'd expect the harshest of school teachers to use for more than merely pointing at the blackboard.

For the purpose of Ken Russell's camera, Zora was pointing at a roughly 14 x 16 grid of single paper sheets stuck to the facade. There were around 200 pieces of paper in all. And when you zoom in on this patchy grid of paper, you see that each is a handwritten or typed note. Each and every one of those paper sheets was a rejection letter addressed to Zora Raeburn. The grid to which this youthful pensioner pointed showed a montage of rejection letters from publishers, libraries, film studios, and radio producers. Yet, here Zora was, in her seventies, still looking for ways to publish one of her six unloved manuscripts.

Your internet search to find this same photograph would tell you of Zora's financial challenges and inventive commitment to spending time on trying to publish her work. In her flat near the British Museum, she rented out two rooms in her home to pay the rent. She also took work as a shorthand typist to supplement her modest pension. That's all you will read in the available captions, but the shorthand typing job Zora took needs more spotlight. Shorthand, or *stenography*, is written on a stenotype machine. Whereas the modern QWERTY keyboard has 104 individual keys, the steno machine has just 22.

If you've ever watched a crime drama where lawyers are verbally sparring during a court trial, the person in the corner, furiously following the action at their tiny typewriter, is the shorthand typist. On the left of the stenotype machine are letters used to symbolise the start of a word. On the right, corresponding keys for the end of words. A row along the bottom gives the vowels, and a singular central asterisk key takes on several functions. Watch any YouTube video that explains shorthand type on a steno machine and you will see this is not a skill to be sniffed at. With the stretch of pinkie fingers, and the beautiful contortions of simultaneously pressed combinations of keys, shorthand type verges on piano virtuosity. Shorthand type is a career skill, not a menial job. Zora had this whole other career path to help supplement her passion to publish her writing!

Beyond the sad picture of Zora that is so easy to paint, there's more to her story than could be met through the eye of Ken Russell's photo collection. More that reveals this story of rejection to be an inspiring one. Indeed, Ken Russell's not the only passer-by to have taken an interest in the cellist trying to sell her book rights on London's streets. Journalist Noel Whitcomb spoke with Zora on at least two occasions in the space of as many years. He wrote about her for his newspaper column. The inventive methods Zora used to earn her rent and subsistence was supplemented by the fact that she lived very modestly. As Whitcomb would capture in his column, Zora was:

"Managing to live decently on less than some people spend on cigarettes" and *"wear a silk shantung dress that once was expensive"*, and from a later report, *"eating became an occasional luxury"*.[86]

Zora's modesty harmonised with her unsung charity. In an interview with Zora, Whitcomb captured the fact that Zora's busking collection box was not for her own needs. She played for the attention of a publisher, not for any money. To quote her own words from the Whitcomb interviews, she wouldn't spend that money on herself *"until I was absolutely forced to"*. Most of the sixpence and shillings she collected went to the blind. With one such busking collection, she bought a bunch of violets from an old man who had struggled to sell anything on a particularly bleak Thursday.

Over a cup of tea in Zora's little abode, Whitcomb discovered that Zora's impressive collection of publisher rejections was not always so gloomy. Quoting Zora once again, she revealed to her curious journalistic audience one reason for why she kept striving to publish her work:

"I don't wish to appear conceited, but I think the publishers are wrong. One of my books was actually accepted by a publisher in 1940. I thought I was in at last. But three days later, he was bombed. After that, no luck. I decided I hadn't much time left to achieve my ambition. So, I had to do something desperate."

This is when our tireless novelist started playing music on the streets. In these darkest moments for Zora, she had actually tried wheeling a piano around before realising the more practically manageable size of her cello. Having been a lifelong orchestra musician, playing alongside her estranged conductor husband, she had instruments collecting dust in her little apartment.

And as she performed, she was met by gleeful children playing around her, by curious photographers, journalists, and other rejected writers, but never a publisher. Yet Zora never let this apparent emptiness stop her. In a mindful reflection of the negativity she could have nurtured, she remembered:

"What this experience has taught me I can hardly tell you. Before I began playing in the street – when things were looking so black – I was beginning to feel hard and heartless…That troubled me, because I've always believed that ordinary people were really decent and kind. All my books have been about small people with big hearts. And now I know again that it's true."

Playing in the streets, for the love of her work, Zora was given donations by a deaf person who could not hear her play, and gifted sweet pink flowers from the man whose livelihood she'd helped save.

Clearly captivated by Zora Raeburn, Noel Whitcomb bade her farewell having borrowed one of her manuscripts. In underlined italicised trepidation, he signed off his first newspaper column about Zora saying, *"I am almost afraid to read it. I do so want it to be good."*

Two years later, Whitcomb returned to speak to the still rejected Zora who, beyond her radical bids to find a publisher on the streets, had now gone one step further. In an act that, today, is normalised beyond repute, Zora had eventually decided to self-publish. Funded by her efforts as a shorthand typist and a subletting landlady, Zora funded the publication of *Disillusioned*, seeking 8 shillings and sixpence a copy (about £10 or $14 (US) per copy today).

Alas, despite achieving what today would yield at least a modest success for anyone with an e-book, this wasn't the end of Zora's rejections. In the 1950s, self-publishing was still exceedingly rare. Some fifty years before Zora's time, Beatrix Potter had successfully self-published,[87] and was later picked up by a publisher who had previously rejected Peter Rabbit, but it wasn't to be for Noel Whitcomb's so-called "bulldog in old lace". London bookstores in the 1950s were unanimously reluctant to sell a work that was self-published. They wouldn't make any shelf space for *Disillusioned*. And yet, on Zora went. She chose herself. She had a poster made, marketing the book's front cover and the bold all-caps lettering:

DISILLUSIONED
BY
ZORA

Through Ken Russell's camera, Zora was captured dragging this poster behind her wherever she went; through winter snow, and through pigeon-covered town squares, but never through the door of another book publisher.

Zora Raeburn was the pen name of Selma Rawlinson. Housewife, musician, typist, and, finally, self-published novelist. She died in Westminster, London, in 1981 at the age of 97, knowing that nothing had stopped her publishing her work. Not poverty, not family break-ups, not 200+ rejections, not a wartime bombing of her one-time accepted publisher, not old age, not the need to entertain other careers, and not the once ridiculous taboo of self-publishing. She recognised the ease with which she could have given up, and the trap of turning the finger of blame on the "hard and heartless" world around her.

Ken Russell's famous image of Zora pointing at her montage of rejection letters is aptly titled with the phrase that anyone facing repeated rejection will have forever burned on their soul:

"We regret to inform you...".

The story of Zora was what I wish I'd found back when I was first collecting my own rejection letters. It's the story that ultimately convinced me to choose myself and self-publish the book you're now kindly reading.

Zora Raeburn knew how to separate the power of what lay in her control from the world whose external forces she was powerless to change.

I struggle to imagine what I could achieve for myself if I had a tenth of the resilience and self-reliance of Zora Raeburn. Can you? The journalist Noel Whitcomb, Zora's champion columnist, leaves all of us who have suffered the self-doubt of repeated rejection with a worthy challenge:

"If all of those authors could have equalled the tenacity of Zora Raeburn, maybe the world would have another library."

More Rejected Writers

If you're in the camp of thinking that academia is uniquely troubled, you're as wrong as I once was. Because, in a profession that demands a lot of writing, you need only look to writers more broadly, outside the universities and institutions, beyond Zora Raeburn, to see that academia is not so special. Repeated rejection is everywhere.

Now, be warned. I'm about to give you more examples of writers' rejections than you might think are necessary to make any point of relevance to rejection, or our imposter discussion. You might understand the point more quickly than I ever did, but I still think it is useful for us to review the handful of failed attempts from the struggling triers of the world that I have chanced upon, those that have helped me challenge my own views on what rejection means, and that I hope will challenge you. Here goes...

J.K. Rowling, of a certain boy wizard fame, was (as a struggling single mother) rejected from 12 publishers before finding a home for *Harry Potter and the Philosopher's Stone* at Bloomsbury Publishing in London.[88] She, for all the controversy that later threatened to overshadow her work, has donated more money to charities than most people ever have money to spend. Stephanie Meyer, who wrote the young adult *Twilight* book series, read 14 '*we regret to inform you*' letters before publishing the book that would later spawn a $3.3 billion (US) movie franchise.

John Grisham, one of the most prolific thriller novelists the US has ever produced, worked through 12 rejections and no fewer than 16 literary agents before being supported to publish his first novel, *A Time to Kill*, in 1988. Since then, he's written a novel every year, peaking at over 300 million books in print across 40 languages.[89]

I'm not even nearly finished. Gertrude Stein submitted her literary works for over 22 years before publishing the likes of the now adored classic, *The Autobiography of Alice B. Toklas*,[90] written in the voice of Stein's life partner, and now considered one of the top 20 non-fiction works of the 20th century.

The famous English novel, *Lord of the Flies*,[91] written by William Golding, is one I'm thankful to have read in my own high school English classes. That book could so easily never have been. It was refused twenty times before its first release in 1954. More than half a century later, even Golding's early rough drafts of his book are now considered museum-worthy artifacts.[92]

It took the keen and teary eye of Doubleday's publishing editor Judith Jones to pull a 15-times rejected diary of a young Jewish girl from the unwanted pile. Despite *The Diary of Anne Frank* being published in Dutch and French by 1950, it spent a further two years in exile until Jones convinced the New York branch of her publisher to print the now-infamous English edition of this most harrowing day-to-day account of a family hoping to escape Nazi persecution.[93]

Stephen King's horror novel *Carrie* was rejected 30 times (some reports say 80)[94] before it ever saw a dust jacket. In his memoir, *On Writing*,[95] King recalled an eerily similar practice to Zora Raeburn, pinning all his writing rejection slips to a wall:

"By the time I was fourteen, the nail in my wall would no longer support the weight of the rejection slips impaled upon it. I replaced the nail with a spike and went on writing."

Jonathan Livingston Seagull is not an author, but rather the eponymous subject of Richard Bach's 140-times rejected novella that later topped the New York Times bestseller list for 37 weeks in 1972.[96]

Even these collected tales of terrifying and repeated rejection look like child's play compared to one William Saroyan, an American-born son of Armenian immigrants, who was orphaned at three years old in 1911. Before selling his first short story (ironically following the woes of a starving young writer) in 1934, he amassed a pile of rejection slips 30 inches tall.[97] That's 14 golf tees, or 55 Aspirin tablets, or slightly over half of a Danny DeVito! Saroyan would later win a Pulitzer Prize and Academy Award for his writing. The list of rejection stories goes on. Jesmyn Ward endured three years of rejection before selling her first novel. She's now the first woman to ever win the U.S. National Book Award twice.[98] Richard Adams endured 26 rejections before sharing *Watership Down* with the world,[99] and it took Margaret Mitchell until her 39th attempt to get any support for *Gone with the Wind*.[100]

All these writers had the discipline to sacrifice comfort to see their projects through to the end. Their projects had a clear end goal, and every rejection was comforted by the clear image they each had of one day holding a hard copy of their own book in their work-weary hands. They didn't focus on a linear career path. They didn't stop writing when the first rejection came in. They reviewed, refined, reworked, and rewrote their pieces, making them better after each 'no' they received.

Yet, there are times when rejection can be overcome, not merely by refining your work after judgement, but by choosing to put your work out there regardless of what certain gatekeepers would have you think. When my daughter was a carefree toddler, we would eat breakfast together, and talk while we watched a delightful animated TV series about a mischievous rabbit dressed in a blue coat.

Those precious memories of laughing with my daughter would not exist if Beatrix Potter, who was also an accomplished scientist and conservationist, hadn't realised that the rejections she received for *The Tale of Peter Rabbit* did not necessarily mean it was game over. After being turned down by six publishers, Potter privately produced 250 copies of her book on 16 December 1901, merely to circulate among family and friends. This tiny offering became so successful inside its first year that one of the six publishers who originally rejected Potter's book helped take it to a much bigger audience. Over a hundred years on, copies of Potter's original self-published story about that naughty little rabbit in a blue coat have sold for upward of £35,000 (about $48,000).

It's easy to assume that rejections of your work are entirely attributable to your initial offering being crap, or not at a quality needed for publication. Just as likely, your rejected work didn't fit a publisher's assumed target audience, track record, remit, image, or ethos. We each fear rejection from a group more than rejection of our work itself. Before considering yourself a failure, a fraud, and a reject, consider all the reasons why you might have been told 'no'.

Consider that these rejections, as painful as they are in the moment, might be your unseeable first round of revisions that helps you reach new heights for the right audience. Consider that there are more routes to success than there are gatekeepers to be rejected by.

A long list of external factors might predispose you to failure. Avoid adding self-sabotage to that list.

Consider that seeking out rejections might be one of the best things you can do on the road to the success you later define for yourself.

If your imposter experiences are driven by the fear of rejection, what happens if you test the fear? What if you could manage rejection by inviting it? What if...you learned to love rejection?

Part 3 - Rejection Therapy

In 2017, marketing manager turned entrepreneur Jia Jiang gave a TED talk in which he told the story of embracing rejection for 100 days.[101] He asked a stranger to borrow $100, asked for a burger refill at a restaurant, and asked his college professor if he could teach the class that Jiang was a student of. These, and 97 other exercises in rejection, Jiang captured on video.

Watching it back, he didn't feel the sickness or spine-chilling fear that consumed him in the early iterations of his rejection experiment. He simply observed the outcome, and realised he was still here, living to be rejected another day. As the experiment progressed, so too did the amount of time Jiang would stand with a person after he got rejected. He would go back for more, call out the doubt and the weirdness he and his unfortunate unwitting volunteer were both feeling. To Jiang, the rejections felt less and less like personal attacks and more and more like the refinement of a new skill.

In rejection therapy,[102] you set yourself up for a fall and then thank someone for it. You don't wait for rejection to find you, you find rejection! You taunt it. Dance with it. Embrace it. And, after all is said and done, thank whoever rejected you. This may sound strange, weird, or downright silly, but challenge yourself on that thought. Is looking for opportunities to be rejected *really* so stupid?

You don't dodge the mental punch of someone saying 'no' to you, you take it! When Jia Jiang ran his rejection therapy experiment, he wasn't anyone highborn or noble. He was simply someone who had faced a paralysing fear of rejection that he wanted to control.[103] He faced the humbling truth that he was afraid of being outcast and left unwanted. His experimental solution was to fight fire with fire, to face rejection by finding it 100 times in 100 days, and in doing so, he gradually realised an important albeit counterintuitive psychological fact.

Most of your thoughts – no matter how dark or foreboding – are thoughts and no more. They have no hidden meaning, no code to crack. They are thoughts that can be recognised and managed. Emotions need not manage you. By inviting rejection, you can materialise the unthreatening reality of rejection rather than predicting its worst possible outcome.

You can face real rejection to avoid the anxiety of forecasting all the bad thing that *might* happen.

Looking back at my first academic fellowship rejection, and my childish outburst, I now shudder to think of how I behaved at that time. Back then, I was so confident that I deserved to be shortlisted for an interview that any other reality, any chance of rejection seemed altogether unfathomable. I've worked damn hard to get to where I am today, and through many broken family situations, any one of which would have been ample excuse to quit. But in pouring my blood into the effort of applying for jobs, my blinkers of focus, my effort, my passion, my hope, my willingness to succeed, all blinded me to one rather obvious possibility that, when whispered to myself, set in motion that earlier stream of tears, pillow punches, and dull screams:

"Someone out there, applying for the same job, at the same moment, was probably more ready, more suitable, more prepared, or more of

an apparent fit for the role than you were."

A full week after my first fellowship rejection news, I didn't want to go to work. I didn't feel worthy to go to work. My once proud, military march was demoted to a hunched hobble of injured despair. It couldn't possibly go on like this...

One of the main things that kept me going was reminding myself of the insane privilege of being here to feel so disheartened by failure. That said, beyond finding Jia Jiang's story of rejection therapy, there was still something missing. I longed for a more career-focused tool to make the mess of rejection more tangible. And it's something completely absent from the résumé we each work so hard to decorate for our job applications.

Part 4 – Your CV of Failures

Your résumé (or *curriculum vitae*, CV) is the piece of paper that gets you in the door, but it doesn't get you the job. Nonetheless, there's a ubiquitous and understandable unspoken agreement among career-minded people that we each must decorate our CVs with honours, successes, society memberships, awards, achievements, papers, experiences, and extracurricular activities. Your CV catalogues what you assume is the best of what you have accomplished. Alas, while you focus on perfecting and polishing your CV, it is only ever half of your story (if that). After all, any tendency you have to think you are an imposter will lead you to conclude that no evidence of your achievements is ever going to be good enough. Remember those top ten Imposter Phenomenon phrases from **Chapter 3**?

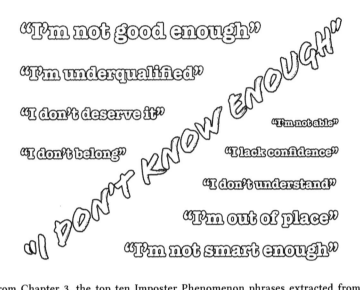

From Chapter 3, the top ten Imposter Phenomenon phrases extracted from participant responses.

Your CV might help collect all those things you think will please the employer you are trying to impress, but the CV falls short of showing the fullness of your efforts. That same CV completely omits any experience of professional rejection the likes of which we've spent most of this chapter discussing. There is, however, another side of your CV that you might never have considered, a sister document that too often remains blank, unused, and uninhabited.

In 2010, neurobiologist Dr Melanie Stefan published a column in the journal *Nature* that sparked a counterintuitive sensation among scientists. Having recently been denied a research fellowship, Dr Stefan reflected on how her hidden rejections compared to her far more visible successes. She emerged from school and university with the grades she needed to be accepted onto the PhD program she wanted. So far, so good. But when she tried to move into a more independent post, she saw the harsh reality of ultra-competitive academia. She was trying to jump from the fish pond to the shark tank.

Academic jobs like the one that Melanie was applying for often have a less than 1 in 7 chance of success. Her CV was good but, in Melanie's own words, it did not *"reflect the bulk of my academic efforts"*. She contrasted her hidden failures against the far more transparent failures of a footballer exposed to constant media criticism. She wondered why it was that we tend (even subconsciously) to hide all those shots at success we take that never pay off. This contradiction inspired Dr Stefan to suggest that we each write an 'alternative CV' to go alongside our traditional CV. That alternative CV idea has now caught a perpetual wind under the name *CV of Failures*.[104]

When I first heard about the concept of a *CV of Failures*, it was a revelation. This 'shadow CV', should you choose to write it, serves to record all the times that you have failed, all the jobs that you were rejected from, all the papers that were tossed aside after peer review, all the grants, fellowships, degree programs, society elections, unfinished works, and attempts to grow your social following.

Whatever you have tried. Whatever hasn't worked out. Every detailed instance where a gatekeeper has said 'no' or your self-sabotage has lost you an opportunity lives in a bullet point on your *CV of Failures*. It is comparatively rare to see any professional make their own documented list of rejections public. Here are some example *CVs of Failure* that inspired me to write my own, and hopefully convince you to write yours.

Example 1: Jeremy Yoder

Before landing his first independent academic job at the California State University, Northridge, ecologist Dr Jeremy Yoder was a long-term postdoctoral researcher on a job hunt. In his early years, Jeremy deliberately targeted certain job posts. He was highly selective. After his fifth year as a postdoc, Jeremy decided that he couldn't afford to be so selective anymore. As he wrote on his blog:

"I had tried to be selective...tried to find positions that fit me well."[105]

When this approach didn't work, it led Jeremy to the realisation that:

"...trying to read a hiring committee's collective mind was futile...Job interviews are unpredictable...better to take as many chances to get it right as possible".

It was like Dr Yoder swapped a laser pointer for a flood light. Once he committed to his new gung-ho job search strategy, he stringently recorded every usable piece of information about his quest: where he applied, how many times he applied, how many times he made the cut for the interview shortlists, and how many job offers he received. The summarised results are spine-chilling.

Before the job offer he finally accepted, Yoder had crafted 112 applications and was invited to just 17 interviews, and even fewer physical campus visits (11 in total). He eventually earned 3 job offers. If you use the offers as the measure of success relative to failed applications, Jeremy Yoder's success rate was 2.7%.

2.7%.

That number alone shows you that Yoder was no academic savant. He didn't claim to be a genius, or to have the world's finest publication record. He really, truly wanted that type of job and he went for it. He tried every experiment, not just those he liked or those he thought would work.

Example 2: Sam Lord

PhD chemist Sam Lord's CV boasts impressive appointments across several top US universities, and career awards ranging from teaching leadership recognitions to postdoctoral fellowships. He has given guest lectures and published in prestigious academic journals.

It is only on Sam's CV of Failures, however, that you'll learn that he has had several articles rejected, eight failed attempts at awards, fellowships, grant applications, a grad school rejection, and a degree application from which he withdrew. Dr Lord became a microscopy expert at the University of California.[106]

Example 3: Sara Rywe

Swedish venture capitalist Sara Rywe, a well-travelled early-stage investor who graduated with an MBA, has a potentially intimidating CV that is decorated with management consulting experience, presidential posts of an entrepreneurship society, and study experiences in the Stockholm School of Economics as well as at several US universities. Her website is sharp and is fronted by a quote of her own:

"No one remembers a coward."

Sara's *CV of Failures* tells the alternative story of the languages she couldn't speak, the computer skills she never had, and all the leadership posts, internships, speaker invitations, summer jobs, and awards she never even heard back from.[107]

Example 4: Bradley Voytek

From Sweden back to the US, I found the research website of cognitive neuroscientist Dr Bradley Voytek. On his research team's website, I found a thirty-page CV, freely available for anyone anywhere to download as a PDF. It's ridiculously decorated. It's the sort of CV that might force anyone who suffers imposter experiences to think, *"Why should I even bother?!"*

From Dr Voytek's eight professorial and leadership roles, to industrial and founding non-profits experiences, over forty papers, book chapters to boot, grant funding totalling a seven-figure dollar sum, multiple TV appearances, popular magazine articles, and more conference appearances than I've ever had hot meals. But the final three pages of Dr Voyek's CV are almost entirely dedicated to the thirty-eight awards and grants he failed to secure, and the

stories behind fifteen of his published works that, collectively, were rejected from fifty-six other journals before they ever saw the light of day.
108

And if you're thinking this exhaustive listing of failures is familiar, trust your instincts. Like the stories of rejected writers, I fully intend to give you as many examples of the *CV of Failures* as I can. Let's keep going.

Example 5: Sam Giles

Paleobiologist Dr Sam Giles worked past six rejections (four before any shortlisting, two after interview) before winning her first junior research fellowship in 2014. She completed her PhD in 2015 and was rejected for another lectureship post in the same year, after her successful junior fellowship application officially started. Then, in attempts to move to a more senior academic fellowship, three more failed attempts came and went before she eventually won a prestigious Royal Society fellowship to expand her research efforts. Dr Giles has now condensed all of these failures into a single presentation slide to share with her students. Understandably, she is also a fan and propagator of the Twitter hashtag #RejectionIsTheRule.

I have four more examples to hammer this point on repeated rejection home. Examples of repeated rejection are plentiful!

Example 6: Anonymous (by request)

I spoke with a multidisciplinary scientist who shared with me (through a Slack channel for UK-based early career academics) a particularly arduous journey to his lectureship at a another UK University. In their own words:

"...about 10% of my applications landed interview invitations, of which about 20% resulted in offers (about 2% overall success rate). I don't remember how many tenure-track applications I did in total

(probably in the range of 150–200, over the period of about six years).
This resulted in about twenty job interviews, with four offers."

This scientist's success rate echoes that of Jeremy Yoder. About 2%.

Example 7: Veronika Cheplygina

Machine learning expert Dr Veronika Cheplygina, as well as producing her own academic CV of Failures – itself composed of 13 job rejections, 19 grant and award rejections, and more than 15 unpublished papers – has also included other "shit I dealt with". In this singularly raw example of the CV of Failures, Dr Cheplygina awards bullet points to her diagnosis with bipolar disorder, a cheating ex-boyfriend who had a secret family, a cervical cancer scare, and fertility challenges.* Almost a year after leaving her tenure-track assistant professorship, she made peace with her arduous past, and moved on to earn a promoted associate professorship at another institution.

Example 8: Alice Soragni

In her first year running her own lab, biochemist Dr Alice Soragni posted a review thread on Twitter about what she wished she knew before starting and what she'd learned in the process of setting up her lab.[109] The first tweet in the thread had been retweeted 158 times when I first found it. It expressed vulnerability with an admirable willingness to cut oneself some slack. On rejection, she said:

"It's the villain you got to fight. Whether it's papers, grants, awards, rejection is all around you.
Learn how to cope.
Learn how to defend yourself and your wellbeing.
Learn how to fight."

---

*In the pursuit of failure, Dr Cheplygina has produced a series of interviews with a growing number of scientists who have each failed and moved on in their own unique way. See: Cheplygina, V. How I Fail - Interviews with researchers about their thoughts about failure. Retrieved on 4 February 2021, from https://bit.ly/3QbjgIo.

The Final Example: Johannes Haushofer

One last example I have for you is the one that, if you have ever heard of the CV of Failures, might just be the case you heard of first. It went viral in 2016, creating a spike in all tweets carrying the hashtag #CVofFailures. It led to articles appearing in *The Guardian* (in the UK)[110] and *The Washington Post* (in the US).[111] Economist Dr Johannes Haushofer took Dr Melanie Stefan's inspiration and ran with it. His rejected papers, failed funding bids, non-awards, and inadmissible degree program applications make up a 2-page list of 33 items. It's perhaps item 34 on his listed CV of Failures that Dr Haushofer is ironically most proud of though. In what he calls a meta-failure, he says:

"This darn CV of Failures has received way more attention than my entire body of academic work."

Part 5 - My CV of Failures

In all of these examples of repeated rejection, all of these professionals, each of whom we'd judge as 'successful' in a heartbeat, each collected all of their career lows all in one place. Naked. Exposed. Out there for all to see. Why? The *CV of Failures* turns the pessimistic notion of rejection on its head. It celebrates the fullness of your effort, not just the shiny bits.

On your CV, you can log all your greatest moments and still think you cheated on the road to now. You might still think yourself a fraud. If, however, you're honest with yourself about all the shit you've experienced en route to your goals, the *CV of Failures* exercise is one that will make you feel both brave and inspired.

The ability to physically hold up your 'shadow' CV against your regular CV is where its use truly takes shape. Every rejection you face can now be an opportunity to hold your head up and write that failure down as another bullet point on the *CV of Failures*. This is how you can empower yourself to learn and improve and pivot.

It's infinitely easier to fail at something once and deem it impossible than to get over the teething phase. When you label yourself as an 'imposter', it's often the result of a quick and dirty assessment; a rough comparison to others and an incomplete, overgeneralized definition of success. Everyone you will ever meet or ever idolise has messed up in ways you know nothing about. They, like you, are undeniably imperfectly human. You are, of course, in part predisposed to success or failure by the uncontrollable facts of where you were born, the era you find yourself in, who raised you, and who you are surrounded by. Predisposed does not mean predetermined. And tools like the *CV of Failures* are all I can offer before the responsibility becomes your own. It is up to you to act.

Your CV is a highlight reel.

For all the successes that decorate your résumé, there are many more failures, near-misses, non-selections, participation medals, and rejection letters. Below is an abbreviated list of some more of my notable career failures along the way to where I am now. The list is ever-growing, and the number of life lessons therein ever-evolving:

2021 - Major research grant (rejected)

2020 - Industrial Snr Scientist (interviewed but denied post)

2020 - Research Fellowship (not shortlisted)

2019 - University Lectureship (interviewed but denied post)

2019 - University Lectureship (interviewed but denied post)

2019 - Business Fellowship (not shortlisted)

2019 - Research Fellowship (not shortlisted)

2019 - European infrastructure grant (cut at first round)

2018 - Research Fellowship (not shortlisted)

2017 - Research Fellowship (not shortlisted)

2016 - University lectureship (not shortlisted)

2016 - Junior Research Fellowship (not awarded)

2015 - Junior Research Fellowship (not awarded)

2014 - International PhD competition (not shortlisted)

It cannot be stressed enough:

This list is *abbreviated.* My full list of failed grant proposals, competitions, and job applications is simply too long to remember. The important thing is that my failures are plentiful. They vastly outrank the number of successes and highlights. In this, I am not alone.

We try again. We fail again. And we try to fail better.

Part 6 – Data on Academic Rejection

In 2020, Assistant Professor of Biomedical Sciences Dr Amanda Haage published a cultural analysis of academic job applications.[112] The 2018–19 survey of over three hundred respondents, predominantly postdocs in the life sciences striving for a first independent academic post, found that job seekers uniformly hated the academic application process.

For what typically requires applicants to include a detailed CV, publications list, research plan, and teaching statement, survey respondents reported the academic job search to be opaque, stressful, time-consuming, and desperately lacking in feedback of any actionable sort. The dissatisfaction is more understandable when you consider just how rare and ruthlessly competitive jobs within the academic market are. From respondents of this study alone, a single job opening in the year 2018-19 could typically attract over 200 applicants from which 30 would make the first cut, 10 invited to remote interview, 6 brought forward for on-site interview, and all to make 1 offer.

Across all respondents in Dr Haage's study, the median number of job applications per person (having anywhere up to a decade of experience) was 15. The range of application numbers for an individual was wild, going from just 1 application up to a bewildering 250! Comparing the third of respondents who went on to receive academic job offers to the two thirds who did not, successful applicants tended to be those who submit more applications.

Those who were unsuccessful, receiving no job offers from any of their applications, may simply not have submitted enough to be in with a reasonable chance of receiving that golden phone call. Any applicant who submitted 15 or more proposals stood a significantly higher chance of being shortlisted for job interviews following initial written applications. An applicant's individual metrics of academic performance, like h-index, did not correlate well with the eventual rate of job offers a candidate received. And the vast majority of applicants had no publication record in the so-called high-impact journals like *Cell*, *Nature*, and *Science*. We'll return to the nature of dubious academic metrics in the next chapter.

Haage's survey represented roughly equal response across gender and showed a statistically indifferent story of success. Men applied 16.5 times to earn 1 remote interview, 2 on-site interviews, and 1 job offer. Women applied 13 times to earn 2 remote interviews, 2 on-site interviews, and 1 job offer. That's a roughly 6-8% success rate overall, with almost no difference between sexes.

A minimum threshold of having a postdoctoral research fellowship and a high enough number of citations (regardless of the specific journal's perceived prestige) together formed the baseline. After that, the sheer number of applications an applicant submitted was all that mattered in achieving a shortlisted place in the subsequent interview rounds.

As a young postdoc eager to start an independent research career, the number of times you apply for rarefied university job posts matters. And if you ever do get in and your hair becomes increasingly decorated with streaks of grey, the number of times you apply for grants (as opposed to job posts) matters, too.

A survey from the US National Institutes of Health (NIH) and related funding bodies showed that, of the scientists applying for research grants in biomedical fields, it tended to be the older scientists who won out.[113] No big surprise, right? The older scientists are seasoned veterans of the delicate art of grant writing. They have larger teams of people generating more ideas that are of superior elegance relative to the younger, arguably lonelier applicants. The easy blame-oriented reasoning here would be to say that the older scientist's name precedes them, and the prestige of a name helps. The older applicants might be seen as more trustworthy and more reliable when it comes to handling larger sums of research funding...especially money coming from the government. As the Matthew Principle goes:

"To everyone that has more shall be given...but from everyone that has not, more shall be taken away."[114]

This mantra of success begetting more success is partly true, but it's not the full story.

The older scientists who won more grants did NOT win because they were necessarily better than anyone else. The older a scientist was, the more comfortable they had become with failure, and the more grants they applied for. So, why exactly do older scientists apply for more grants than younger scientists? For one, the experience of time is likely to uncover more gems from under more rocks, more good ideas from an accumulation of bad ones. This is one case where age may actually breed wisdom. From my own Imposter Phenomenon study, there was some intriguing evidence to suggest that older participants recorded lower imposter scores. What, then, of the components of such wisdom? What helps us fail better?

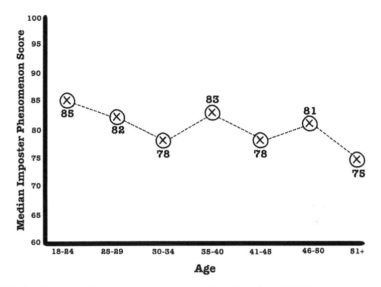

Median Imposter Phenomenon scores as a function of age. While scores across age (for this study group) remain high, there is some evidence to suggest that the imposter experience becomes less severe as we get older.

Part 7 – The Components of Failing Better

Be it Jia Jiang's rejection therapy, Zora Raeburn's road to self-publishing, or Melanie Stefan's *CV of Failures*, all these professionals are examples of people whose drive to achieve a specific goal helped them persist in the face of constant rejection. But the commonality between these stories goes further than the seemingly lazy explanation that they were merely persistent.

Crucially, they all refused to view rejection as *failure*. It was experimentation and comfort with viewing each rejection as an experiment that saw them through. With every rejection came a refinement of an idea. With every 'no', a creative step was taken towards finding (or making) a 'yes'.

Jia Jiang sought out 100 rejections and slowly tamed his fear of failure. Zora Raeburn collected enough book rejection letters to cover the side of a building before choosing herself. Melanie Stefan navigated rejection as the norm in academia by documenting the fullness of her efforts, successful and otherwise.

The point of these rejection stories is not to glorify failure. And you will hear more stories beyond those we've explored in depth. Stories like those of James Dyson, who generated over 5,000 prototypes before marketing the first in his now-famous line of bagless vacuum cleaners, and Thomas Edison, who was often (wrongly) thought to have failed 10,000 times before getting his electric bulb working, are stories that can be mistaken for applauding failure. This is what the writer and entrepreneur James Altucher calls *Failure Porn*.[115]

I have struggled to understand why I was once content to act like a spoiled brat when I received a single job rejection, but have grown more stony-faced when a new rejection emerges...

Together, the following traits help us understand the strength to persist through rejection.

Grit

The most successful people are rarely those with the most potential. It matters (more often than not) what you do with your potential. Psychologist Dr Angela Duckworth has studied successful people in different settings to understand why they stayed the course of their chosen path, beat the competition, and managed to gain the job or position or lifestyle that might have first looked impossible.

Duckworth's approach aims to dispel the easy explanations for success. For Duckworth, a one-word metric, though far from the full picture, helps tell us what drives the most successful people, the sort of people we might compare ourselves to when falling into another instance of our imposter experiences. That metric is *Grit*.[116]

Grit is composed of two key components: passion and direction. It's about having a very specific, very personal, and very clear idea of what you are trying to achieve. It's a little like self-control but different from the kind you need to sit down and do your taxes, or study for an exam in a subject you care nothing for. It is part of an attempt to deconstruct some elements of goal achievement rather than settling for the cult of 'genius'. For that most prized of your goals, *Grit* is similar to what Finnish people refer to as *sisu* – the act of digging deep and doing it anyway, even when you don't feel like it.[117]

To formalise the scientific study of Grit, Duckworth developed a ten-point questionnaire that defines a Grit scale, ranging from 1 (not at all gritty) to 5 (as gritty about a goal as anyone can be). The test is freely available on Duckworth's website, in her book Grit, and in the scientific publications describing the scale. The questions include:

(1) *New ideas and projects distract me from previous ones.*

(2) *Setbacks don't discourage me. I don't give up easily.*

(3) *I often set a goal but later chose to pursue a different one.*

(4) *I am a hard worker.*

(5) *I have difficulty maintaining my focus on projects that take more than a few months to complete.*

(6) *I finish whatever I begin.*

(7) *My interests change from year to year.*

(8) *I am diligent. I never give up.*

(9) *I have been obsessed with a certain idea or project for a short time but later lost interest.*

(10) *I have overcome setbacks to conquer an important challenge.*

I scored about a 3.9 out of 5 at the time of writing this chapter. Setbacks don't discourage me easily. I am a hard worker, and I have conquered important challenges after setbacks, yet there are still occasions where I get bored with old projects after a month and chase something new. I've definitely had occasions where I fail to finish something I started.

But just like Clance's Imposter Phenomenon Scale (0–100), your *Grit* score is particular to the time you measured it. I am a 70 on the imposter scale now, but would have been closer to 85 just after my PhD, when I moved to another research lab for the first time in four years. And while I was a 3.9 on Duckworth's scale during this book's creation, I was easily sub-3, maybe sub-2 out of 5 during my undergraduate years in my early 20s. Back then, I was far more distracted, far less committed to any one goal, not yet passionate about anything in particular. As Duckworth explains in her book, *Grit* can grow, and this is consistent with Amanda Haage's study on postdocs applying for rare academic jobs. The growth of *Grit* with age is also consistent with the hypothesis that older professors win more grants because they simply apply and get rejected more frequently than their younger counterparts.

Resilience

Beyond the formally defined Grit from Angela Duckworth's work, Dr Meg Jay, a clinical psychologist from the University of Virginia, has reflected on the origins of another commonly referenced trait of success: *resilience*. Of 400 people studied in a 1962 study by Victor and Mildred Goertzel, 300 of them were found to have suffered and survived through childhood trauma.[118]

The musician Louis Armstrong grew up poor and left school young to support his struggling family. Starbucks founder Howard Schultz also grew up in poverty. Business magnate John D. Rockefeller's dad was a con man and not often at home. TV icon Oprah Winfrey was sexually abused by family members as a youth. *Resilience*, like *Grit*, is often too simplistically defined. *Resilience* is not merely an ability to bounce back from hardship. It isn't simply a trait, it's a way of thinking, a way of living. It's using everything you have, no matter how little, to your advantage. It's determination, it's problem-solving, it's persistence. *Resilience* takes many forms. What is consistent from case to case is what breeds resilience. Namely, exposure to intermittent stressors.

Learned Optimism

In the early 1990s, psychologist Dr Martin Seligman shared the concept of *Learned Optimism*.[119] Seligman explored a person's explanatory style, essentially whether they tended towards pessimism or optimism. In short, pessimists lean towards thinking bad events are permanent, final, and hopeless. Optimists, conversely, see the same troubles as temporary hiccups on the road to success.*

Whether you are fearing failure or the rejection you associate with failure, there are four reminders and questions to investigate when the dark cloud of your imposter thoughts rolls overhead:

(1) *"It's how I cope with my failures that ultimately matters."

(2) *"Are there distractions I could be handled more quickly?"*

(3) *"What's really going to happen if I don't do this perfectly?"*

(4) *"Does my feeling guilty [about success] help?"* (It doesn't!)

Antifragility

Some rejections can seem random, uncontrolled, unpredictable, and largely at the whim of a panel of human subjectivity. It is this sort of unknown that can contribute heavily to stressful imposter experiences. Yet facing events of this random nature is

---

*This has strong parallels to Professor Carol Dweck's concept of fixed versus growth mindsets. See: Dweck, C. S. (2006). Mindset: The New Psychology of Success. United States: Random House Publishing Group.

what is needed for many systems, including you, to grow. Just as intermittent stress builds resilience, we are one example of a class of systems that stand to gain more from random stressors than predictable perennial protection. Some systems, like a wine glass, are genuinely fragile. If you knock one over, it smashes, and does not benefit or get better in any way as a result of being knocked over. If you instead drop a kid's plastic cup, it doesn't smash but, at the same time, that plastic cup doesn't improve its function as a result of the fall to the ground.

You, on the other hand, are a biological system, born in an incomplete form, ready to grow and built to learn. With exposure to knocks, you learn from the feedback and adapt. Without any exposure to such knocks or stressors, you can never learn from them. Author, former trader, and no-nonsense risk practitioner Nassim Nicholas Taleb coined the term *antifragile.* He did this to conceptualise the hidden truth of systems that stand to inherit more gain than pain when exposed to random stressful events.[120]

Sociologist Dr Jonathan Haidt became a strong advocate for the concept of *antifragility,* showing how it helps with the understanding of the dangers of overprotective parenting.[121] Well-meaning parents do physical and mental damage to their children if they clear out or watch over every obstacle their child might face, from the womb through to adolescence. So, too, might those who stop applying themselves to a particular goal after the first rejection be channelling the fragility of the wine glass.

The Dip

In **Chapter 4**, when we discussed genuine imposters, we looked at the closest thing we have to an opposite of the Imposter Phenomenon – the *Dunning–Kruger Effect.* Those who are incompetent and don't know it will learn a little to reach the apparent peak of new learning and then stay right there on 'Mount Stupid'.

The rest of us come crashing into the chasm, the Valley of Despair, from which we slowly and, with consistent effort, surely climb towards expertise. That chasm is what marketing legend Seth Godin alternatively calls The Dip.[122] In the same-named book, Godin explores the idea that the period when pursuing an ambitious goal seems too tough, it seems easier to quit. In such cases, progressing through a dip is about visualising the remarkable advantages to be gained by sticking it out.

On the flip side, there is skill in knowing when to quit. There are times when you are not in a dip but in a *cul-de-sac*: a stale, flat, unproductive march to nowhere. This is where your investments in time and energy can be emotionally as opposed to rationally driven. We are forever at risk of falling prey to the *Sunk Cost Fallacy*, where we feel like we need to keep investing in something because we are keen not to lose the precious resource we have already put in.[123]

Is the problem that you're working on at a true dead end? Do you have something more pressing or worthier of your valuable time, money, and energy? If so, bin the problem. Quit with confidence. It's a *cul-de-sac*. Is your problem tough? Is the end in sight but agonises like a mirage? Do you feel like quitting but see improvement with every rejection that comes your way? Keep going. It's a *dip*!

Collectively, Grit, Resilience, Learned Optimism, Antifragility, and the Dip can help grow in you the resolve of Zora Raeburn and the experimental vulnerability of Melanie Stefan. So, here we are, having considered failure and our imposter experiences. Allow me to imprint on you one more message on this topic...

Part 8 – Summary

When I fail now, I don't punch the pillow. I don't mount a pathetic private protest, even though the temptation remains. And I do not think anything of how much or how little I might have deserved to be considered for whatever opportunity I've just been rejected from. At most, I might let out a mumbled curse word alongside a deep sigh. As I have tried to persevere in the goals that matter most to me, my once fragile inability to handle failure has been tempered into an antifragile growth state. The stories of repeated rejection that I've found along my way led the charge.

If you forget everything else that I have shared with you in this chapter about rejection, remember this unavoidable truth:

You will fail.

As scary as that might sound, the more important realisation here is not that you will fail, it's that you *can* fail. Again and again.

If you throw enough shit at a wall, the good stuff will eventually stick. Don't procrastinate about applying for grants. Don't convince yourself a job isn't worth applying for. Don't stop yourself from founding that business. Don't entertain the thought that putting your pen to paper is a waste of everyone's time. It's all good practice. If you don't give it a go, you will open yourself up to even more imposter experiences, and an endless line of lazy excuses for why someone else is apparently more deserving of an opportunity than you are.

If your first attempt at your goal comes and goes, no big deal. That failure will never be as big a deal as it feels to you in that first, most painful moment. Your first failure has levelled the ground and laid the intellectual foundations on which you can build something stronger for next time.

Just as accounts of suffering imposter experiences are not exclusive to the bubble of academia, so too do the experiences of repeated rejection affect everyone, from all walks of this human existence we find ourselves a part of.

And if you're not traditionally successful by making someone else's cut, channel the story of Zora Raeburn, London's "bulldog in old lace". Choose yourself. If you really want what you're going for, find a way. Find *another* way.

When failure makes you feel like an imposter, the challenge is to avoid jumping straight to the excuse that the world is out to get you. Don't let the easy explanations of someone else's success populate your conversations with bobbleheads of polite agreement that everything is unjust. It is rarely if ever the 'genius' or the smartest of the smart that goes on to succeed. That person who both inspires and intimidates you has probably suffered their own rejections along the way. Rejection is often the rule. Try to waste as little time as possible being jealous of someone else's success when the chances are that you have never really considered what it took for that person to be successful. After all, time spent on jealousy is time you are never getting back.

You need to be smart enough and have enough directed determination to really ascend to where you want to be. Do not assume endowed talent. Question whether your panicked point of view is an accurate one. Write a *CV of Failures* to accompany your CV. Note the lessons you learned from each rejection. So focused are most of us on creating the positive versions of our career paths that we simply don't show just how much work, effort, grit, imperfection, and perseverance it has taken to write the CV we assume everyone wants to see.

Sharing ideas can be like breaking open your chest and baring your shivering soul to the world. But share your ideas you must! People are willing to help if you let them. Show your idea to people you know, trust, and respect. Your inner thoughts of being a fake can be managed if you allow other voices, external voices, to speak to you. If they don't love your idea in its draft form, welcome the rejection as if they'd just congratulated you.

What feels to you like a beat-down is really the first step towards building up your work to a state of something better than before. Something you can put out there. Not perfect, but valuable to those who need what you have to offer. You need your ego to get your work out there, but you need to put that same ego to one side and spill your ideas onto someone else's canvas if you want to improve how your idea is packaged.

By sounding out ideas, sharing them with those you trust, submitting them to the panel that scares you, you can chip away at the rough edges to sculpt something that looks like a masterpiece to those who need it, even if your perfectionist tendencies still twitch inside. If you're the only one checking your work, you might think you are keeping up with your secret perfectionism when, in reality, you are delaying the chance to help those who need you most. How valuable the feedback on your work is will depend on how you decide to use that feedback.

Fail often to hone your craft.

Rejections are experiments, not embarrassments. Rejections are experiments, not discouragements. Rejections are experiments, and they provide all the feedback you need to progress.

Don't give up the game because victory isn't immediate. Someone somewhere needs what you have to give.

Your Chapter Challenges

1. Expect rejection as the norm. Seek it through your own form of rejection therapy.

Use the template provided in the book's journal resources to:

(i) record scenarios in which you need to ask for something. A combination of more serious goals and silly examples for the sake of the rejection exercise is ideal here.

(ii) write down all the anxious thoughts occurring before you made the ask in each scenario.

(iii) document what happened, and whether or not your request was successful. What was the result of acting in spite of the thoughts that would once have paralyzed you to the point of inaction? (Hint: if you survived the rejection long enough to write it down, you're onto a winner).

2. Stories of repeated rejection before success are plentiful, in and outside academia. Many an 'overnight' success is instead the result of many an hour's work! In this chapter, you learned about a small sample of writers whose work was rejected multiple times before it was either successful or the author chose to do things their own way.

Choose one person who's successful (however you define 'success') and dig deep on how they got to where they are now. Watch their interviews, read their biographies, and scroll their socials. Even reach out to them!

Record what you assumed about that person's success then compare that assumption to what you found out when you went digging.

Tell the others! Post a photo of your exercise online using the book's hashtag #YouAreNotAFraud. This way, you might even find some more surprising stories of rejection turned triumph from fellow readers.

(Spoiler alert! This chapter challenge will go a long way to helping you with what you learn in the next chapter.)

3. Celebrate your rejections and failures as experiments towards your goal.

Record each career rejection or failure as a bullet point on your CV of Failures. A template is provided in the available journal resources.

As a minimum, print your newly-created CV of Failures and your standard CV.

If you want to use your example to help others do the same, take a photo of your CV and CV of Failures printouts and share it online.

If you want to go further and post your CV of Failures on your website, go for it. You can find a printed version of my example in the book appendix, or head along to www.dr-marc-reid.com/cv-of-failures to see the living (and growing) version of the document.

Chapter 7: Social Comparisons

When comparing yourself to others, are you aware of all the assumptions you are making? These assumptions, whether you're aware of them or not, help lead you down the dark path towards thoughts of being an imposter. Consider, for example, the following curious result from my own research. When participants were asked about their feelings on performance evaluations, there was a split in the room. About as many people wanted to avoid performance reviews as attend them. It's one of the few questions in the Imposter Phenomenon study whose collective answer did not yield a strong agreement in one particular direction. Why?

It's here, in this chapter, that I share with you the Imposter Phenomenon's most notorious double-edged sword. Whenever I've had the privilege to talk about this subject with an audience, one question consistently comes back time and time again:

Is there anything about the Imposter Phenomenon that is good?

Social comparison is the case in point. As you'll soon learn, comparisons you make between yourself and others can be the fuel that lights the fire of your ambition. If taken too far, the same comparisons can reduce your ambitions to ash.

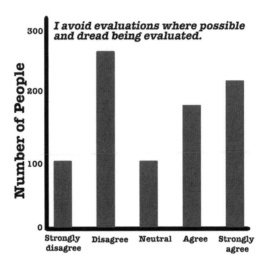

Imposter Phenomenon score question focusing on the role of evaluation in triggering imposter experiences. A rare example of a question producing a divide among participants.

A full 730 days of my academic career passed before I faced my greatest embarrassment. And it's here that we meet the very heart of the Imposter Phenomenon – this insatiable drive to compare ourselves to others around us. In my study, relative terms of comparison ("than me", "compared to me", and so on) appeared in around 29% of all imposter experience stories. Stories citing parents only appeared in 23% of cases. Comparisons, therefore, are also core to feelings of being a fraud, concerns about perfectionism, and the fear of failure. So, whilst I figure out how to tell you my side of the story, I ask you to think about the world of high-end gourmet cuisine.

Part 1 – The Chef Who Cared Too Much About His Reputation

In 17th century high-society France, François Vatel was an impressive guy. He worked for the country's Superintendent of Finances, and later became maître d'hôtel (manager of the château) for a prince. Vatel was a well-known figure in the lofty world he inhabited. He was respected and valued; the prototypical event planner of his day. Vatel was held in such high esteem that he carried his own ceremonial sword and had his own bed-chamber in the castle where he worked (both blade and bed being clear status symbols for the time).

Alas, Vatel's earned position and regal responsibilities ended when he threw himself on his sword. The story of François Vatel is one of someone who was petrified of dishonour and the imaginary judgement of those to whom he compared himself. Working hard only to be attacked by the perennial panic of upholding a reputation resonates with me more than I dare admit to you. You, like me, might not be a chef of any description. Nonetheless, as we continue this story, try to keep track of how Vatel's interpretation of events in his life failed to match the reality.

Where might the comparisons you make serve to exaggerate your imposter experience?

Vatel was born Fritz Karl Watel to a working-class Swiss family living in Belgium.[124] Following his cooking apprenticeship in a pastry kitchen, he shot to the upper echelons of French cooking. He wasn't so much a cook or a chef but rather a leader for the grand kitchen teams he commanded. He had eccentric royals to please. Extravagance was the name of the game, and Vatel excelled at it.*

---

*The Superintendent of Finance, by whom Vatel was once employed, was one Nicolas Fouquet. After Fouquet's displays of opulence, which Vatel helped with on the culinary front, Fouquet was thrown in jail by King Louis XIV, for whom Fouquet's actions were both threatening, ambitious, and ultimately must be tantamount to embezzlement from the government.

His signature events included stage illusions, plentiful banquets, and dazzling fireworks displays. This was event planning – 17th century style.

In April of 1671, Vatel's then employer, the Prince of Condé, announced a dubious honour. Louis XIV, then King of France, would soon be visiting the Château de Chantilly. Two weeks before the visit from the overbearing king (who built the Palace of Versailles, the largest royal residence ever built, just to keep his minions all under one roof), Vatel was asked to plan a three-day banquet...for an entourage of five *thousand* people. This almost impossible banquet was placed solely on Vatel's shoulders. He didn't sleep for twelve straight nights.

Renaissance banquets could be ridiculously opulent. These shows of self-importance were believed to turn the humble requirement of eating into a transcendent experience. It was recognised that good cooking wasn't enough to make such feasts a success; genuine masters of ceremony were an essential part of the workforce for the upper classes who commissioned such events. So utterly exacting were the demands of a Renaissance gathering that, two hundred years before Vatel's time, the guidebook *Du fait de cuisine* was written by a medieval master chef to help event planners calculate what they would need for a good party.[125]

Imagine you have to prepare food for several hundred guests, with no fridge, no freezer, no electricity, and poor lighting. Your guests must be well-fed, and might even stay for a few days longer than expected. There's no internet and you don't have the luxury of a car or *Click and Collect*. What do you think you'd need? According to the event planning guide from 1420, you'd be looking to source around 200 lambs, 100 calves, and 2,000 chickens. Per day. And, just to make it a little more interesting, on the Christian fast days, Friday and Saturday, fish was essential. No meat allowed on those days.

For the visit of King Louis XIV to Château de Chantilly, François Vatel was organising a three-day event, Thursday to Saturday, not for several hundreds of people, as was delineated in the *Du fait de cuisine* planning guide, but for five *thousand* people. Oh, and I've not even hinted at the quantity of dairy products, spices, kitchen staff, wine, and musicians that would be needed to pull off this behemoth celebration, but you get the idea. These banquets didn't need menus, they demanded blueprints.

During preparations for the king's visit, things went from bad to worse for Vatel. He was a perfectionist; a working-class man forever in the company of regal superiors. Comparison between himself and others was likely never far from his mind. He was eager to please, and compelled, by a trick of his own mind, to work non-stop.* Just before the start of the event, it was announced that an additional *seventy-five* guests would be joining King Louis XIV for the banquet. That didn't fit his plan.

As a result, he was forced to leave two of the banquet tables without any roast meat. He hadn't allowed for shortages or last-minute changes to his precise execution of the proceedings. More strangely, Vatel remained haunted by the roast beef mistake even though his direct employer, the Prince of Condé, tried to console him, asserting that the food shortage was *not* Vatel's fault. Remember, all the while, that one of the core tenets of the imposter experience is to feel that way even when the evidence and others around you see it differently.

After Thursday evening's apparent failures, Vatel stayed up into the small hours of Friday morning. Remember, he hadn't slept for twelve nights, agonising over the thought of preparing this festival for his perceived superiors. For the main banquet on Friday, fish had to be the centrepiece (in 17th century Catholic France, no meat could be eaten on a Friday). Around 4am that same Friday morning, Vatel met with a merchant delivering fish to the castle. But here, Vatel faced another terrible problem. The fish delivery was tiny, nowhere

---

*In the letters of Madame de Sévigné, Vatel was described as having *"too nice a sense of honor"*. See the English translation of the original French letters at: Retrieved 30 March 2020, from https://bit.ly/3BSySgb.

close to being enough to feed all the guests. When Vatel asked the merchant if this was all the fish that was coming, the merchant nodded.

Several hours passed as Vatel waited, in hope and terror, for more fish to arrive on site. That fish never materialised before Vatel's eyes. Three apparent failures – the extra guests, the tables without a roast, and the fish shortage – in the service of those he held above himself was too much for Vatel. He went to his bedchamber and shut the door. Mounting his ceremonial sword at an angle on the ground, he stepped back and then ran into the point of the blade. Like the three festival planning failures that depressed him, Vatel fell into his sword three times before the steel connected with his weary heart. Under the pressure of perfectionism and the will to please the highborn royals to whom he compared himself, Vatel's release was to let his blood run cold on stone.[126]

What Vatel hadn't understood from the fish merchant he spoke with was that the particular delivery in question was not all the fish that was going to be delivered that Friday morning. The first delivery at 4am was just all the fish that the first merchant had. Others were to follow. No more than a few hours after Vatel's suicide, the remaining fish deliveries arrived for the banquet. Left without the master of ceremonies who would oversee its preparation, that fish was never eaten.

Vatel's story survives through a prolific letter-writer of his time. For the failure of the first evening, Vatel is reported to have repeatedly said:

"I have lost my honor! I cannot bear this disgrace."

So focused was Vatel on his failures that he simply couldn't believe the Prince, his employer, who tried to reassure Vatel with the words:

"Everything is extremely well conducted, Vatel; nothing could be more admirable than his majesty's supper."

The prince continued to offer support but it just did not land with

Vatel, who replied:

"Your highness's goodness overwhelms me; I am sensible that there was a deficiency of roast meat at two tables."

For crying out loud! Vatel was told directly by the person he worked for that everything was fine. More than that, the meal wasn't just fine, but rather *"nothing could be more admirable"*. And yet, what stuck with Vatel? The *"deficiency of roast meat"*. When Vatel learned of the apparent fish shortage, some of the last words he ever uttered for outside ears were:

"I can not outlive this disgrace."

François Vatel compared himself to those around him and cared deeply about what they thought of him. Him, a working man from humble Swiss beginnings who worked hard to get to the top of his profession, versus the royals of France. Perfectionism clouded reason, and he paid the ultimate price. François Vatel died on a Friday. His banquet continued on the Saturday.[127]

Alas, these dark days in April 1671 did not mark the last time that France and Switzerland would be connected by the mental struggles of culinary superstars. There is a more modern story to tell of chefs bound by comparison and perfectionism.

Part 2 – The Poison of Comparative Perfectionism

Southeast of Paris, about a three-hour drive from the site of Vatel's demise, lies the small town of Saulieu. Sun-bleached terrace houses and cobbled brick walls fill its narrow streets. The singular steeple of the village chapel overlooks unassuming cars whose factory colour has long since faded. A quiet graveyard rests the town's ancestors. On one of those graves rests the blackened sculpture of neatly folded chef whites, emblazoned with the interwoven letters "B. L.".

Drive approximately 270 kilometres (168 miles) due east of Saulieu and you arrive at the Swiss lakeside town of Crissier. It is a town with a cosmopolitan palette of buildings: square, three-storey abodes with wood slats, crisp paint finishes, and rows of perfectly aligned windows. Per square mile in Saulieu, you'd find seventy-five people speaking French; in Crissier, you'd find fourteen hundred, conversing in French, Italian, Portuguese, German, and Romansh.

Should you ever wish to escape the terabyte terrors of modern city life, Saulieu and Crissier would each offer tranquillity by their own characteristic ladleful. What ties these towns together, however, is not the bright blue lines of directions on a Google map, but something far darker. Both Saulieu and Crissier are home to renowned hotel restaurants thought to be worth a special trip just for the pleasure of eating there. Both superstar head chefs of both restaurants in both towns have died by suicide.

The letters "B.L." on the tombstone chef whites in Saulieu commemorated the late Chef Bernard Loiseau. He was the 3rd generation owner of La Côte d'Or, an infamous old building which now bears Loiseau's name. He worked tirelessly to obtain the rare and coveted Michelin three-star status. Since his teenage apprenticeship days in the 1970s, watching his mentors rise to the godly three-star status, three Michelin stars was all Bernard Loiseau wanted. In 1991, that dream came true.

But the time came, at the turn of the new millennium, when Loiseau's culinary status seemed to be reaching its sell-by date. In 2002, a meeting with Michelin officials suggested that Loiseau's three Michelin-star restaurant might slip to just two stars.[128] What's more, a competing restaurant guide had recently downgraded Loiseau's main restaurant from 19/20 to a still highly respectable 17/20.[129]

Let's be clear: in the world of cuisine, the almost divinely-inspired third Michelin star is what raises your restaurant in the guidebooks from a worthy detour to a life-affirming pilgrimage.[130] It has the power to add (or subtract) zeros to the bottom line of any restaurant's revenue. In the pursuit of a boyhood dream, Michelin stars had brought Bernard Loiseau fame, fortune, endorsements, and stability for his family. His chaotic charisma fuelled an empire. If one star had to fall from his restaurant's name in Michelin's annual guide, everything Loiseau had built would be compromised.

In his prime, he had helped pioneer *Nouvelle Cuisine*: a clean and elegant style of cooking that avoided lashings of butter and heavy sauces to instead draw out the natural flavours of each ingredient.

On 24th February 2003, Chef Bernard Loiseau was running his normal lunchtime service at *La Côte d'Or*. Guided by empty eyes, he went to his home office for a break, and never came back to the restaurant. Later that same afternoon, Bernard's wife, Dominique, found him in their bedroom. He lay lifeless next to a hunting rifle that she had once gifted him.

Fast forward from 2003 to 2016, and three Michelin-star Chef Benoît Violier of Restaurant de l'Hôtel de Ville in Crissier, Switzerland is found dead in his home, lifeless from shotgun wounds sustained in a presumed suicide.* At the time of his death, Violier was the chef of the best restaurant in the world.[131]

So, what do we have? Two superstar chefs, separated by thirteen years and 300 kilometres, connected by a profession that drowned them in so much stress that they each fired a gun at their own head.

In a drive towards the three Michelin-star status, they each burned fumes to achieve perennial prestige in comparison to their peers.

In the end, the ultimate connection between Loiseau and Violier, and to poor François Vatel three centuries before them, remains their untimely, avoidable deaths in the service of perfectionism. But it's more than that.

---

*Benoît Violier, like Bernard Loiseau, was a keen hunter. The irony of their similar deaths is not lost in this fact.

What's particularly revealing about Loiseau and Violier, in a way that wasn't possible in Vatel's time, is their tie to a restaurant rating system. Vatel obsessed about the number of roasts and fish. Loiseau and Violier counted stars. But to understand just how bizarre it is that a restaurant rating system would drive these men (and other chefs besides) to constantly compare themselves to others, you have to understand where the Michelin Star system came from in the first place.

Part 3 – Michelin and the Birth of Maddening Metrics

You may have heard of the old saying, *"What gets measured, gets managed".*[132] It was originally uttered with positive sentiment: if you find the appropriate way to keep track of a task, you will be able to observe progress in an objective fashion. On the more cynical side, *"What gets measured, gets managed"* can also take on a more totalitarian purpose. If a boss wants to control their employees, they'll hold those employees to particular metrics of performance.

In your own work life, you might have come across some metric that strikes eye-rolling indifference into those – including you – who may be bound by it. You sigh in the name of annual 'accountability'. But let me more directly ask you this.

For any metric that you have ever been measured against, or that's ever caused you to compare yourself to someone else's score on that metric, do you have any idea where that metric came from?

Do you ever ask who came up with it, why it exists, or what happened before everyone around you took the metric for granted? Until I started looking deep into sources of imposter experiences, I had never asked myself these questions about metrics. And yet, as the data in the opening of this chapter shows, there are about as many people who dread evaluation as those who are perhaps driven by it. I thought even more about the real influence of metrics when I started reading about the world's greatest chefs killing themselves. So, what about the endowed Michelin stars? From where in the night sky did they fall upon the world?

Michelin's main logo is of a ghostly white, cartoon figure, rotund on account of the concentric tyres that make up its torso. This is, in fact, the same Michelin company that produces the now-infamous red-covered restaurant guide and three-star rating system. The three-starred metric that can make and break the careers of the chefs who pander to it. That is to say, the Michelin company of tyre fame and the Michelin company producing the little red book that rules the world of high-end cooking are *one and the same.*

If this connection of tyres and restaurants sounds strange, ridiculous, or odd to you – good! Trust your instincts. This connection was an eye-opener for me, and it blew a hole in how much I cared about the academic metrics that I, as a scientist, otherwise unconsciously lived by. Some of these metrics have exaggerated how often and how closely I compare myself to others and how often I have felt under-qualified in my workplace. Before we get to academia, I want to share with you the deeper story of how Michelin stars came to be, and how understandably tragic it is that any chef lives (and dies) by that little red book.

Nowadays, cars are on all roads, everywhere. But in the early 1900s, cars were still pretty rare and, for a time, shared the roads with horse-drawn carts. So, here's a question for you: how would you feel if you owned a company selling what car owners needed but knew that cars themselves were rare? Put another way, if you had a great product to sell at volume but only a tiny customer base, do you think your company would be likely to succeed? Such questions were at the heart of a problem faced by French brothers Édouard and André Michelin. Building their business at the turn of the 20th century, their vital question was:

How do we get people to buy more tyres?

In a more cunning guise, the ultimate goal of the brothers Michelin revolved around the question:

How do we convince more people to buy cars that then lead them to buy the tyres we are selling?

In the Michelin brothers' time, there were fewer than 3,000 cars on the roads of France (compared to about 32 million cars at the time of writing this sentence over a hundred years later). Back then, most people couldn't yet imagine the world of possibilities that a car could open to them. This problem of how to sell one product to improve sales of another is the sort of challenge that a marketer's dreams are made of, and the Michelin brothers were more than up to the task. Their solution? If your potential customers don't yet know what a car can do for them, you *educate* them. You give them a *guide*.

In 1900, Édouard and André published their book of maps, tyre maintenance instructions, tourist locations, and restaurant recommendations for the very first time. It was the *Guide Michelin*, a compact collection of inspirations for aspiring motorists, Édouard and André's answer to making their tyre business boom. They were the pioneering content marketers of their day.

The first 35,000 copies of the Michelin guide were published free-of-charge; a gift to the people of France, inspiring them to seek out life-affirming experiences in their cars. The marketing gamble paid off. The guide's success was such that, by 1904, it was expanded from France to Belgium, and then to several more countries around Europe.

By 1920, the Michelin brothers stopped paying for the guide with advertising pages and started charging $2.15 per copy, removing any perception that the little red book was merely a door stop. Six years later, in 1926, the *Guide Michelin* changed the restaurant business forever. Having noticed that the restaurant section of the guide was the most popular, the Michelin company hired their first *mystery diners* to covertly rate the restaurants and hotels of France.

The reward for impressing a mystery diner was to have a single star stamped next to your listing in the guide. In the eyes of the guide and those reading it, you (as the restaurant owner) were now deemed especially worthy of a motorist's time. For logistical reasons, the rating system was later focused on fine dining establishments only, and, in 1936, the one-star stamp became the three-star Michelin rating system known the world over today. Here's how you are supposed to count those stars listed against restaurants in the guide:

- **1 star** = *high quality cooking, worth a stop.*
- **2 stars** = *excellent cooking, worth a detour.*
- **3 stars** = *exceptional cooking, worth a special visit.*

Other restaurant rating systems exist but, in the immortal words of late great chef, Paul Bocuse (a household name in France):

"The Michelin guide is the only guide that matters."

Nowadays, when the *Guide Michelin* is published in January each year, the media buzz rivals that of the Oscars or the Nobel Prize. Newspapers announce the stars earned, retained, and lost from the previous year. The ingenious marketing trick that urged more people to buy tyres now commands the respect of restaurateurs in twenty-four territories across three continents. Those earning a new star rejoice for their lucrative badge of honour and advertising exposure that the star brings to their business. The losers, on the other hand, those shunned or stripped of their star(s), hang their heads. In some cases, the losers even take the Michelin company to court.* But you now know that the fear of losing a Michelin star

*French chef Marc Veyrat's Alpine restaurant, La Maison des Bois, was awarded its third Michelin star - the highest possible rating - in 2018, and downgraded back to 2 stars the following year. Veyrat tried to sue the Michelin company and lost. Michelin called him a "narcissistic diva".

can mean something far worse than bad press. Bernard Loiseau and Benoît Violier found this out the hard way.

So, why does a rating system, born as a marketing gimmick, command the respect and, alas, the lives of so many chefs? I think it's for some of the same reasons that François Vatel threw himself down on his sword.

For good or bad, secretive and subjective metrics like Michelin stars nonetheless supercharge our temptation to compare ourselves to other people.

The definition of 1, 2, and 3 Michelin stars seems completely clear and boastfully transparent. When you have these ratings, you know what it means. It's printed in glorious red and white on the Michelin website and printed guide. What it does *not* tell you is *how* to earn a star. All the chefs know is that some ethereal level of performance consistency is expected. The methods of the Michelin institution itself are shrouded in deep secrecy. How exactly Michelin's mystery diners watch and judge these chefs is unknown.

In 2003, Pascal Rémy, a former Michelin inspector (a mystery diner), published his exposé on the institution.[133] It sent palpable shockwaves through the industry. Rémy contested the ability of Michelin to annually inspect all restaurants in their guide. There are just too many high-quality restaurants and not enough inspectors. By the same stab of the knife, Rémy accused Michelin of treating some superstar chefs as untouchable. By heightening the demigod status of some chefs, it helped maintain the legitimacy of the Michelin brand.

The curious and unclear notions in Michelin's mystery inspections run deeper still. In 2002, a year before his death, Bernard Loiseau had a secret meeting with representatives at Michelin, who were concerned about the consistency and quality of Loiseau's cooking. Later, Michelin would try denying this meeting ever happened, but documented meeting minutes made the effect clear. Loiseau was noted as being *"visiblement shocke"* (visibly shocked).[134] Alas, while Bernard and his wife exclaimed that Bernard would dedicate himself to maintaining the restaurant's three stars, Michelin said nothing about how this maintenance of quality should be achieved. The rating system remained opaque to Loiseau right up until he pulled the trigger on his hunting rifle.

Gaining or losing a Michelin star can seriously impact restaurant income.* When chefs are caught in the bright headlights of the Michelin metrics, they don't see the freight train that is hurtling toward them.

Earning status with a metric is one thing, but the pressure to maintain that quantified status can be crushing.

As well as pandering to a mysterious set of standards, judged anonymously by people with less culinary skill than those they judge, some chefs live with the constant fear of going out of fashion. What is innovative and revolutionary one year might be judged boring and chased out by younger chefs the next. Yet, there is one innovation from a particular chef that helps turn these dark tales into a tool for managing the sorts of comparisons we so intrinsically connect to the Imposter Phenomenon.

Part 4 – The Street Urchin

Over the course of his career, chef Marco Pierre White ascended from dish cleaner to dining royalty. He battled all the way to winning the coveted three Michelin stars. In 1995, at age just thirty-three, he was the youngest ever British chef to be deemed worthy of Michelin's highest rating. He is *Grit* personified. Hard work and measured risk have earned him coveted and lucrative roles as a TV chef and brand ambassador.

---

*Two-star Michelin Chef, Raymond Blanc once launched a scathing attack on Michelin for the power they have over the amount of money a chef's business can earn. Similarly, in his book *Wine Snobbery*, wine writer Andrew Barr exposed the truth behind some apparently prestigious vintages, more inflated brands than delicious blends. Amidst it all, there are some sage chefs who have seen the *Guide Michelin* for the metricised gimmick it has (to some) become.

After a sixteen-year journey to earn his stars, he held them for five years, proving that what he could earn, he could retain. Consistently. Then, seemingly against all sense, he retired and handed the stars back to Michelin. A chef with three Michelin stars, a man on top of the world with the highest rating from what was the most revered metric in fine dining, handed back the chef's equivalent of a Nobel Prize. To those still reaching for their own stars (including White's arguably most famous protégé, Gordon Ramsay), this was madness. A cheap publicity stunt. Michelin itself rushed to claim that handing back stars was not in even in White's authority to do so. But why did Marco Pierre White do it at all?

The 2012 documentary *The Madness of Perfection* explored the highs and lows of Michelin-starred kitchens and what it takes to earn and retain the Michelin stars.[135] When chef White was asked about his experience, he said winning three stars was like *"the end of the race"*. More importantly, when he was asked about why Michelin puts such pressure on chefs, he corrected the documentarian by saying that chefs put this pressure on *"themselves"*.

There is a very thin line between the external pressures imposed by a system of metrics and the internal pressure induced by adherence to such metrics.

White could see that earning and maintaining his Michelin stars were not the same thing. At that level, maintaining three stars is all about doing the same thing, over and over, consistently to the undefined levels that Michelin expects, charging three-figure bills to diners for the pleasure. White even went so far as to call the process of three-star maintenance "boring", and he's not the only one to have smelled the Michelin rat.

Skye Gyngell, Alain Senderens, Joël Robuchon, Marc Veyrat, and Olivier Roellinger are just some of the Michelin-adorned chefs who have since said thanks...but no thanks.[136] They are all doing their own thing, by their own rules, no longer marching to the judgemental beat of the mystery diners who have far less technical skill than they do.[137]

Vatel, Loiseau, Violier, and others besides* something deeply striking hit me when I looked into these chefs. They were all high-achieving, all at the top of their game. François Vatel was an innovator in his time, a master of ceremonies for royalty. Bernard Loiseau brought a failing hotel back from the brink of collapse and became a household name in France. And Benoît Violier, author of a triumphant 1,000-page opus on cooking game meat, was running a restaurant recently celebrated as number 1 in *La Liste*, a curation of the thousand best restaurants in the world. Number 1.†

There was a spine-chilling familiarity borne from these stories of chefs. High-achievers in a competitive landscape were aiming for unattainable perfection. Innovators were being judged by ill-defined metrics that drove them to over-value external opinions. They were reaching for stars that left nothing but mental scars. This is a problem that runs much deeper than the world of high-end cuisine.

Part 5 – The Grandfather of Google

The Sticky Paper Metric

Like the life-weary chefs chasing stars, academics have their own version of the Michelin metrics trap. Again, whether you are in academia like me or not, I'm willing to bet that you're able to draw your own parallels between the Michelin story and the metrics that exist in your workplace. More on that later, in your Chapter

---

*In 1966, chef Alain Zick completed suicide by gunshot after Michelin stripped his 2-star status. And in 2003, the same year as Bernard Loiseau's death, chef Gérard Besson suffered a non-fatal heart attack on hearing the news that he was to lose his third Michelin star.

†La Liste is France's answer to another restaurant ranking list that the French feel is biased against French restaurants, perhaps because the converse feeling exists for bias for French restaurants in the Michelin Guide. In La Liste, the algorithm used is named Ciacco, after a gluttonous soul damned to eternal punishment from a three-headed hound in the third circle of Hell.

Challenges. As to how this relates to Imposter Phenomenon, 30% of participants in my study cited journals, publications, and their metricised ranking as a source of their own imposter experience (versus 23% for parents). Here's what a mere handful of them reported:

"When I see colleagues publishing in top high impact journals and I can't get one, I feel it's my fault I'm not as good as them."

"In my PhD, some of my peers were publishing high-impact papers, graduating early, and getting impressive grants to continue their stellar trajectories...It was easy to focus on these people rather than the vast majority who were like me..."

"Any time anything remotely related to publications comes up I feel like an imposter."

"I believe I feel so overwhelmed with information and people bragging about publications and how well they are doing, that I just feel like a loser."

Once more, you might be one of these people, you might not. But one of these people could be your son, your daughter, your sibling, or among those who you'd look to recruit into your business.

The old saying in academia is that you *"publish or perish".*[138] As an academic, you develop your research like a fine dining meal, then serve it up in a journal paper. The better your papers are perceived, the better shot you have at attracting ambitious students to your lab, and winning lucrative grants. Are you seeing the parallels between chefs and academics yet?

Here's the contradiction. Just as many great restaurants exist without necessarily being decorated in Michelin stars, there have been prize-winning discoveries reported in apparently 'lower tier' journals.* Where the Michelin story helps us see how easily a gimmick

---

*The 2016 Nobel Prize in Chemistry was jointly awarded to Fraser Stoddart, Ben Feringa, and Jean-Pierre Sauvage. Sauvage's award-winning work was originally published in what is now considered a low impact journal (*Tetrahedron Letters*). What's more, the article was published in French!

becomes gospel for chefs, so too is there an eye-opening history behind how academics in universities became part-governed by an immortal journal metric called 'impact factor'.

At a similar time to when Zora Raeburn was trying to get published, no one had a computer at home. It would be several more decades before the number-crunching power of laptops and smartphones got into the hands of, among the rest of us, librarians. Far from being a sedate, silent, and unassuming profession, librarians are tasked with cementing the retrievable archives of our combined human knowledge. They are the original information scientists.

To find books, articles, letters, theses, and tomes from over the world and across the ages, it has been the job of librarians to come up with the methods of classification that make knowledge of documented history retrievable. Using limited budgets, librarians need to figure out which literary materials to stock, subscribe to, and to ignore.

Before the Google search bar was even a twinkle in Larry Page's eye, the work of sorting was still in the realms of paper databases, punch cards, and periodicals. Far from the page-ranked platforms of the Internet age, information scientists of the time knew there were serious problems for academics looking to find sources of ideas in the literature. The origins of a particular idea might rest in that academic's own field or well outside their perceived realm of interest. This 'sticky' problem of connecting ideas to information turned out to have a rather sticky solution.

In 1875, salesman Frank Shepard needed a way to help lawyers understand when and why one legal case would refer to another. Using sticky gum paper, he stuck notes inside hardbound case files, acknowledging other sources citing the particular case to which the notes were stuck. The ideas and content of a case could thus be linked to ideas and content from *other* cases, without either case having to occur within the same published source. A higher number of sticky notes on the case file, the more cited it was, and the more perceived value it had. The legal profession has used Shepard Citations for over one hundred years. The original business has since been acquired and modernised through a lucrative business merger.[139] Yet, making use of Shepard's sticky note innovation in libraries as opposed to law firms required an ideological leap in its own right. Enter, Eugene Garfield.

Our natural desire to categorise everything is muddied by the fact that the axioms of one subject often cross-fertilise with those of another subject. There are bridges between physics and chemistry, chemistry and biology, poetry and history, and so on. When Garfield, an information scientist, started tackling this library problem in the pre-computer era, he brought one crucial intellectual insight:

Researchers looking in the literature aren't primarily motivated by a well-defined subject; they are driven by *ideas*.[140]

Garfield developed his insight into a sorting index that offered the best compromise for collecting the largest number of connected ideas in high-quality articles, and minimising the citation of poor-quality data. It helped librarians choose which journals to stock on the shelves! Garfield formulated what could easily be called an *association of ideas* index. Today, he is remembered as the *Grandfather of Google*.[141] He, in turn, introduced the *Journal Impact Factor* (JIF), the academic equivalent of placing sticky notes onto legal files.[142] Despite the eminently legitimate reasons for which it was created, JIF, like Michelin Stars, can easily be contorted into a comparison-inducing nightmare.[143]

Interpreting Impact

The nut that Eugene Garfield cracked with his journal ranking metric was to base it on the number of citations earned by papers in a particular journal. More sticky notes on the case file was all that mattered, not so much where those sticky notes came from. The Journal Impact Factor (JIF from here on out) doesn't care if the citations came from within your field or far outside it. The bigger the JIF number, the better quality the collected research papers in a journal are likely to be. It's simple. Quantified. Elegant. Right?

Well, you now know that the viciously prestigious Michelin stars were originally invented to sell cars rather than fancy meals. Do you think the JIF metric was ever going to be *that* easy to work with? Just as stargazing chefs have embattled themselves with the pressure of Michelin fame, and like so many of the Imposter Phenomenon study participants desperate to avoid evaluation, so too has academia taken JIF far beyond the innocence of sorting library shelf space. The first problem with the JIF lies in its interpretation.

The main problem with the JIF metric is that it is reported as a type of average called the *mean*. But (here's where it gets statistical) this assumes that the graph showing how many articles have a particular number of citations is bell-shaped. By contrast, the real article citation data are not at all bell-shaped and are instead squished to the left, shaped more like a bell that's been melted on one side. And when you have such skewed data, it's not the *mean* that is the most valuable statistic for making sense of the 'middle value' in the spread, but rather the *median*, a more robust cousin of the *mean*.[144]

While the more robust *median* metric is just as available as the *mean*, the *mean* of the data is what is used and marketed on journal web pages. Why? Well, if you had the choice of reporting your own journal's impact factor as 26 (the mean) or 16 (the median),[145] which would you choose as a way to market your journal?[146]

In one wonderfully ridiculous case, a niche chemistry journal's impact factor once jumped from 2 to 42 in a year because of a single very highly cited article that appeared in that journal. That same journal's impact factor has, at the time of writing, now settled back down to around 2.*

What ties all of this to the Imposter Phenomenon is how the innocently invented journal impact factor has led to offspring that, rather than trying to measure the quality of a journal, tries to objectify the professional worth of an individual.[147]

The Contortion of Academic Metrics

In 2005, around fifty years after the introduction of Garfield's Journal Impact Factor, physicist Jorge Hirsch invented what is now eponymously known as the *h-index*. Whereas Garfield's metric was aimed at sorting a *journal*, Hirsch's metric aimed to assess the individual contributions of a *person*.[148]

An individual academic author's *h-index* tells you that they have at least *h* papers with *h* or more citations each. To Hirsch, this was a way to fill the loophole left by using raw citation count as the traditionally preferred way of measuring a researcher's productivity. The problem with raw citation counts is that if one person had a single paper with a huge number of citations, a scientific *one-hit-wonder*,[149] that would be enough for them to be deemed a success. Such outliers are unpalatable to the scientific community who, in the main, value steady, consistent contributions over singular stratospheric hits. Hirsch designed the h-index to help the theoretical physics community better understand productivity, but the influence of the h-index has spread far beyond its roots. This one individualistic metric is now used to assess academic job applications, and it's one of only a few sticky labels made plainly visible on an author's Google Scholar profile.

In several review articles explaining the history and meaning of Journal Impact Factor, Eugene Garfield acknowledged that JIF had

---

*In balance, within chemistry, there does seem to be some validity to impact factor versus the proportion of articles in a journal achieving a certain number of citations. But the trend remains that most single articles in a journal achieve less citations than the glorified impact factor would suggest. See, for example: Cantrill, S. (2014, December 5). Nature Chemistry's 2014 impact factor citation distribution. Nature Chemistry. https://go.nature.com/3vA8rYo.

evolved to determine author as well as journal impact. He did not shy away from the fact that it is dangerous to conflate a journal's impact factor with the impact of a single researcher. In his own words:

"The term 'impact factor' has gradually evolved, especially in Europe, to describe both journal and author impact. This ambiguity often causes problems. It is one thing to use impact factors to compare journals and quite another to use them to compare authors."

In academia, it's this shift towards individual metrics that plays a big part in driving the wrong types of comparisons between ourselves and others.
150

Metrics and Money

When I read Garfield's personal accounts of Journal Impact Factor, I found something fascinating beyond the core content. On the opening page, tucked neatly into the bottom-left corner in a tiny font, you find Garfield's correspondence address. In these articles, Eugene Garfield is not listed at some university, as a scholar might normally be, but as *"Chairman Emeritus of Thomson Scientific"*. If you search online for *"Thomson Scientific"* now, you won't find their website.

The company merged with Reuters Group in 2008. The Science & IP division of Thomson Reuters was then later sold to a private equity firm that, in turn, established the journal analytics company Clarivate. One of the products under the Clarivate umbrella is Web of Science (basically Google for scientists). The original company that Garfield had been chairman of had, through his insight, created means of storing, curating, and indexing the world's scientific knowledge. So valuable were these data that Thomson Scientific was able to amass that, through the iterations of acquisitions and mergers, the company sold, on 3rd October 2016, for $3.55

billion (US).* Cash. While metrics madden many, they make others millionaires.

I'd always thought that a career in academia was the pinnacle of achievement. Harking back to being a first-generation university student as a root cause for my imposter experiences, I've always placed the possibility of being an academic on a pedestal.

Understanding the business model behind the science of Eugene Garfield's work was an eye-opener for me. Before reading his last correspondence address, I had naively assumed such bibliometric work would have remained academic. It instead gave me a crystal-clear perspective on just how tragically silly it is to get wrapped up in the metrics that would have us compare ourselves to one another even more so than we otherwise might. Why compare myself to others through a metric that has been distorted beyond its original purpose? Why waste my thoughts and breath on a hyper-individualised branding iron that says nothing of the teams I've worked with, the area I work in, or use of my work beyond the pages of my journal articles?

It needs to be stressed. Prestigious journals publicly acknowledge the limitations of these metrics. At the same time, however, they recognise the attraction of the rejection-fuelled scarcity the metrics have enabled in the name of marketing. It's like chef Marco Pierre White said. The Michelin company doesn't put pressure on chefs to work to their metric, chefs do it to *themselves*.

And so it is in academia. Journals don't force scientists to stress themselves out over perceived high-impact factors and rocket-fuelled h-indices. Scientists do it to *themselves*. And it has alas resulted in similarly dark days to those that shook the world of the chefs. In 2014, toxicology professor Stefan Grimm ended his own life when his employers at Imperial College London warned that his

---

*Part of the intellectual property in the company that was once Thomson is the more complex calculation behind Journal Impact Factor, linking an article to its unique citations by other researchers in other papers.

grant income (indirectly tied to the apparent metrics-determined quality of Grimm's papers) wasn't high enough.

The modern dangers of JIF and the individual metrics that have been born from it have driven several organisations to construct manifestos on how to make research assessment fair. *The San Francisco Declaration on Research Assessment* (DORA),[151] for example, directly calls out the deficiencies of JIF in its text, urging researchers and assessors to take this infamous metric with a firm pinch of salt.

More recently, the Leiden Manifesto offers ten principles on the responsible use of metrics, and encourages assessors to adopt a flexible approach to assessment, based on the field of research, and the tangible assets of impact developed as a result of the papers under scrutiny.[152]

Vatel, the Michelin brothers, Loiseau, Violier, Garfield, Shepard, and Grimm – all of it brings me to the story I have avoided telling. Until now.

Part 6 – The Story I Didn't Want to Share

It was a rare sunny morning, rays pouring into my university office. I opened my emails and read that a promising young scientist was coming to my department to present their recent work. The email advert revealed that this particular early-career scientist* had been so successful that they had published a series of more than ten papers in just over a year. I had published one. This person was a year ahead of me, in a similar academic position, and on what seemed, at first glance, like a similar career path.

Immediately and without warning, I grew desperately short of breath. All my familiar thoughts of academic worthlessness came

---

*"Early career" in academia is commonly conflated with raw age. However, the term is more broadly defined as including anyone who is within the first 3 - 5 years of their first academic appointment.

flooding back. Before I could draw any air, I automatically rushed to compare my career, pound for pound, paper for paper, metric for metric, against this emerging star...who was visiting my department! *My office!* As I dusted my table and repositioned the chairs just so, I reached the conclusion, neglecting logic or consideration, that I was a fraud. Somehow, it felt that nothing I had done in my own career could possibly stand up to anything this other budding academic had already achieved.

My focus was on the fallible metrics that I had allowed to be judge, jury, and executioner of all my efforts. I scrolled through this imminent visitor's website. I cross-compared our publication impact factors and h-indices, never once questioning what these metrics meant or where the hell they had come from. I wondered if I should quit while I was ahead. In this blindingly stupid panic, I stared at the email announcing the visitor's schedule, and silently dissolved.

That compulsion to compare myself unconsciously and unjustly to one of my peers was the first and only time I have ever come close to thinking that things might be better if I weren't here at all...

I really do not think the darkness that consumed François Vatel, or Bernard Loiseau, or Benoît Violier, or Stefan Grimm, or anyone else is within my constitution. Nonetheless, that experience of metric fixation unearthed a side of myself that scared me. I'm not sure that I could ever be driven to fall on my own sword, but that doesn't really matter. The way I felt when I compared myself to that visiting academic left me staring down a dark road with only unanswered questions for company.

What might I have been convinced to do? What if I felt there had only been one way to end my worries? What I share with you here, now, is my ultimate embarrassment. This most desperate instance of my imposter experiences was triggered by comparison through academic metrics. The metrics, however, are not entirely to blame.

These tempting comparisons are far more foundational than

the metrics we construct.

Early 20th Century physicist Paul Ehrenfest shot himself after years of tormented self-criticism. Working at the time of giants like Niels Bohr and Paul Dirac and Albert Einstein, and despite being a celebrated communicator, Ehrenfest saw his own contributions to physics as petty by comparison.[153] Writing to his doctoral students, he once confessed:

"Every new issue of the Physical Review immerses me in blind panic. My boys, I know absolutely nothing."[154]

Ehrenfest died in 1933 and, like François Vatel before him, did so long before modern metrics gripped his profession. He didn't have Eugene Garfield's journal metrics feeding these depressive imposter experiences. The social comparisons he made to his peers happened anyway. Indeed, whilst wrestling with how to manage the comparisons that led to the very worst of all my own imposter experiences, I learned that comparisons aren't simply at the heart of the Imposter Phenomenon. No, no. Comparisons are at the very heart of who we are.

Part 7 – The Psychology of Comparison

François Vatel became depressed for the apparent dishonour of failing the royals to whom he compared himself. Bernard Loiseau fuelled his Michelin-starred rise and untimely demise through maddening comparison to his fellow three-star chefs and an unattainable perfectionism. Paul Ehrenfest couldn't reconcile his wonderful teaching ability with research giants like Einstein.

Terry Crews, whose story inspired the opening to this book, almost never became an actor because he panicked whilst working with established superstar Arnold Schwarzenegger. And stressed-out academics, myself included, compare their intellectual worth against their peers through the contorted frame of journal metrics.

This entire chapter boils down to what is arguably the main feature of all imposter experiences: our natural desire to compare ourselves to our peers. In my own study, no question was answered with more emphatic agreement than that attending the toll of comparison between ourselves and our peers.

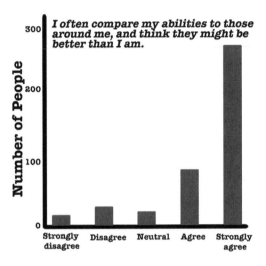

Imposter Phenomenon score question focusing on the role of comparison in triggering imposter experiences.

Notice that I said 'peers' and not simply 'people'. Because, what you have to realise, as I now have, is that this drive for comparison runs much deeper than the Imposter Phenomenon. Because the Imposter Phenomenon itself, I would argue, is the birth child of a sociological phenomenon that was first coined during the study of US soldiers and airmen in World War II.

Imagine, for a moment, that you're out for a drink to catch up with two old friends. Conversation turns to how things are going at work. Both friends (let's call them Alex and Andy) work in the same large company but in different departments. Their departments are in separate buildings and they never see each other at work.

Over drinks, Alex explains to you that his rather swanky and well-resourced department is one with rapid promotions, whereas Andy's department has very few promotions up the ladder.

As you sip your drink and listen to what Alex and Andy have to say, you know they're both hard-working, both high school graduates, and both worthy of the jobs they hold, but who do you think is most satisfied in their job? Alex or Andy? If, understandably, you assumed Alex, being the one in the best-funded department with reportedly highest chances of promotion, you would be wrong. Why is it that the person we expect to be more satisfied in work is not? And why have I made no mention of Andy, in the less illustrious department, being at all jealous of Alex?

When sociology professor Samuel A. Stouffer studied the morale and motivations of over half a million soldiers in wartime, he and his team observed a curious difference between servicemen in the Military Police and those in the Air Corps.[155] Stouffer surveyed over 2,000 men across these two divisions of the Army, and asked the following question:

"Do you think a soldier with good ability has a good chance for promotion in the army?"

The results, published in a two-volume tome called *The American Soldier*, unearthed a pervasive concept that now ripples through psychology, sociology, economics, and beyond.[156] Stouffer found that the Military Police answered the promotion question more positively than did the Air Corps. The Air Corps (like Alex's department) was better paid, with better conditions, and more frequent promotions than in the Military Police (Andy's department). Why was it that the assumedly worse-off Military Police group felt more satisfied than their loftier Air Corps colleagues?

Like your friends Alex and Andy, working in the same company but in distant departments, the two different sections of the Army rarely encountered one another. We expect that, because the Air Corps had the better set-up, that the Military Police might see their chances of promotion more negatively than their esteemed airborne colleagues. But that's not what happens at all.

Military Policemen worked closely with other Military Policemen who shared the rarity of ever being promoted. Air Corps members compared their position versus all their other colleagues in the same rapid promotion environment. How would you feel to work in a place where lots of promotions are happening but you don't get yours? When two related groups of people are distant, people in one group compare their situation only to others within the *same* group. Andy in the poorer department is more satisfied at work than Alex in the wealthier department because Alex and Andy never have the chance to compare themselves to one another. They each have more immediate comparisons to make.

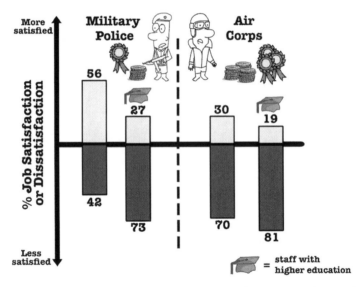

Left of the vertical dashed line: job satisfaction data for Military Police. Right of the same line: comparable data for the Air Corps. Whether you compare the whole or the more educated subset of each group, in all cases, the Air Corps reported less satisfaction than the Military Police, despite having better conditions and more chances for promotion.

Stouffer realised that comparisons are relative, not absolute. The unexpected result led him to formulate a concept now known as *Relative Deprivation*.[157] And it's a concept that pervades many fields because, when applied in a specific context, *Relative Deprivation* overlaps with several other psychological phenomena that go by different names.

In 1954, Leon Festinger published an influential paper on *Social Comparison Theory*: a fundamental psychological mechanism influencing our experiences, behaviours, and judgements.[158] When you want to understand where your abilities or opinions stand, you look to those around you. But you don't look to just anyone to learn about yourself. When you make these comparisons, you behave like the Military Police studied by Samuel Stouffer. You make comparisons locally, to those closest to you, those within reach. You don't make comparisons that are intangibly distant. If you're in the Military Police, you don't care about the Air Corps.

Festinger's *Social Comparison Theory* was built on nine principles. Among them, most importantly for our concerns on the Imposter Phenomenon, one of the nine principles recognises that, when you assess your abilities, you will naturally compare yourself to someone whom you perceive as being ahead of you. That is to say, there is a natural upward drive when comparisons are made to establish ability level. You compare yourself to other people as part of your attempts to figure out how to raise your game. And the further someone else's level is from your own, the less you compare yourself to them. Comparisons are most fierce, most potent, when they are close.

It's often impossible for us to determine our skill level or the validity of our opinions by reference to the physical world. For all those times when you're left searching, *social comparison* becomes the next best thing. It is often the only thing. You will seek out others similar to yourself, and slightly further ahead in ability. You will compare yourself to other people, even if a hypothetical database of all possible comparisons to the physical world existed. Alas, nearby social comparisons are simply much easier than investing the extra mental resources needed to assess the objective list of every possible comparison. Social comparison helps us fulfil our goals by providing an energy-efficient mechanism for self-evaluation and self-improvement. On why we compare ourselves to others, Festinger himself said:

"The holding of incorrect options and/or inaccurate appraisals of one's abilities by reference to the physical world can be punishing or even fatal...".

But more than that, the language of comparison helps us communicate effectively. The distance from here to the sun is about ninety-two million miles, but that doesn't make much intuitive sense on its own. Saying instead that the distance from here to the sun is the same as walking from the North Pole to the South Pole over seven thousand times starts to give you a deeper sense of the scale of the journey, right?

From Stouffer's *Relative Deprivation* to Festinger's *Social Comparison Theory*, the reason why imposter experiences always seem to be linked to comparisons was becoming clearer to me. Yet, the most important of these comparison theories – to me, to my working life, to the Imposter Phenomenon – uses a metaphor of fish in ponds.

In the 1960s, James Davis investigated the academic confidence and achievements of college graduates.[159] He found that the calibre of graduating students' career choice correlated more strongly with grade-point average (GPA) than with the ranked quality of the school itself. Davis' core argument was that students attending higher-ranked colleges felt worse about their individual ability, and thus achieved a lower GPA at the point of graduation than students in a lower-tier college. Davis even likened his proposal to Sam Stouffer's *Relative Deprivation* work on Military Police and the Air Corps:

"The theory of relative deprivation suggests a plausible explanation, that students' career decisions are affected by their self-judgments regarding their academic abilities, and that, like soldiers, students

tend to judge themselves by comparison with others in their unit, that is, in terms of GPA."

Davis' paper was titled *"The campus as a Frog Pond".* It leads us to a profound question about comparisons, and something I think is at the heart of the Imposter Phenomenon:

Is it better to be a big frog in a small pond, or a small frog in a big pond?

Some twenty years after James Davis first proposed this question, it evolved into one about fish rather than frogs. In 1984, Australian psychologist Herbert Marsh ran a study to look at the relationships between socioeconomic upbringing, academic achievement, and *academic self-concept.*[160] Academic self-concept (or ASC), simply put, is how you assess your own ability. The value of ASC cannot be overstated. How high or low you score on such a scale can have a profound influence on what you choose to do with your professional life. You can think of the academic self-concept as being a pie cut into four slices:

Absolute ASC: performance unrelated to any internal or external reference.

Critical ASC: performance evaluated against an objective measure.

Individual ASC: performance compared to past performance.

Social ASC: individual performance compared to peers.

Of all the slices of pie that make up the ASC, the social ASC is the biggest. Marsh found that for every 1 unit increase in average class grade, there was a near equal unit decrease in social ASC.* For the same 1 standard deviation increase in average class grade, the absolute ASC decreased by only 0.2 standard deviations. In other words, a student's propensity to compare their performance to those around them is the surest way to decrease their academic

---

*I've deliberately avoided talking about this point in the more academically rigorous term of *standard deviation.*

self-concept. The better your class is, the worse you feel, regardless of how well you actually perform.

Marsh's findings get weirder still. You might think that a student from a wealthier background would feel better about their academic ability than a student from a poorer background. The wealthier child would presumably have stable family circumstances, more opportunities for extracurricular academic support, and more opportunity to feel confident in their academic ability than a child of a lower-income household.

But according to Marsh's study, this intuition is false. Kids from the wealthiest households had the *lowest* academic self-concept of all. And whilst the students in the higher-ranked schools felt worse about their ability than students in lower-ranked schools, the *teachers' assessment* of these students gave the opposite trend. When the teachers had to assess the students' academic self-concept, they scored the students from higher status schools as having a higher opinion of their academic ability than students in the lower tier schools. The students and the teachers were assessing academic self-concept through very different lenses. This overall negative correlation between class average performance and a student's own academic self-concept is what is now known as the *Big-Fish–Little-Pond Effect.*

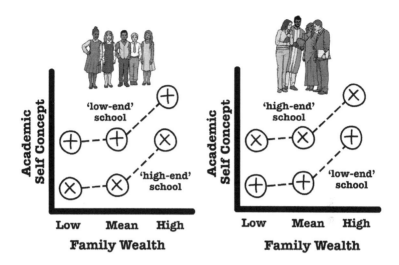

Left: when students report how well they see themselves doing academically, it's worse in seemingly higher ranked schools, regardless of socioeconomic status. Right: when the teachers estimate the same students' academic self-concept, the trend switches, wherein the teachers rank the kids in high-end schools more able than those in low-end schools, again regardless of socioeconomic factors.

A major follow-up study by Marsh in 2003 found evidence for the *Big-Fish–Little-Pond Effect* across 26 countries, with 24 being highly significant.[161] In 2018, a Stanford University study reported the most compelling evidence to date, showing a clear negative causal link between class average grade and an individual's academic self-concept. From the study crossing 33 countries, the *Big Fish Little Pond Effect* was found regardless of social class, subject of study, and gender.[162] The study presents the most definitive evidence to date that, as individuals, competitive academic environments provide a strong driver for self-comparison. And in terms of how you feel about that, it's much better to be a big fish in a little pond than a little fish in a big pond.

It has to leave us wondering:

Do the 'best' schools help us to reach for our highest ambitions, or do they encourage the type of comparisons that make us pick only the lowest-hanging fruit? Personally, I'm just grateful to have learned about the dark side of social comparison before it was too late...

Part 9 – Summary

In many ways, the story of the Imposter Phenomenon is the story of social comparison. If you've ever felt like an imposter, I'd be willing to bet it is, at least in part, because you have endlessly compared yourself to the best in your business, the big shot a few ranks above you who is famous and showered with fandom. Their success seems so close and yet so far.

When I think back now to that sombre and sunny day before the young superstar academic visited my office, I look again at the comparisons I made on autopilot. I think, now, about what I didn't know then. I think about François Vatel and the perils of overwork in the service of a perfect banquet. I think about Bernard Loiseau and Benoît Violier, haunted by their attainment of a star-branded metric originally designed to sell car tyres; a metric that made them compare often, and stress always. I think about academics like Paul Ehrenfest and Stefan Grimm, haunted by the trappings of academic competition. I think of all the students whose academic self-concept is blighted by the school and college rankings that society perceives to be the cradle of career success. And I think about you, because if you're still with me, you've recognised experiences of comparison in yourself. So hear this.

There are myriad pressures, systems, metrics, and games that would have you – consciously or not – compare yourself to other people. The incentives of the game can make you lose sight of what matters most. You take on the game's definition of success and forget all about your own. You try to tick **their** boxes, not your own.

Feeling like an imposter often arises from people trying desperately to find their unique place in the crowd. You feel like such a rip-off because you have so many opportunities to think of yourself as the small fish swimming into a shark-infested ocean. Stave off imposter experiences by finding your niche. Face uncharted waters.

Don't be the big fish. Be the only fish.

Comparisons between ourselves and our peers is unavoidable. From war, from sociology, from psychology, comparison is part of the human condition. Metrics of our classrooms and workplaces can drive these comparisons beyond a means of improving ourselves towards a deranged means of concluding that we are always underqualified. Understanding where a metric comes from, where it was born, can help us take it off the pedestal on which we hopelessly placed it. Whether it's Michelin Stars or paper citations or grade point averages, appreciating the origin stories of why these numbers exist can help take your mind away from the madness of metrics and onto the only game of comparison you can ever win...

Making you *now*...better than you *then*.

Your Chapter Challenges

1. Not everything that can be counted counts. The origins of a metric can reveal their limitations. We've covered Journal Impact Factor and Michelin stars here. Now it's your turn.

What is your version of attaining three Michelin stars or publishing in a journal with a high impact factor? Consider the metrics in play in your own workplace.

If the metric involves a numerical scale, write it out.
Note what 'good' is supposed to look like according to that metric.

Dig into the origins of your chosen metric. Finalise your challenge template by documenting any historical facts about the metric that differ from how it is now used or interpreted.

2. Beware of your environment. You will always compare yourself to those around you. Moving from one stage or place in your career to another is a strong trigger for imposter experiences.

Write down a notable study year or employment transition you've experienced in your career. To be clear, as discussed in regard to the Big-Fish–Little Pond-Effect, the career move in question could be anything from a move from school to university, to moving company, team, or rank.

On an arbitrary scale of 1–5, rate your confidence in your own abilities before and after said study year or career move. A template is available in the accompanying journal resource.

How did the move affect how often you were tempted to compare yourself to others in your work?

Chapter 8: Questioning Your Brain

If your imposter experiences involve you jumping to the conclusion that you aren't good enough, what happens if you try to prove that you aren't good enough? What if you started to write a stepwise plan to move towards 'good enough'? If we challenge the negative thoughts in our heads with external evidence, we can start to cultivate the self-awareness needed to keep moving forward.

Part 1 – The Diary Days

This entire book project started as something that wasn't meant for anyone else. It began during my transition from my PhD lab to my postdoc lab, from one organisation to another, from one group of colleagues to another. The panic induced in me then poured out into a diary. That diary became the book you are reading now. Because it was back then, in that first big career move, that I learned, first-hand, that I couldn't handle the thoughts of intellectual inferiority circling in my head. So, that's when I first put pen to paper.

After those first few days in my new postdoc role, I went home to my rented bedroom in the quaint little house across the road from the building I worked in. I quietly bounced upstairs, kicked off my shoes, and cracked open my laptop. I opened a new file and wrote. Daily. For two years.

That daily writing exercise was my first attempt to drag my thoughts out of my head and place them in front of my eyes. Painfully and persistently, I tried to manifest each thought as words and analyse each one. After that move from one lab to another, rather than focus on my work, I was consumed by thoughts of how smart I thought all my new colleagues were compared to me. All of what I have said to you in previous chapters emerged at a time when every moment felt like an accusing finger was pointing right at me, revealing me as a fraud, ready to cast me out of my workplace.

Had I never written down all those moments where I thought I was a fraud, this book would never have existed.

I wouldn't be talking to you now. I might not be here at all.

But as dramatic as that may sound, it serves the purpose of allowing me to share with you one last set of tools for managing your own imposter experiences. In self-reflection, self-awareness, and an ability to disconnect from the instantaneous melee of your thoughts in the present moment, there lies the resilient magic with which to manage your fights with the Imposter Phenomenon.

Before we dive into one last story, I want you to consider the following short review of all the previous chapters so far and have a think about what links them. Here we go:

In **Chapter 1**, we reflected on the unknown, unlabelled, unmanaged emotions that can leave us convinced we don't belong in the workplace. We also dove deep into the origins of the Imposter Phenomenon and how family upbringing can play a well-meaning and unintended root cause of feeling like a fraud.

In **Chapter 2**, we gave these troubling experiences a name: imposter experiences. Here was the first time we looked into the history of the Imposter Phenomenon as it was first articulated by Pauline Rose Clance and Suzanne Imes. Perhaps, just as importantly, finding the origin of Imposter *Phenomenon* helped us learn that it is not Imposter Syndrome, as is now pervasive in our online culture.

Chapter 3 challenged the assumption that any of us are ever alone in feeling like an imposter, and **Chapter 4** challenged us to think more about the meaning of the word 'imposter'.

For **Chapter 5**, we looked at the real story of luck – a favourite excuse for success among Imposter Phenomenon sufferers – and the incredible unlikeliness of our existence.

Then, in **Chapter 6**, we turned the tables on how to view rejection, to see that failures are oftentimes experiments in persistence towards our goals.

And in the previous chapter, **Chapter 7**, we dealt with a better understanding of the comparisons – good, bad, and ugly – that are so often at the heart of any imposter experience.

What links all the other chapters? In a word: awareness. Now, we will look specifically at some of the techniques we can use to improve self-awareness, and call into question your self-labelled status as an imposter.

Let's call a spade a spade. The Imposter Phenomenon is, at its core, a psychological wonder. Thoughts driving behaviours, driving more thoughts and more behaviours, round and around. But have you ever stopped to consider what a thought, a *single thought*, actually is? Is your Imposter Phenomenon a sad result of seemingly misfired logic? Are these thoughts fixed, unchanging, deeply rooted truths from your ancestral past, or are they flexible predictions of a brain starved of data?

One of the most surprising findings from my own study came down to the themes identified in the participants' experiences. When asked to describe a personal situation of such an experience, many cited obvious factors like social comparison, demographic barriers (age, gender, ethnicity), and working environment. Still, significant portions of the study population cited matters of anxiety, depression, post-traumatic stress, perfectionism, and low self-esteem in their answers. From some 40% of respondents came the necessary reminder that the Imposter Phenomenon is, in part, entangled with other affairs of the mind.

Over time, I've found that knowing just a little bit about how our brains work (and don't work) can be extraordinarily empowering. Learning how our emotions are made, as if from an out-of-body experience, can help stop us from panicking in the moment, each and every time a new imposter experience arises.

Part 2 – The Problem with Psychoanalysis

Stray thoughts appear in our minds all the time. But what about those streams of conscience that shock us when we snap out of a daydream?

Dr Sigmund Freud, arguably the 20th century's most famed psychologist, was the father of psychoanalysis. He took the view that dreams and associated human behaviours could be rationalised. To Freud and his followers, our dreams, nightmares, thoughts, ticks, and other actions could all be linked to an unconscious primal urge or a forgotten trauma. Psychoanalysis inferred that all thoughts have meaning.[163] The efforts of the psychoanalysts to clinically treat patients focused on bringing unconscious thoughts to the conscious realm. For the Freudians, free will did not exist. Everything about the human mind was predetermined.

In a nutshell, psychoanalysts assumed that humans were driven entirely by unconscious biological urges like sex and aggression. Why does any of this matter to you? Well, let me walk you through an instance of one of my thought streams during an imposter experience when I moved from my PhD to my postdoc lab:

"Oh, God, I wish that person would stop talking. I really wish I had what they have. I wish I was better. I won't ever be as qualified or as successful as they are! I wish I could do more. Ugh, what's the point? Maybe I'm no good at this. Maybe my work will be hated by everyone. No one will ever understand this feeling. I will always be alone. I'm not worth anything to this job. I'm a phoney. I'm going to get found out soon..."

"Why does the Freudian position matter?" I ask you. If someone is suffering from crippling thoughts that threaten to become a serious

psychological condition, telling the person that their thoughts have a neatly defined meaning, that it all rests on unchangeable biological urges, can be extremely dangerous! What could possibly make you feel more helpless than being told that your therapy is nothing more than an attempt to reveal what lies preconfigured inside the black box of your head? In other words, there is a problem with the Freudian approach to treating people living with psychological problems.[164]

The idea that thoughts are connected to real, tangible, explanatory events, instantly raises a hurdle to getting past these thoughts. Despite the infamy of his name, Freud's psychoanalytic approach to treating mental struggles has now lost its once unflinching grip on psychology. So, what has taken Freud's place?

Your thoughts are more in your control than you might think.

Part 3 - Cognitive Behavioural Therapy

In the late 1800s, physiologist Ivan Pavlov was studying salivation and digestion in dogs.[165] When presented with food, the dog would drool. But when, by chance, Pavlov spotted that his dog was slobbering in excitement at the sound of the footsteps of an assistant approaching with food, it inspired a series of now-infamous experiments leading to the phrase you may have already heard: *Pavlov's Dog*.[166] The now-famed physiologist later found that he could 'condition' his dog to associate the ringing of a bell with food approaching. At peak conditioning, he could ring the bell and the dog's mouth would moisten, ready to eat, even if no food came.

This work birthed a massive movement in early 20th century psychology known as behaviour therapy. More broadly, the psychological movement of *Behaviourism*, coined by John Watson in 1913,[167] led to a dark period in psychological treatment where internal thoughts were ignored. Only measured responses to stimuli were considered.

In the 1940s through 1970s, American psychologist Dr Albert Ellis and psychiatrist Dr Aaron Beck each worked on bringing rationality back to the treatment of psychological disorders, focusing on (rather than ignoring) a patient's internal thought processes. Ellis was originally trained in psychoanalysis (Freudian-style thinking). Unconvinced by the effectiveness and scientific validity of established psychoanalytic practice, he broke with tradition, and pulled no punches doing so. In 1950, Ellis published a monograph that dared question psychoanalysis, saying:

"Although the art of psychoanalysis is now over a half-century old, a comprehensive formulation of its scientific principles is still far from being realised. Such a formulation, which will strip from analytic theory and practise all trappings of dogmatism, unverified speculation, bias, and cultism, and which will leave standing only those principles and procedures which are, or seem well on their way to becoming, clinically validated, has been partially attempted, but by no means as yet systematically executed, by several neo-Freudians..."

He followed that verbal jab at psychoanalysis with a crushing uppercut:

"With advocates of unscientific psychoanalysis there can be essentially no argument...Most contemporary psychologists and psychiatrists agree, however, that thorough going scientific knowledge is the only valid basis for analytic (and other) therapy, and that rigorous criticism of non-scientific psychological methods is quite justified."[168]

Albert Ellis developed *Rational Emotive Behaviour Therapy* (REBT).[169] It marked the first big shift away from the unfounded woo of psychoanalysis towards more active cognitive methods of managing psychological issues.

Aaron Beck, working only slightly later than Albert Ellis, was working with patients suffering from depression when he started to notice commonalities across individual patients' thought patterns.[170] He noticed that his patients expressed several categories of what he called *automatic negative thoughts*. In the blink of an eye, Beck's patients would draw distorted, hopeless, and unfounded conclusions about themselves, the world, and the future. But rather than trusting these thoughts at face value, Beck tried to have his patients *reassess* the evidence to the contrary of what their automatic thoughts made them believe. This one insightful pivot from Aaron Beck – to reassess thoughts rather than assuming they had deeper meaning – helped him notice something profound.

Over time, his patients were able to think in more balanced and realistic ways, lifting their depression, and changing how they processed their thoughts. In what became known at the time as *Cognitive Therapy*, the focus was on understanding how we, as humans, think,* and applying that understanding to processing psychological challenges.[171]

Neither the behavioural therapy derived from Pavlov's dog nor the cognitive therapies of Ellis and Beck paint a full picture of human thinking and behaviour on their own. For over twenty years, in the period where both behavioural and cognitive therapies were available, there was an open and intense research debate over the use and validity of cognitive therapy versus behavioural therapy. It was only in the early 90s, when two separate global conference gatherings of these two therapies started receiving overlapping research papers, that the commonalities of cognitive and behavioural therapies became obvious. Today, they are combined into what is now called *Cognitive Behavioural Therapy* (CBT).[172]

Here's how to think about CBT in the context of the Imposter

---

*In 1979, family psychologist Dr Alice Miller's book *The Drama of the Gifted Child*, focusing on childhood trauma, provided a complementary and equally powerful vehicle for exposing Freudian psychoanalysis as an unfit tool for effective psychological treatment. Freudian psychoanalysis put the human mind in a black box and treated it like an unchangeable automaton. The likes of Ellis, Beck, and Miller showed that there was much to be gained by lifting the lid on the box.

Phenomenon:

You're among a group of your peers and experience a saddening thought. That small seed grows and quickly casts a shadow in your mind. It persists, it spirals, it grips, and you eventually conclude that you are a fraud. You are convinced that these people are only seconds away from discovering that you are not good enough to be there with them. You nod along with the conversation, you smile and you laugh when you're supposed to laugh. Inside, your heart is clattering off your ribcage, and your sweat could boil a river.

That thought might subside, you might calm down. Maybe. But the fact that you *recognise* the thought means you've had something like that experience in your past, and it could very well happen in your future. But now what? Rather than simply accepting that this is the way things are for you, this is where CBT could come in.

The innovative approach offered by CBT for managing your moments of anxiety is not to ask what the origin of the thought may be, or what subconscious desire it represents. No! That's what Freud and his followers would have you do. Instead, ask yourself this:

What is the evidence that supports the conclusion drawn from the imposter thought you experienced?

Think back to that hypothetical situation where you're standing in a group of your peers. If you think yourself a phoney, a fake, or a pretender, present your evidence for it. Have you *really* made it here by sneaking your way through the system, driven by luck alone? Is your success (however big or small) truly immaterial? Did your friends miss a wily, deceitful trick of yours? Soon enough, the lack of evidence in favour of you being an imposter slowly unravels the nonsensical nature of your imposter-based thoughts.

You can think of CBT as an evidence-based 'talking therapy' that helps you reassess identifiable distortions in your thinking processes.* It has been found to be as effective as medication in the early stages of treatment for some psychological disorders (social anxiety,[173] depression,[174] post-traumatic stress,[175] agoraphobia[176]), and often more effective than medication in providing long-lasting change. CBT is proven to be a positive contributor to treating low self-esteem,[177] bipolar disorder,[178] and psychosis.[179] It instils a sustainable practice that has the potential to remain a part of your routine long after any doctor's appointment ends, or prescribed medication runs out.

The negative distortions of thinking that CBT enables you to spot can, ironically, tempt some to dismiss CBT as a mindless exercise in positive thinking. This is not the case. Through structure and practice, CBT helps you to re-evaluate your initial assessment of a situation. You then work towards a more *realistic* and *actionable* interpretation of what happened in the moment.

Ultimately, the goal is to help you pivot to more measured and mindful responses when you find yourself in similarly stressful situations in the future. In essence, CBT gives you a framework in which to see how your thoughts, feelings, emotions, physical sensations, and environment all interact to account for your behaviour (be it for an imposter experience or some other psychological struggle). If you're not yet convinced, good. There are some exercises and thought experiments coming up. I encourage you to reflect on these when you can.

Another way to understand how CBT can help you reassess automatic negative thoughts is by using a related three-letter acronym: *ABC*.

- A is for *antecedents*, which is really just a fancy way of saying trigger events or something that happens to start a domino-

---

*If you want to go further, you might want to consider CBT alongside CFT, Compassion Focused Therapy, developed by Paul Gilbert. The CBT that has helped me and that I'm sharing with you centres on behaviour and thinking. CFT takes a more emotion-centred approach. See, for example: https://bit.ly/3d1ilGy.

like process of other thoughts and physical sensations that follow.

- **B** is for *behaviour*; quite simply, what your brain chooses to do physically and mentally as a result of the initial event. Physically, your heart might beat faster, your stomach might churn, your palms sweat, your breathing deepens. Mentally, you might experience a negative event with emotions such as fear, terror, or nervousness.

- **C** is for the *consequences* of those behaviours. What happens as a result of your behaviour? Do you forget to say something important? Do you shy away from a negotiation? Do you not bother showing up?

What threads this ABC model together is the B in the middle. How you *behave* as a result of a particular event will lead to certain consequences. If how you automatically behave can't be identified, engaged, and slowly changed, new instances of the *antecedents* (A's) will lead to similar or perhaps worsening variations on the *consequences* (C's). The implicit inevitability of behaviours in the frame of Freudian psychoanalysis was ultimately what led to the downfall of that approach to psychological treatment. CBT, on the other hand, helps you process how certain events or triggers (the antecedents) have, in the past, led to you responding in a particular way (the behaviours), and bringing about seemingly unavoidable outcomes (consequences).

Think about a time when you felt like an imposter. What was it about the *antecedent* (or trigger event) that you interpreted as a threat? Consider again that hypothetical group of peers I asked you to imagine standing with, from the story earlier in this chapter. That peer group was an example of such a threat. Your resulting thoughts of being an imposter represent one of the *behaviours* that follows on from the moment you stepped towards that peer group.

Cognitive Behavioural Therapy enables you to question your original interpretation of any event that you might have at first

deemed threatening.

It encourages you to examine, very closely, why you see the event as a threat. To be clear, this is not the Freudian version of asking 'why?'. CBT is not about finding some immutable, unconscious, unmentionable desire that you've supposedly been harbouring in the deep recesses of your monkey brain. Far from it. Here, with CBT, you are asking 'why' in order to start the search for evidence of you being an imposter that does not exist. You think you're a fraud? Okay, why is that? And where is the proof?

CBT was tremendously powerful and completely revolutionary for how I approached my own imposter experiences. So, let's take the story I told you in **Chapter 7** about the young superstar academic who was coming to visit my office and to whom I compared myself in the most terrible of terms. Here's the ABC of what happened:

- **A** - the *antecedent* was the first email I received announcing the visit of the young academic to my university.
- **B** - my *behaviours* following the email announcement included searching for this person's profile and academic performance metrics. This online career stalking then led to a series of automatic thoughts wherein I paid no mind to the distinct differences between my career path and the visitor's. I assumed this person was better than me in every conceivable intellectual respect, meaning then that I was a fraud, and very likely to be found out during my forthcoming conversation with this person in my office. As if on autopilot, I then glided into endless self-comparison. My breathing deepened and my heart droned.
- **C** - the *consequences* of these behaviours were that, when I actually met this person, I spoke quickly, laughed nervously, and struggled to be mindful of what they were saying in response to the research I was telling them about. I felt terrible about myself after the meeting. Frustrated. The diagram below shows a breakdown of what happened.

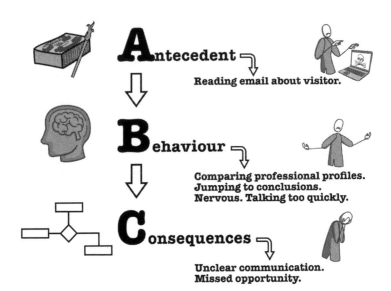

Antecedent

Reading email about visitor.

Behaviour

Comparing professional profiles.
Jumping to conclusions.
Nervous. Talking too quickly.

Consequences

Unclear communication.
Missed opportunity.

Visual summary of the antecedent (A), behaviours (B), and consequences (C) that played out to manifest the worst of my comparison-led imposter experiences. Cognitive Behavioural Therapy (CBT) and related tools are what can help spot such patterns of activity and help you edge towards more positive behaviours and more constructive consequences from similar future antecedents (or trigger events).

In this example from my own imposter experiences, where is the 'why?' behind my imposter thought process? Look again at what I wrote against B of the ABC process. I *"assumed this person was better than me"* and I *"paid no mind to the distinct differences between my career path and [theirs]"*.

With the help of CBT, I've learned, slowly but surely and increasingly quickly, to recognise that my very first response (B) to an announcement of any such visitor (A) is yielding to the temptation to look at a series of metricised summary stats that tell me absolutely nothing about that person's path to now (C). The experience did everything to reinforce my horrid assumptions of being a fraud when the evidence of my achievements pointed to the contrary. Revisit **Chapter 7** if you need a reminder of why not everything that can be counted counts.

Let's now move away from the history of CBT and my experience of using it, to look at more of the tools of CBT that you can use to more mindfully recognise some of your own behaviours. In the course of CBT's development, certain common so-called 'distortions' in thinking have been identified that can play out in any *antecedent-behaviour-consequence* (ABC) process. Recognising these distortions is what kick-starts your ability to change the automatic physical and mental behaviours that you otherwise assume to be out of your control. Nine of the most common distortions in thought are as follows:

1. **Mental Filtering** – you focus on the negative aspects of feedback or event outcomes, ignoring anything positive, complimentary, or redeeming.

2. **Over-generalising** – not only do you focus on the negative, but you frame those negatives as global, fixed, and unchangeable. You use words like *'never'* and *'always'* as if to encapsulate each and every aspect of your life. You fail to use more realistic and practical terms like *'right now'* or *'in this instance'* which would instead remind you that nothing is set in stone.*

3. **Catastrophizing** – for you, the worst-case scenario seems to be the only case scenario. You envisage all the terrible things that could happen after an event as if they definitely *will* happen. You do this before anything has *actually* happened. This is closely linked with another distortion in thinking known as **Future-telling**.

4. **Black-or-white Thinking** – you think along the lines of being a failure if you're not 100% perfect. There is no in-between, no shades of grey for you. You are either the right person in the right place at the right time, or you're a fraud.

5. **Mind-reading** – you jump to conclusions about what someone might be thinking based on little or no evidence. You amplify the possible negative criticisms the person might have of you, and seldom consider alternative positive interpretations of what this

---

*Before looking at your own behaviour, scroll through any series of angry posts on Twitter and I'd be willing to bet you find over-generalising without much effort.

person could *actually* be thinking of you.

6. **Emotional reasoning** – how you feel and how things actually are can be easily mixed up. Here, you jump to the conclusion that having a negative feeling is, in and of itself, evidence of wrongdoing. In your mind, the physical evidence and your emotional experience are one and the same.

7. **Discounting positives** – you dismiss positive events that you feel are irrelevant and somehow 'don't count'. This is a particular variation on **mental filtering**.

8. **Blaming** – you focus on external factors as the ultimate cause of your troubles and pay little attention to how you might take responsibility for what is in your control. If you find yourself blaming the world for all your problems, it's always worth remembering that when you point your finger at someone, there are always three more fingers pointing back at you.

9. **Labelling (of traits)** – an extreme form of **over-generalising** and **black-or-white thinking**, where you label yourself with highly emotive labels. *"X happened, therefore I am a fraud"*.

How many of these thought distortions did you recognise? I felt like I'd won the worst game of bingo when I first saw this list. Whenever you reflect on an event that led to a distorted thought, you can now *name* that distortion. You can call it out for what it is. It's just a thought, and it's not necessarily a reflection of reality.

Linking CBT to our earlier discussion on loneliness from **Chapter 3**, try to find one person to whom you can say out loud, *"I feel like a fraud"*. You will hear how it sounds and they, your trusted confidant, will tell you the same. Thoughts in our heads take up arms until we throw our voices into the silence for someone else to catch.

While Cognitive Behavioural Therapy might sound like a 20th century revolution, it has some of its origins in Ancient Greece. And it's there we find a CBT-style exercise that can help you avoid the worst consequence of feeling like an imposter...failing to act for fear of failure.

Part 4 – Fear Setting

Imposter experiences are driven by a fear of the unknown and thought distortions like catastrophizing, future-telling, and emotional reasoning that we named when discussing *Cognitive Behavioural Therapy*. But what I didn't mention about the development of CBT was that it was inspired by the ancient wisdom of Stoic philosophers. Especially for Albert Ellis, the CBT pioneer who rejected the Freudian psychoanalytic approach, the Stoic philosophy played a defining role in him realising that not all thoughts are rational or even meaningful. From Marcus Aurelius, the philosopher who most resonated with Ellis:

"If you are distressed by anything external, the pain is not due to the thing itself but to your own estimate of it; and this you have the power to revoke at any moment."[180]

Serial entrepreneur and author Tim Ferriss has also been hugely influenced by Stoic philosophy. Before we get to that, understand that Ferriss' success doesn't mean he hasn't faced failure and mental challenges (we looked at the assumption of success closely in **Chapter 6**). He has bipolar disorder and has a history of suicidal depression. He also came close to killing himself during his college years. To maintain strength, focus, optimism, and forward momentum, Ferriss created a three-page written exercise called Fear Setting, distilled from the Stoic exercise *premeditatio malorum* (meaning *the premeditation of evils*).[181] Ferriss is cited as having performed this Fear Setting exercise at least once every three months.

My own attraction to this particular exercise lies in its overlap with the many similar exercises in CBT. Fear Setting is simple, repeatable, and very useful for confronting the sort of procrastination that your imposter experiences can bring about.

Like CBT, Fear Setting helps you question how you are feeling about a particular situation in a given moment. It puts the spotlight on the things you're thinking of trying but, at the same time, think you're not good enough for. For the worthwhile risks that have you frozen in procrastination, here's how Fear Setting works.

On page one of the exercise, you write down, in vivid detail, the worst-case scenarios of the action you're fearful of taking. You do this in three parts:

> (1) **Define the action**. What are you thinking of doing but are fearful of trying?
> (2) **Consider the prevention of disaster**. What proactive action can you take to reduce the chances of failure?
> (3) **Consider repairs**. If the worst-case scenario plays out, what can you do to limit the damage and make the most of the apparent failure?

In Ferriss' TED talk on Fear Setting (viewed over nine million times when I wrote this chapter), he asks one very powerful follow-up question:

"Has anyone else in the history of time, less driven or less intelligent, figured this out?"

The answer, as I hope you would agree, is almost always "yes"!
In page two of Fear Setting, you are encouraged to ask another question:

"What might be the benefits of an attempt or partial success?"

Just like Zora Raeburn and the writers we met in **Chapter 6**, what happens if you give it a go and fail? What might you gain from facing what you fear the most? What if, for example, you took the chance to make a speech or give a presentation, even though you didn't feel ready for it? Your community will learn who you are and what you do. By standing on the stage or sitting in front of your webcam, you've given everyone a chance to start a conversation with you, the speaker. You aren't squirrelled away in the corner and out of the way. You're there. You're visible. You're invested and giving yourself the practice that you need to refine your approach.

In the third and final part of the Fear Setting exercise, you ask perhaps the most important question (and one relevant to imposter experiences):

"What is the cost of inaction?"

Ask this question in three parts:

- What is the cost of inaction in *6 months*?
- What is the cost of inaction in *1 year*?
- What is the cost of inaction in *3 years*?

You will always, always, always regret the things you did not do more than the things you did.[182] How painful might your regret be if, later in life, you look back and ask yourself:

"What if I had just given it a shot?"

By using Fear Setting to write down and make tangible all the things going on in your head, you give yourself a better chance of managing the fray. Like the ABC of CBT, the framework of Fear Setting prompts you to meditate on the *antecedents* (triggers) that could lead to *behaviours* that result in negative *consequences*. You, through this cognitive exercise, learn to place the premeditation of evils under your mindful control. Let me share with you one story of when I applied the Fear Setting exercise.

When I was working as a postdoctoral researcher, not yet running my own research team, I wanted to start applying for funding to help me take that next big step in my scientific career. You can think of this example like trying to pitch for investment in your first start-up company, fundraising for a charitable cause, or stepping up from being an instrumentalist to being conductor of the orchestra.

When the idea to apply for independent research funding first came to me, the application forms terrified me. I stared at the screen.

The only part of me that moved was the cold sweat slowly seeping upwards from under my skin. There were what felt like a thousand funding options to try, and I knew how precisely none of them worked. It all seemed too complicated, too alien, too much to try, too far beyond my meagre reach.

Then the inevitable happened. I thought about everyone else that *could* be trying to win the same grants, and then focused on justifying why they were more worthy applicants than I could ever be. Whether it was the number of published papers they had, where they came from, where they studied, whatever. It all gave me the fear that everything I could do to win a grant and start up a research group was doomed to spectacular failure. I was scared shitless. Through the practical scaffold of Fear Setting, however, I framed my premeditated grant application worries as follows.

First, I asked myself the direct question related to what I wanted to try:

(1) **Define the action.** *What are you thinking of doing but are fearful of trying?*

> MY ANSWER: Writing and submitting a grant application to help me start my own research group. I'm afraid because it is a complex and highly competitive endeavour. I can't help but think that there are too many unknowns to get my head around, and too many other people more worthy of applying for this funding than I am.

(2) **Consider the prevention of disaster.** *What proactive action can you take to reduce the chances of disaster?*

> MY ANSWER: A 'disaster' in my case would be having my application rejected. I would feel stuck, worthless, and left wondering if there was any point ever trying

again. To give me the best chance of success, I could speak to older colleagues and mentors who have been in a similar situation. I could learn how they applied for such grants, learn what worked for them and what didn't. For any funding body that I apply to, I could study the application guidelines and make sure I don't miss any compulsory points in my final application. For the research ideas I'm looking to include, I could ask my colleagues to sense check the science. Similarly, I could seek their help to dictate my ideas back to me, allowing me to see just how clear my own writing is. The list of these proactive actions goes on, but I think you get the idea.

(3) **Consider repairs.** *If the worst-case scenario plays out, what can you do to take the edge off the damage?*

MY ANSWER: If my email inbox flags up the dreaded 'Dear John' letter, telling me my application was unsuccessful, I will be tempted to run, hide, and cry in the coldest, darkest corner I can find. To focus on practical action, I could first request some feedback from the funding body itself to see what their reasoning was for not supporting my bid on this occasion. If that's not possible (which is often the case), I could take the final grant application back to colleagues and mentors and ask them – very directly – what they might have done differently. I could also take a minute to celebrate the fact that I gave it a shot at all! I'm not having to suffer the pain of wondering what might have happened if I applied. I have a result. It's not what I wanted this time, but I now know for certain what the outcome was. I now have a completed application to work from, improve on, and resubmit on a future occasion. If I had convinced myself not to apply, I would be holding a blank page.

With the action, prevention of disaster, and possible repairs all considered, the next thing to do was ask myself the question that Ferriss posed:

"Has anyone else in the history of time, less driven or less intelligent, figured this out?"

Asking this question is tough and bold at the best of times. But it's arguably worse for me or you, who suffer from imposter experiences, to be so forthright as to answer 'yes'! You might be tempted to think that everyone you know is more driven and more intelligent than you are. Instead, try asking a related question that is just as useful:

"Are there steps I can take today that will mean I am more knowledgeable about this problem tomorrow?"

For my grant writing fears, I asked this question so that I could focus on the 'how' and worry less about the 'anyone else' from the original question. Still, the answer to this alternative question is almost always 'yes'! There is almost always something you can do today to make yourself more aware, more prepared, more excited, more eager, more able to tackle the problem tomorrow. In the beginning, I didn't have the first clue what some of the grants I could apply for were even called. I didn't know where to find them, or what a final application might look like. I was afraid of the unknown.

Continuing this example, next came the question in Part 2 of the Fear Setting exercise:

"What might be the benefits of an attempt or partial success?"

As I started to convince myself that an application was worth a shot, I used the Fear Setting exercise to write down what I might gain from the experience, even if I didn't win the funding. In my case, I used the 'partial success' question to nudge myself towards listing what I would have tomorrow even if I failed in my application today. Without being exhaustive, trying and failing to win a competitive grant would:

(1) Make me aware of at least some of the other funding options that are available.

(2) Give me a sharper understanding of the amount of work involved in writing such an application.

(3) Help me understand how many weeks or months of preparation might be optimal for taking my next funding application from awful, to fair, to good, to great.

(4) Give me ideas of where to find previous grant winners that I could try to connect with and learn from.

(5) Place in my hands an application from which to build, refine, rework, and reapply. If I didn't apply, I would have nothing to work from except my original fear.

(6) Help me understand if this is something I even want to do. If it is, I've now made my mentors aware of the direction I want to take. The more they know, the more they can help. If I decide after trying the grant writing that it's something I don't want to do again, I've just taken the first step towards a pivot onto a new career path.

And finally, after listing the partial successes that would come from a failed attempt at your goal, comes Part 3, and perhaps the most important question from the entire Fear Setting exercise:

"What is the cost of inaction six months, one year, and three years from now?"

If I don't try this first grant application, I could procrastinate for another six months before convincing myself to make a start. By then, I could be near the end of a short-term job contract and otherwise consumed with more practical worries of cash flow. A year from now, I wouldn't have amassed all those research papers, videos, and seminars that feed into the creation of new ideas. A full three years down the line, I could have convinced myself that I have no ideas worth trying. I might have left my career behind altogether. I could be sitting wondering, *What if I had given it a shot?*

Whereas CBT helps you reflect on thought processes in your recent past, and Fear Setting helps you step into your future, there are other tools that I've found essential for making me more aware of what is right here, right now.

Part 5 – Mindfulness

In the closing months of my postdoc position, I commuted by bus across cities. Every morning, the first orbs of car light would bounce off the periodic clouds of my breath seeping out from under my scarf. I paid little mind to the silhouettes lined up in front of me at the bus stop. There was nothing to say except share in the silence that spoke for our collective desire to be anywhere else but there. On those cold bus-burdened mornings, my shivering body yearned for warmth, and my head burned with the fire of ever-present imposter thoughts.

The groan of the bus was heard before it was seen. And each morning, as the yellow door hissed open, the driver invited me (and the silhouettes) aboard where I would spend two hours with my thoughts. Most of those rides to work were focused on all the people I would greet later that day. All the people I thought were waiting to find me out and throw me back on the bus. Same imposter thoughts, different day. Every single day. But I did find a way to quieten the chatter in my head when I tried something I once naively thought was reserved for Buddhist monks and quacks. I meditated.

The idea to meditate grabbed me when I heard it mentioned on a podcast. Some celebrity was singing meditation's praises and

I was automatically set to reject the premise as some sort of homoeopathic horseshit. That said, the cold mornings in my constant frets of fraudulence were dissolving my sense of professional worth. I was desperately seeking quiet and decided that maybe this meditation stuff was worth a shot.

I squared myself onto my seat on the bus. Feet planted flat; my chin parallel to the floor. All I could see were the fine grey threads that composed the seat cover in front of mine. The odd flicker of my peripheral vision snapped into action as if to monitor the possible embarrassment of someone else looking at what I was up to. My scepticism stopped me from trying this meditation thing alone, so I used an app on my phone to guide me through it.

Hand in audio hand, I listened as I was gently instructed to breathe in through my mouth...then out through my nose. The whistles of air through my red nostrils stretched the time between my chest puffing up...and deflating. I closed my eyes and switched back to my normal direction of breathing. In through my nose...out through my mouth. In through my nose...out through my mouth. In through my nose...

Behind me (I'm not sure how far), I picked up the faint whisper of a phone call, periodically drowned out by the click and clatter of the bus toilet whose uninviting clinical aroma met my quivering nose. I noticed my knee itched through the rattling of the bus wheels on the motorway. Through those same vibrations, the metallic high-pitched harmony of the axles and pipes underneath the bus rang in my ear like tinnitus. The deeper groan of the diesel engine rippled through the windows. It was funny. The constant chorus of the bus sharpened the jovial conversation the bus driver was enjoying with a passenger up front. I hadn't noticed that before. Nor had I noticed the daylight. Or that I missed my bus stop for work. I did notice, however, that I didn't care. As I gently opened my eyes, I opened my mind to what meditation could offer. For what seemed like the briefest of experiences, I was merely there, in the moment. In every moment.

For the first time since I left my PhD lab, some two years earlier, I hadn't thought about what an imposter I was. This was the bewildering reality of the meditation I had previously been so dismissive of. I was stunned that this simple exercise could, at least temporarily, silence the exhausting thoughts in my head. And the controlled breathing that I tried is just one flavour of meditation. There is a whole gamut of meditations out there that you could try: yoga, journaling, loving kindness, body scanning, gratitude, zen, mantra, transcendental, and doing absolutely nothing at all for twenty minutes a day.

Whatever it is for you, pick a task that demands your attention. CBT, Fear Setting, and Mindfulness worked together to map out past, future, and present thought patterns. But with this awareness of how thoughts can be managed came the wonder of what thoughts are at all.

Part 6 – The Only Person in Your Head

If tools like CBT cover the *what* and the *how* to manage your brain, the remaining question is: why can the brain be managed at all?

Why were the Freudian psychoanalysts, with their passive treatment and assertion of no free will, wrong? Why, then, were the practitioners of *Cognitive Behavioural Therapy* so much more effective than practitioners of psychoanalysis for the patients in their care? In coming to terms with my imposter experiences, brain training techniques have been amazing, but not everything. I've found that knowing just a little about how the brain in our heads works – and does not work – has been a necessary complement to the practices of mind management.

Looking back on everything I've shared with you on the Imposter Phenomenon and my experience of it, one thing has been very difficult, near impossible, to avoid. It has been easy to describe imposter experiences as if they are embodied as a little demon inside my head, or yours; a looming, grooming, dooming creature that haunts and corrupts our thoughts, convincing us that we are frauds. We are evolved to visualise two things very well: routes through space and agents of action embodied as people. In Joshua Foer's book, *Moonwalking with Einstein*, such visualisations of people and place are used by Foer to win a memory championship.[183] Using such maps of meaning are useful for teaching difficult concepts, and useful for survival. Useful...but ultimately flawed, and possibly dangerous.

In 1980, cosmologist and master communicator Carl Sagan brought the documentary series Cosmos to our TV screens.[184] As part of this far-reaching magnum opus of science education, Sagan told the up-to-date story of how everything, everywhere, and everyone came to be. Part of Sagan's story involved the evolution of our brains. Through erudite prose and the gently booming base notes of his voice, Carl Sagan educated a generation of the general public on what makes us human. To 500 million viewers across 60 countries, he explained that our brains hold in their structure the clues of the three main stages of evolution through which they have passed. This particularly popular evolutionary story of the brain was of an 'inside out' model, explaining how these wondrous cranial organs reached their current state of complexity and size. Like peeling back layers of an onion, the three chapters of Sagan's brain story started with the brain layer closest to the touch of our hand – the *cerebral cortex*.

Thought to be the youngest part of the brain, the *cerebral cortex* was said to have evolved most recently in our ancestral primates. It was identified as the seat of creativity and calculation, of conscious-ness and criticality. Everything you think of as *you*. Whilst this presumed human part of the brain was said to have evolved some millions of years ago, the second of the three layers of the brain was said to have evolved earlier, tens of millions of years ago. The so-called *limbic system* evolved in earlier mammals, not yet primates.

Here, this middle brain layer, Sagan narrated, was the producer of our moods, emotions, and care for our children. Going deeper still, looking to the third and final chapter of the brain story Sagan told in *Cosmos*, you find the *R-complex* or *reptilian brain*. This deepest part of the layered brain structure was said to direct the darkest parts of our unshakeable character: raw aggression, hierarchy, ritual, and territoriality. Evolved hundreds of millions of years ago, the *R-complex* of the brain is likened to the brain of a crocodile.

The story Sagan told of our brain's evolution is part of what is known as the *Triune Brain* model. That's just a fancy way to say three-layers-in-one. Sagan educated us through our TV screens and in his Pulitzer Prize-winning speculations on brain theory titled *The Dragons of Eden*.[185] Scientifically, the three-in-one brain model was developed, in large part, by the neuroscientist Paul D. MacLean.[186]

Starting in the 1940s, MacLean worked from the inspiration of earlier 19th century giants like Charles Darwin and Paul Broca.[187] In doing so, MacLean was empowered to progress a linearly staged model of our brain's evolution, with its regionalised responsibilities of what we ultimately experience in day-to-day life. The most compelling, pervasive, and arguably intuitive part of MacLean's *Triune Brain* model was its assertion that our brains evolved in an additive fashion, from reptile to mammal to human, leaving us in an uneasy truce between our evolved logical selves and our caged ancestral predecessors. Following MacLean's model of the brain, there are two people in your head – the person you know to be you, and the instinct-driven cave dweller your bloodline used to be.

The beautiful, sensible, and tragic *Triune Brain* model marries with our sense that not everything we do is under our control. It is strangely comforting to think that there is genuinely a feral version of ourselves inside our head, battling for control, absolving us from the responsibility of what looks like our most impulsive reactions and embarrassing behaviours. Not only that, the three layers in MacLean's brain model marry beautifully with successful management models like Professor Steve Peters' *Chimp Paradox*.[188] In this model, he clearly points out that it is a useful simplification of the underlying truth. Peters has applied the simplified three layers of the brain to successfully help top athletes, as well as the general public, understand that the would-be *'chimp'* in your head can be controlled. He goes on to show this self-control can be exercised through regular, mindful thought processes that update the *'computer'* in your brain. In this way, the inner cave person is kept calm, giving you more time under the control of your logical *'human'* self. The three-layer model of the brain also fits masterfully with psychoanalyst Sigmund Freud's parallel psychological model of the mind,[189] containing the *Id* (our instincts), the *Superego* (our moral compass), and the *Ego* (our realistic negotiator between the dialectic pull of the *Id* and *Superego*).[190]

The only problem with MacLean's three-layer brain model, which Sagan so poetically retold, is that it is completely wrong. You and I, as humans, are not as unique as MacLean's *Triune Brain* model would lead us to believe. MacLean gathered some compelling evidence in support of his model, like victims of accidents changing their behaviours after having a part of their brain removed or damaged, yet he didn't slow down to consider counter models or arguments against his theory. It is not my aim here to fall into the rabbit hole of neuroscience, but rather to show you enough of the promising picture that you can use in your struggles with imposter experiences.

Before we get to that, let's try to understand why the *Triune Brain* model, and any notion that you are battling with an inner insecure ape, is false. Firstly, MacLean's idea that the cerebral cortex, the supposed outer layer of your brain, was the 'crowning glory' of a linear evolution and newest of the three brain layers, doesn't match the scientific record.

Early mammals already had well-formed cortices,[191] meaning some high-level thinking predated humans altogether.[192] Other high-level operations thought to be reserved for humans in this outer part of the brain, like tool-making and complex language, can also be claimed by the industrious nesting and beautifully communicative songs of birds. Definitely not human. In evolutionary terms, it is far more likely that a common group of existing brain structures evolved in different ways along different paths at what was once a shared prehistoric fork in the road.

Myths about the central *limbic system* of the brain can also be refuted. Some reptiles, crocodiles for example, exhibit so-called *paleomammalian* behaviours, like childcare, rather than abandoning their young after egg-laying, as many other reptiles do.[193] As you dig deeper still into MacLean's three layers of your brain, the evidence for us having an *R-complex* (or reptilian brain) inherited from early land-crawling lizards, is also on shaky ground. There exist early jawed fish that possess the more technically labelled *basal ganglia*, revealing that such deep brain structures predated the reptiles from whom we were supposed to have inherited our most inhuman and inhumane components. Together, all of this evidence points to an alternative truth.

Your brain does not exist in three semi-independent layers fighting for control of your body. There is no 'you versus the ape'. Instead, your brain acts as a unified whole, with a structural constitution like that of a shark, a frog, an ape, and a lamprey, just evolved along a different path to become a more cognitively effective size.

What, then, of the chances to ever truly understand our thoughts? What remains when you can't blame your irrationality on a perpetually protesting chimp inside your head? Asking these questions led me to a fascinating modern view of the brain, and one that has contributed massively to my ability to question my imposter experiences. If you remember nothing else after reading the next part of this story, remember this:

The emotions you connect with your imposter experiences are built, but they are not built in.

Part 7 – The Theory of Constructed Emotion

When it comes to thinking about how brain structure is tied to mental struggles, MacLean's intuitive but flawed *Triune Brain* model tempts you into blaming a survivalist chimp for everything that might feel to you like a flawed reaction to the world outside your head.

The fictitious three layers of the brain urge you to ask where your emotions are made when there is a more helpful question you can ask; a question that has since enabled me to stop talking about imposter experiences like they are a monster in my head. Stop asking where your emotions are made. The better and more empowering question is asking how your emotions are made. This is the mind-changing magic of the *Theory of Constructed Emotion*.[194]

There is a constant conversation between your body and your brain. Your body is forever sending sense data to your brain for interpretation. Crucial though it is, your conscious self is not wired to experience this body–brain conversation in high definition or with surround sound.

Rather than being acutely aware of the fine details in the body–brain conversation, you experience a blended banquet of blurry feelings like pleasant, unpleasant, comfortable, uncomfortable, and so on. This mood or *affect* is the equivalent of little status lights and symbols on the dashboard of your car. If something is wrong, you will be alerted. Further investigation will be needed to understand what exactly is wrong and why the warning lights lit up in the first place.

The sense data collected from your eyes, nose, ears, skin and tongue are the result of your body's encounters with the outside world. Your brain, on the other hand, is locked away, encased and protected inside the black box of your skull. And when your brain receives the collected information from your senses, it has essentially just received a raw data dump. The crude oil. There is no refined information yet, no detailed report, nothing but the kaleidoscopic chaos of the sights, smells, tastes, touches, and sounds of whatever your body just encountered out there. What can your brain possibly do to make sense of the messy data it has just received? Well, it guesses!

Using past experience, your brain looks at all the new sense data and tries to match it to the closest past experience from whenever similar datasets were acquired. Slowly but surely, over the course of time, when your organs send your brain similar collections of raw sense data, your brain develops a concept for that particular class of experiential data. Each and every instance of an experience involving that stored *concept* will be different – the data varied, the exact numbers different from the time before – but there will be some sort of pattern that your brain starts to recognise.

When all is well, your brain's guesses become more like educated predictions. You might even say such guesses become expertise. The very act of being able to read the words over which your eyes now scan is because your brain has collected so many past experiences of squiggles, matched to sounds spoken by another human, that the squiggles now naturally hit you as letters and words and spoken prose. Yet, if those same squiggles written in your native language were translated into another language, you would not have the same experience of instantaneous recognition. Instead, you would be experientially blind. For example, you will probably be less clear of the phrase *'Tu probabiliter non intelligis linguam Latinam'* than the phrase *'You probably do not understand Latin'*. But such experiential blindness isn't just manifest in a lack of linguistic skill. The guessing games played by the brain have profound consequences on our understanding of emotions.

Your emotions are not universally expressed and recognised by others, nor are these emotions primitively automated reactions to the outside world. Emotions have no irreducible fingerprint shared by everyone everywhere. Unless you're from Portugal, you probably have never experienced the exact emotion of *desbundar* (to shed your inhibition and have fun). If you're not German, you might never have been able to exactly express *sehnsucht* (a feeling of longing for an alternative state of affairs). And if you're from outside certain regions in the Middle East, it's likely never occurred to you to say you're feeling *tarab* (a musically induced state of pure ecstasy). The same goes for facial expression. In the West, a simple smile might express happiness, whereas in the East the same expression is more likely to be used as a sign of respect, or to hide some other emotion. In countries like Japan, people read faces with the eyes more so than in the West, where the eyebrows and mouth do more of the heavy lifting. This is why it's harder to fake a smile in the East than in the West.

In my Imposter Phenomenon study, the variability of emotional concepts came through in a rather surprising way. Earlier, we discussed the Clance Imposter Phenomenon Scale, where scores closer to the maximum of 100 denoted the most chronic and severe imposter experiences. In addition to this scoring, and beyond the open answer stories the participants shared, each was also asked to relate their experience to one of a choice of nine possible emojis. Be it a crying face, a frown, a straight face, a grimace, a closed smile, an open smile, tongue-out zaniness, rosy-cheeked bashfulness, or knowing smirk, every participant linked one of these yellow emojis to their own story. What would you expect might happen to the emoji choice as the Imposter Phenomenon scores reached higher and higher values? If, like me, you expected higher scores to yield exclusively gloomy emoji choices, you'd be wrong. Check out the following graph for some examples of what actually happened.

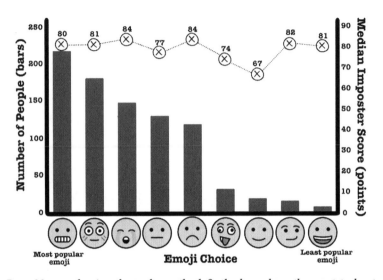

Bars: Measured using the scale on the left, the bars show the most to least popular emoji choice from participants asked to pick from 1 of 9 emojis when describing their imposter experience. The grimace was most popular, the open smile was least popular. Datapoints: Across the board, the median ('middle') Imposter Phenomenon Score associated with each emoji choice was high. In other words, a person's choice of facial expression cannot reliably predict how they are feeling. We should not judge an emotional book by a deceptive facial cover.

Just as there is no 'cheat sheet' to reliably summarise instances of emotion or facial expression, modern neuroscience holds that there are no distinct emotion circuits in your brain. You can't hold a brain mould in your hand and point a finger to where an emotion was made.

If this all sounds odd or counterintuitive, it should. Some of the three-layer brain myths that now pervade many cultures are simply overhanging hypotheses from the most compelling but defunct science of the past.

There is no reactive cave dweller in your head.

There is no one mandating the appropriate emotion for you to express at a given time. Your emotions, every last variation of every last instance of every last one, are guesses constructed by your prediction-building brain. None of your emotions are built into your head at birth. Instead, they are simply built.

Using past experience, your brain continually builds and refines concepts to draw from. Past experience is used to predict how your body will behave in the present. As you read the words 'toothbrush' and 'lemon', your brain will draw on your past experiences to create new instantaneous experiences of refreshing mint and sour citrus. You might even synthesise a new concept of a sour-tasting toothbrush, using the combinations of lemon and toothbrush.

While emotions themselves are constructed, variable, and predicted, there are (at the same time) legitimate 'inward looking' feelings that detect basic pleasantness and unpleasantness in the body. These blurry, ill-defined feelings, collectively known as *Interoception*, aren't like the emotions we label as anger, fear, excitement, exhilaration, terror, tension, sorrow, security, pessimism, or panic. Interoception is a sort of sixth sense that enables you to detect if something is 'wrong' internally. It is a feeling, but it isn't tied to any one emotional concept. It's not something that can have an emoji slapped on it. Part of *Interoception* is the mood or *affect* mentioned earlier.

We experience emotions as if they happen to us, but they are, in fact, created by us. Past experience leads to predictions of present experience, and present experience fashions the concepts your brain will use to make future predictions. And round and round it goes. But here's the beautiful thing. We are architects of our own experience. If we take baby steps to change our experiences today, we prepare our brains for more favourable predictions tomorrow. This is why passive Freudian psychoanalysis failed, and why active therapies like CBT can work. But with such a beautiful realisation comes something truly scary – you have more responsibility for your emotions than you think you do. Not a chimp, not the outside world, not anyone else. You!

It's on each of us to update our stored concepts so that our brains can better avoid inaccurate predictions that lead to energy-draining behaviours.

We're not directly in control of our emotions, but we are in control of how we view and interpret each experience.

Therein, you can take small but deliberate steps away from blind, data-starved brain predictions in your future. So, if today's experiences contribute to tomorrow's predictions, how would you want to view today's imposter experiences ahead of tomorrow?

While the predictive nature of the brain places the responsibility on you, that's not to say external social factors don't matter. Imagine you are (once again) comparing yourself to someone else. You collect the sensory clues about that person. You conclude that you are a fraud and, in that moment of familiar terror, you physically exhaust yourself.

What do you think will happen the next time you start to compare yourself to someone else? And the time after that? If the cycle continues, and you tire yourself out with one such experience after another, where does such weariness lead? It can lead to it becoming more difficult to drag your heavy body around. It might lead to you thinking it's too hard to get out of bed. In your imposter experiences, you are subconsciously reinforcing the collection of concepts in your brain that will lead to future refined predictions that you are indeed a fraud. You are sharpening the knife that will plunge deeper and deeper wounds into your back.*

Since learning about the *Theory of Constructed Emotion*, I have constantly tried to view imposter experiences through this enlightening lens. The imposter experience is another pigeon-holed concept that our brain uses to build the way we see and feel the world. When you go round the Imposter Cycle that we spoke about

---

*The original title of this book was *Pull Out the Dagger*. Depending on when you read the book, the remnants of that title may be preserved in the original book cover as a non-fungible token (NFT)...

in **Chapter 2**, you reinforce these negative concepts and facilitate wrong predictions for each and every new situation that, for similar situations in past times, initiates a new instance of your imposter experience.

Part 8 – Summary

Each of our realisations in previous chapters were steps towards a more mindful, reflective, measured view of imposter experiences. But now you have the psychological stories from this chapter to strengthen the foundations of how you manage the Imposter Phenomenon. I didn't need to earn another degree for the bite-sized nuggets of actionable knowledge from this chapter to be helpful to me. Nor do you.

Cognitive Behavioural Therapy (CBT) triumphed over Freudian psychoanalysis and Behaviourism because it placed the power, insight, and responsibility for thought management in our hands. No longer is the fictional monkey in our mind to blame. If you can use CBT to speak out loud or, on your own, write down what you're going through, you are actively training yourself to turn once automatic negative thoughts into points of constructive reflection.

Couple CBT with meditation – guided, chanting, or simply sitting still – and you are well on the road to developing an unstoppable level of self-awareness. Step back to consider your reactions as if you were outside yourself, outside your body. Nothing calms your mind like being able to observe it as if from a bird's eye view. The book you are reading right now is, in part, a result of over one hundred thousand raw, unfiltered thoughts being spilled onto a page, for two whole years, whilst I struggled with self-comparisons, failure, ego, and forever feeling like a fraud. You can be your own outside observer.

If you then combine your new tools of mind management with even just the top-level knowledge of how (not where) emotions are made in your mind, you can become kinder to yourself. At the same time, you will take on more responsibility for what is in your control to change.

The traditional view of emotions and where they come from is wrong. Emotions are real, but they are predictions rather than built-in reactions of a caged ape. They aren't fixed labels, nor are they universal. Not every culture has the same concepts of emotion and there is no set facial expression of the common emotions like fear, anger, anxiety, happiness, excitement, or ecstasy. The old view of a three-layered brain remains compelling because it's almost intuitive, even though it has long been scientifically disproven. Why does this matter? Because what you experience as an instantaneous emotional reaction does not necessarily reflect reality. Ask yourself in moments of imposter angst:

"What assumptions am I making that have caused my brain to make the prediction leading to my imposter thought?"

Your overwhelming feelings of not being good enough are orchestrated by a predictive brain, not a reactive one. You use your past to predict how you behave in the present. That present behaviour builds and reinforces the concepts your brain will use for a future instance of that category of experience.

How you experience the world today will influence how you experience the world tomorrow.

When you are able to more deliberately self-reflect, you are more likely to question your brain's predictions and use tools like CBT and Fear Setting to build new concepts and new responses. Once you're able to re-examine yourself, you can re-examine so much more.

There is space for both specialists and generalists.[195] You can consider option C when everyone else is ferociously arguing for option A or B. You can learn to understand the temptations of groupthink.[196] You can learn to question every personal and social cue that once led you to feel like you were a fraud.

The icing on the cake? If you keep with you the knowledge of how your brain constructs your experience of the world, every time you feel like a fraud will be less severe than the last.

Whether it's learning a language, learning to ride a bike, or learning to better manage the Imposter Phenomenon, understanding just a thin slice of the *Theory of Constructed Emotion* can go a long way. If you can harness tools like CBT, Fear Setting, and Mindfulness to better interpret your experiences, if you simply become aware that your brain is predicting rather than reacting, you also arm yourself with the ability to have your brain make more meaningful, useful, and accurate future predictions. Over time, you can move from the red text on the cover of this book that reads 'You Are a Fraud', to being able to read the scribbled correction...

...You are *NOT* a fraud!

Your Chapter Challenges

1. The related tools of Cognitive Behavioural Therapy and Fear Setting enable you to take a structured written approach to observing your thoughts.

Consider again the instance(s) of your imposter experience(s) that you wrote about in earlier Chapter Challenges.

Reframe such stories in terms of the antecedents (triggers), behaviours (actions), and consequences (outcomes).

A template of a modified version of the original Fear Setting exercise (which integrates elements from previous chapters of this book), is available in the journal resources. Firstly, write out how the exercise might have impacted your behaviours, and thus the consequences, had you known about CBT back then.

Next, complete the same exercise for something you have yet to achieve. What might the antecedent or trigger event be? What are the negative and more proactive behaviours that might result from that trigger event? What are the possible consequences emerging from the negative behaviour versus the possible behaviour?

2. The stillness of meditation and mindfulness can cultivate your ability to take a 'top down' view of your behaviour. See yourself as if you were the observer.

Find a meditation method that you want to try. This can be one of the classic examples (like yoga or simply sitting still) but what matters most is that it is an exercise that focuses your mind on a particular task.

Document the changes you observe in yourself after sticking with the exercise for around one month (at least).

3. The brain predicts more so than it reacts. There are not two people inside your head and there is not an ancestral ape

version of you calling the shots. Use this knowledge to drive your use of the tools in Challenges 1 and 2 immediately above.

Reviewing your written answer(s) to Challenge 1, identify the elements of the behaviours you documented that are reinforcing the brain concept that you are an imposter.

Identify the part of your story that exemplifies what is triggering your brain to predict the feeling and the threat of being a fraud.

As a collection, your 18 Chapter Challenges completed across all 8 chapters of the book should serve as an individual journal. The actions you've taken here will, I hope, serve to improve your awareness, understanding, and first steps to managing your imposter experiences. Whether you keep it entirely private, share the social components of the challenges, or complete the whole exercise in group form, what matters most is that you do it. You give it a shot. That way, you prepare yourself not only for managing your own imposter experiences, but rising to my biggest challenge to you...

Epilogue: The Responsibility of Leaders

In the late 1700s, Joseph Black delivered his last lectures on chemistry at the University of Edinburgh. He did not start the course with a lecture on this subject. Instead, Professor Black, the same man who invented Scotland's premier scientific society, who was among the first to tame carbon dioxide gas, and who developed the first analytical balance, decided to warn his students against the imminent threat of imposter experiences. In transcripts of his lectures, you can read that Black began by offering his students *"a few general cautions and remarks with regard to this subject"*.

He was specifically addressing those who *"have not the advantages of experience for their direction"*.

Most importantly, Joseph Black told his wide-eyed audience that *"even those who have been most distinguished by their learning, have frequently met as much difficulty in their first setting out, as most others"*.[197]

Two hundred years before Dr Pauline Rose Clance coined the Imposter Phenomenon, Professor Joseph Black was warning those in his care about the likely trials of self-doubt. He warned his students about the possibility of them each, in their own unique way, feeling like a fraud. He made sure they knew that not even the most revered scholars of the day were immune to feeling like they were going to be found out and stripped of their robes. And he instilled in his students an empowering awareness before such threatening feelings could ever truly take hold.

It is in these closing pages where a book summary might normally be thrown at you. But that's not what is needed. Here's why.

My story is no longer the only one I am personally responsible for. I now have students, mentees, and younger colleagues in my care, not to mention my own beloved kids. All of that scares me senseless. I share this, imagining that you and I are sitting across a table from one another. And with that privilege, I end by addressing you not as the wandering soul burdened by unmanaged feelings of being an imposter. I instead address you, the growing leader. Because one day, maybe even now, the responsibility of leadership will fall on your shoulders. It will be in your gift to guide, to listen, to encourage, and to elevate those around you. You, not I, will help someone who is suffering from the feeling that they are not good enough to be where they are. Those people need you, not me.

Leaders are more than a boss.

They are confidants, pastoral carers, advisors. When asked for advice, leaders are in the position of utmost responsibility. They are comfortable with being critical as well as caring. The aim of a true leader is to be as helpful as they are direct. They are not enablers or validators or avoiders of woe.

Given all the ways we have looked at managing the Imposter Phenomenon, I now leave you with seven principles to consider as you carry on this journey in your own way.

Principle 1 – Charitable Leadership Begins at Home

Before you try to help anyone else suffering from imposter experiences, first address your own. As a leader, don't for a second pretend that you've got it all figured out. You don't have all the answers, and you don't wear a skin of stone. Yes, I've written this book on managing imposter experiences, but that doesn't mean I'm somehow 'cured'. I still have moments when I feel like a fraud, but such feelings no longer knock me out. I no longer want to run to the nearest bathroom and lock the door every time I'm comparing myself to the person I'm talking to.

These imposter experiences still pop up in my life, as they may well do in yours. If we falsely lead our embattled colleagues to believe there's a way to irreversibly extinguish all of their imposter thoughts, we set them up for the inevitable crushing disappointment triggered when their imposter thoughts return in a new setting.

The inner battles you will confront before leading others are not necessarily battles that you will win. As you take more and more life-affirming risks, the world outside might bring about another instance of the conditions that once made you feel like a fraud. Countless books will sell more copies than this one. Almost guaranteed. That is partly because of the promise many of those books make to enable you to cure, or smash, or defeat, or overcome your imposter 'syndrome'. Reject these false promises.

As entrepreneur and podcaster Peter Shepherd puts it, your imposter experiences are to be 'danced' with.[198] Consider imposter experiences dormant but never dead. Pinned down but never entirely shut out. Your imposter experiences are to be understood, acknowledged, and managed. Whenever you take your life into exciting unknowns, consider your imposter experiences as an old friend rather than a fervent enemy.

Only when you have managed your own imposter experiences can you ever hope to help someone else with theirs.

Principle 2 – Learn What Your Brain Is and Is Not

Consider the person in your care who thinks they have two people in their head. That person might otherwise be doomed to procrastinate on all their goals, and to blame a mystical mind monkey for every panicked imposter experience. You, as a leader, can be there to listen to what antecedents (or triggers) are causing the behaviours that lead to the ultimate imposter consequences for this person. Share with them the concepts of CBT and Fear Setting, not so you can do the work for them, but so that you can point to the frameworks that (and maybe even the qualified therapists who) can help them grow the self-reliance they need to best manage their self-doubt.

You're running brain software that gives you the false sense that there are two people inside your head. There's a feeling of having the logical you and the reactive ancestral cave dweller on whom you can blame every fear, every overprotective inaction. But there aren't two people in there. You know that now. And those in your care need to know this, too. Remember that your brain uses past experiences to construct what it judges to be the best physical and emotional response in that moment.

When the person in your care is tempted to point the finger of blame, this is your chance to show them the three fingers pointing back at them.

Principle 3 – Listen more than you speak

When you become the person sitting across the table from someone suffering the familiar woes of the Imposter Phenomenon, consider the following:

Listen.

The late Larry King, master of the journalistic interview, conducted over 60,000 interviews in his career. He believed that, in order to have an interesting conversation and to learn from someone, you have to understand how to ask the right question.

How many times have you asked someone how they are but not really stopped to listen? It's just something we say. *"How are you?"*.

It's cocktail party chat. On the flip side, how many times have you been asked how you are and you've mildly responded, *"Fine"*, or *"I'm OK, how are you?"*? The answer is as mundane as it often is untrue.

As a leader, it is your responsibility to be able not just to hear but to listen intently to the people in your care. In order to be *interesting*, we have to be *interested*.

You have two ears and one mouth for a reason. While sharing the vulnerability of your own experience with those in your care, do not equate your story to theirs. Individual struggles deserve your individual attention. Don't disrespect the privilege of someone being open with you by lazily reciting platitudes of your sameness. And whatever you do, don't tell them that you know *exactly* how they feel. You don't. Empathy is not impersonation. Consider encouraging your struggling colleague to reflect deeply on their own experience in the non-judgemental space you have created for them. Learning is often emergent, not imparted. Learning is more by experience than by instruction. Don't steal their revelation. Lead them to the place where they reveal it for themselves.

Principle 4 – Don't Let Them Forget the Unlikeliness of Being

I wrote everything on family trees and the perspective that helps manage imposter experiences around the time my first daughter was born. I wrote her the letter you saw in **Chapter 5**. In a more general form, it brings me to a fourth principle. One you must share with anyone struggling with imposter experiences, looking into their eyes as if into those of your own child.

Finding a lost toy in the bath is easy. Finding the same toy in an Olympic swimming pool is much tougher. But finding that very same toy in the ocean, with its coverage, currents, and colossal depths, is virtually impossible. Improbable, but not wholly impossible.

Keep in mind, for yourself and for those who seek your counsel, that we are all that improbable bath toy.

And for anyone in your care who is drowning in those horrid feelings of being a fraud, remind them that the odds of them ever being here are so ridiculous that there is no time to waste. The chances of being alive are about 1 in $10^{2685000000}$.

Whether those in your care know it yet or not, they've won the lotto. And you are the catalyst that will open their eyes before they can blind themselves to what's possible.

Principle 5 – Save Their Work from the Fires of Perfection

Consider closely the value of 'good enough' over perfect. The Imposter Phenomenon is a weapon expertly crafted for inaction. In the throes of self-doubt, opportunities are missed, chances will not be taken. The Imposter Phenomenon manifests the ultimate excuse to keep you and your work hidden from the world. And so, too, might this happen to someone in your care. This is where your generous mentorship comes in.

Alexander Pope was a poet and satirist. His landmark works swept Great Britain in the 1700s. Such was his influence on literature that Pope is now enshrined at Westminster Abbey in London (UK), bejewelled and celebrated in death. He's buried next to Sir Isaac Newton. The literary contributions of Pope are unquestionable. Still, this giant of the written word was not free from his own battles with self-doubt.

From 1728 – 43, Pope released three versions of his satirical poetic masterpiece, *The Dunciad*.[199] Written first anonymously and with pseudonyms before Pope ever put his name to it, the poem mocks the advances of tastelessness in Britain. It's an unsubtle and un-apologetic jab at human nature.

But the entire work almost never was.

Immersed in unfathomable hatred of his own work, Pope came close to throwing his original draft of *The Dunciad* in the fire. This was the 1700s...there was no back-up copy, no USB locked away, no ethereal cloud storage. Pope wanted to get rid of his work from existence. Period. To history's aid, however, came Alexander Pope's dearest friend (and fellow literary giant) Jonathan Swift.

Swift – most noted for his authorship of Gulliver's Travels – was a friend of Alexander Pope for almost thirty years. It was during some of their time together that Pope acted to banish his Dunciad draft to the flames. Swift acted...well, swiftly. He thrust himself from his armchair, pulling the pages from the grip of the fire. *The Dunciad* was saved from an irretrievable fate.

Pope had produced one of the finest satirical works of his time, something still celebrated today. Yet, it took a deep friendship and the objective sense of another human being to avoid Pope's self-sabotage. Pope did eventually reflect on this event with gratitude, etching Swift's heroic action in the introduction to *The Dunciad* saying:

*"...without you it had never been"**

So, whose work might burn if you're not there to stand watch over the fire?

---

*Famed author and screenwriter Steven Pressfield wasn't as fortunate as to have Jonathan Swift by his side. While Pressfield became famous in his 40s, he penned his first novels in his late 20s. Those drafts saw the bottom of a bin before they could ever see the eyes of an audience.

Principle 6 – Turn Awful Comparisons into Awe-inspired Action

Help those in your care to see that their working environment (or changes thereof) can be a source of imposter experiences.

As a leader, you must listen intently for the unfounded comparisons someone might use as a catalyst for thinking they are a fraud. In **Chapter 7**, we discussed the systems and metrics that feed the unhelpful comparisons that can take imposter experiences to even darker places.

Someone in your care might compare themselves to others and *immediately* race to the conclusion that they are not and could never be as good as that other person.

As the leader, you can help your colleagues look beyond the *'what'* and more at the *'how'* of a peer's success. Help them see how that other person came to be successful. Consider helping them pivot away from feeling awful and more to feeling awe-inspired. Read that again: awe-*inspired*.

Successful people, despite endless distractions, know how to get shit *done*. They can realise that multitasking is not all it is hailed to be. They set their minds to a task and don't stop till it's done. Then they move on and move up. Next, next, next!

The position of leadership need not mean a direct, hierarchical relationship, where the person seeking advice is your employee, student, or assistant. It could equally be a stranger, someone recognising or perceiving your advanced knowledge on a subject. A particularly useful example of this comes in the form of Rainer Maria Rilke, a Bohemian-Austrian novelist and poet revered as one of the most influential German language writers during the 19th and early 20th centuries. In 1902, Rilke received a letter from a young poet, Franz Kappus, a young man seeking critical advice on his poetry from Rilke. In Rilke's thankful and measured reply, he urged

Kappus not to focus on the approval of and comparison with other people:

"You ask whether your verses are good...You have asked others before. You compare [your poems] with other poems, and you are disturbed when certain editors reject your efforts. Now (since you have allowed me to advise you) I beg you, give all that up."[200]

Rilke's advice on avoiding external comparisons is first and foremost. He continues with what Kappus should do in place of the insidious search for external validation:

"Search for the reason that bids you write; find out whether it is spreading out its roots in the deepest places in your heart...Delve into yourself for a deep answer."

Unless you do it for you, there is no hope of being happy with what you produce. Rilke is essentially asking, *"Is this really what you want to do with your life?"*. Be damn sure. If not, you'll continue to seek the praises of people for work you don't truly care for.

And, as a by-product of over comparing with other people, Rilke urges Kappus to avoid the trap of becoming derivative:

"...avoid at first those forms that are too facile or commonplace."

Compare yourself to other people and you will live in their shoes rather than your own. If you are able to peer into yourself and be truly, genuinely comfortable with what you do, then you will release yourself from the urge to please other people with the results. This last point from Rilke to Kappus reads as follows:

"And if out of this turning inward...verses come, then it will not occur to you to ask anyone whether they are good verses...looking outward and expecting from the outside replies to questions that only your [innermost] feeling in your most hushed hour can perhaps answer."

For those people in your care, you have a duty to spot such traps of unhappy behaviour. These traps are what contribute strongly to feelings of being an imposter. Quashing thoughts of comparison in people who seek advice from you may seem cruel at first when you call them out. In effect, it's the most admirable kindness you can bestow as a leader.

Consider helping those in your care to focus on what is in their power to change, rather than what they feel makes them powerless compared to someone else. Help them to focus on making the version of them that exists today better than the version that existed yesterday.

Principle 7 – Look Out of Other Windows

In the movie adaptation of Harry Potter and the Order of the Phoenix, Harry leads the training of school friends in essential skills needed to fight their foes. Their enemies are bigger than them, stronger than them, and more experienced in the same magic as them. In a secret gathering room, Harry helps train his classmates, day and night, whenever they have the chance to gather. Some pick up the skills and the spells quickly, others have to persevere beyond repeated failures. Everybody, no matter the initial skill, has to practice and practice and practice. To ward off feelings of mass self-doubt among his peers, Harry remarks that every great wizard who ever lived started out as a student.[201] Such greats were made, not born.

Someone can easily get stuck in a cycle of imposter feelings if they judge their life choices as either A or B. Black or white. Zero or one. Great wizard, or forgettable footnote. Looking at binary decisions discourages anyone from ever looking beyond that realm. The *Overton Window* tells us that any debate which lies on a spectrum of two extremes can blind us to options outside the window of those extremes. While the world rages in two camps over A or B, encourage those in your care to consider options C, D, and E. Breed comfort with heterodox thinking. Lead them towards being dissatisfied with the imposter view they have framed for their distorted world view.

A Well-timed Phone Call

Towards the end of writing this book, I was contacted by an old colleague from my PhD days. They had gone off to a life in industry and were now looking to pursue an academic career.

When the phone rang, I was pleased to hear their voice – a blast from the past, and one that I respected greatly. But where I initially thought the chat would steer towards finding logistical routes back into academia for this colleague, the call took a rather different path. Instead of mere practicalities, we discussed my colleague's primary concerns about coming back to academia. They were scared. Having compared their knowledge and ability to previous supervisors, to other students of their generation, and even to me, they couldn't help but wonder:

"Why am I even thinking of going back there?"

"Do I have the same level of knowledge as the others?"

"Could I really do this job?"

"Am I good enough?"

As they asked these questions, I didn't have a sense of déjà vu but rather a sense of growth. Relief, even. The conversation carried the now not-so-intimidating familiarity of thoughts that once consumed me.

Balancing a knowing smile with the quiver of a tear, I knew, uncountable years into my own exploration of the Imposter Phenomenon, that I could now help someone other than myself. This moment, this phone call, showed me that learning to cope with imposter experiences, learning to recognise them, acknowledge them, and manage them, had all been worth it. The monster that once threatened my livelihood and my life was now an old friend.

On the tip of my tongue now sat the knowledge that feeling like an imposter is not a syndrome, that we're never alone in feeling like a phoney, and that we are wrong to talk about ourselves in the same breath as the genuine fraudsters. There, too, rang the realisations that our very existence is ridiculously unlikely, that failures are experiments, and that comparing ourselves to earlier versions of ourselves is the only game of comparison we can ever win. No monster or mammoth-slaying caveperson lives in our heads. And our emotions, those triggered by imposter experiences or not, are built, not immovably built in.

My attention turned back to the phone.

"Don't worry", I said to my troubled colleague.

"You said you feel like you might not be good enough. You might even feel like an imposter. If that's the case, here are some things you might want to consider..."

Acknowledgements

Over the course of writing You Are Not A Fraud, the support grew from a handful up to a small village of people. I was, at times, silly enough to believe I could write this book all on my own. That one-man-band approach to the work couldn't have been further from the truth of how the book eventually came to be. To everyone who helped me avoid this book becoming a bumbling, embarrassing mess, I am forever grateful.

I thank the first person who ever heard me toy with the idea of turning my secret writings into a book: Dr Calum Forsyth. Calum, thank you for turning your patience and conversational presence into the motivation I needed to let that first seed grow. Little did I know, back at our Mini Grill meal in 2016, that I'd need that motivation to help carry me through five more years of bringing this thing to life.

To my beta-readers – Amanda McFarlane-Reid, John-Paul and Elaine Rafferty, Ross and Colette Batpie, Mark McLaughlin, Paul McClair, Kenny Doherty, Heather Walton, Jimbo McKee, Dr Katherine Geogheghan, Dr Ella Gale, and Dr Tommy Reilly – I struggle to comprehend the selfless kindness with which you gave your time to read the draft of the book I naively thought was 'final'. Not only did you each provide wonderful encouragement, but (rising to my challenge of not being a cheerleader) also provided truly insightful written notes to help bring the book to the more concise clarity I hope I've now been able to deliver. A special mention here, too, goes to fellow author Dr Claire Jarvis: Claire, thank you for sharing your writing research gift with me. You helped spark what would later become the Epilogue I truly wanted to write.

To Drs Stuart Cantrill and Elizabeth Gadd – thank-you for taking the time to be a sounding board to my difficult realisations on the academic metrics that I might otherwise have struggled to write about...at least in balanced terms.

To my wonderful editor Kirsten Rees, I'll be forever grateful that you decided to take on this project. It was a random delight to have found you through the Glasgow podcast circuit. And it was an immeasurable privilege to have your challenges raise the bar of what I could otherwise have hoped to produce. Here's to our next project!

I opened the book with a Preface that made plain that I'm not a professional psychologist. In that vein, I am indebted to my dear friend, best man, and lifelong confident Paul Reynolds-Cowie. PRC! From the very earliest notes I took on this book idea, you were there to lend me your expert lens. You kept my research questions balanced, my assertions referenced, and my recommendations clear. To have come through school together and eventually collaborate on this book, two decades later, has been a full-circle joy the likes of which I would never have predicted.

And from the inspiration of an expert psychologist in PRC came the courage to reach out for more research support, especially in the guise of Iona Craig. While early in your undergraduate Psychology degree, you showed me a wisdom and professionalism I didn't even know existed when I was your age. Your passion, patience, and perseverance to help analyse one of the most gruelling data-scraping tasks of the research in this book will never be forgotten. Ever. Thank-you, Iona.

To Francesco Gentile and Tolga Burcak, my Argentinian and Turkish coding wizards, respectively, thank you for turning my early scripts and ethereal ideas into useable tools. Your programmatic insights have helped mine more information gold from the crude and raw research data that would ever have been possible on my own.

Perhaps the most joyous penny to drop for me was that which

came from the study of family history, family trees, and all things genealogy. To the immortal Pete Berrie, I thank-you for opening my eyes to the world of the census. Thank you for introducing me to the real Zora Raeburn. Your guiding hand through the cracks of history filled the gaps on an otherwise meandering Chapter 5!

To Isaac, Valentina, Zoltan, Kelly, and Ali, thank you all for your small but seminal parts in helping me research the imposter stories from history. You showed me the true magic of building a freelancing team.

To David Colon, the graphic designer who designed the original Pull Out the Dagger book cover, thank you for helping me see that the project had to grow from there to something altogether different.

For professionally and patiently polishing the audiobook sessions, producer Paul Shields at the Green Room in Glasgow deserves my enduring thanks. Thanks for keeping the red light on while I turned the air blue in the Green Room.

To my mum May, late dad Mark, brothers Joni and Jamie, and grandparents Joe, May, Archie, wee Meg, and to Carol, Joe, Sharon, and Demi, much about our family is far from picturesque, but you were never far from my mind in thinking how lucky I am to be here, now, anywhere at all.

And last but by no means least, to those for whom this book is most dearly dedicated...Amanda, Adaline, and Lachlan. Without your love and support, scarce little of me (never mind the book) would remain. Thank you for keeping me facing forward. I'm putting the laptop away now. Promise.

About the Author

Marc was born and raised in Glasgow, Scotland.

He completed his Masters in Chemistry at the University of Strathclyde in 2011. In 2015, he completed his Carnegie Trust-sponsored PhD in Chemistry at Strathclyde. From 2015-16, Marc was a postdoctoral research associate at the University of Edinburgh. During that time, he was inducted into the SciFinder Future Leaders in Chemistry programme.

In 2016, Marc won the prestigious Leverhulme Trust Early Career Fellowship and rejoined the Department of Pure & Applied Chemistry at Strathclyde from 2017-20. This position was supported by GlaxoSmithKline, and he was thus the first Strathclyde-GSK Early Career Academic. In 2018, Marc was selected to participate in the Scottish Crucible leadership program, the Merck Innovation Cup, and was part of the Converge Challenge Entrepreneurship Competition Top 30. In 2020, Marc became a Lecturer for Innovation in Education at the University of Bristol.

Most recently, Marc was awarded a UKRI Future Leaders Fellowship, joining the Department of Pure & Applied Chemistry at Strathclyde in 2021.

He has held visiting lectureships at the University of Bristol and the Hunter Centre for Entrepreneurship at the University of Strathclyde. In 2021, Marc completed Seth Godin's altMBA.

His research interests include physical organic chemistry, computer vision, virtual reality, process safety, and the psychology of the imposter phenomenon.

He lives with his wife, two kids, and border terrier in 'sunny' Glasgow.

Contact the Author

If you enjoyed the book and think someone you know would benefit from reading it, please consider sharing details of the book.

Tweet Your Challenges!

For those who might learn from your example of completing the book's **Chapter Challenges**, share your experiences on Twitter, or any of the other platforms listed below.

The hashtag for this book is **#YouAreNotAFraud**

Find out what other people are saying about the book by searching for the hashtag on Twitter.

Connect with Marc

Marc's main social and correspondance channels are as follows:

Twitter - https://twitter.com/reid_indeed (@reid_indeed - with one underscore!)

LinkedIn - https://www.linkedin.com/in/dr-marc-reid-18974554/ (search "Dr Marc Reid")

Instagram - https://www.instagram.com/reid__indeed/
(@reid__indeed - with two underscores!)

TikTok – https://www.tiktok.com/@reid_indeed

Medium - https://reid-indeed.medium.com/

Website - https://www.dr-marc-reid.com/book

Email – https://www.dr-marc-reid.com/contact (Add the subject "You Are Not A Fraud")

For a list of all ways to share this main book and the journal resource accompaniment, scan the QR code below:

https://linktr.ee/reid__indeed

Notes

Preface

1 Alma Mater Studiorum: the University of Bologna: Throughout History. (2019). Italy: Alma Mater Studiorum - Università di Bologna.

2 Stokes, H. (2011). The Emblem, the Arms and the Motto of the University of Cambridge: Notes on Their Use by University Printers. United Kingdom: Cambridge University Press.

3 Levecque, K., Anseel, F., De Beuckelaer, A., Van der Heyden, J., & Gisle, L. (2017). Work organization and mental health problems in PhD students. Research Policy, 46(4), 868-879.

4 Shackle, S. (2019, September 27). 'The way universities are run is making us ill': Inside the student mental health crisis. The Guardian. Retrieved December 2, 2021, from https://bit.ly/2nDTfcD.

5 Oswald, A. (2018, June 28). Middle-aged academics are at Greater Suicide Risk Than Students. Times Higher Education (THE). Retrieved December 2, 2021, from https://bit.ly/3OOf3cp.

6 Haidt, J., & Lukianoff, G. (2019). The coddling of the American mind. Penguin Books.

7 Kinman, G., Wray, S. (2013). Higher Stress: A Survey of Stress and Well-being Among Staff in Higher Education. University and College Union.

8 Guthrie, S., Lichten, C.A., van Belle, J., Ball, S., Knack, A., and

Hofman, J. (2017). Understanding mental health in the research environment: A Rapid Evidence Assessment. Santa Monica, CA: RAND Corporation. https://bit.ly/2sDmFtM.

9 What researchers think about the culture they work in. Wellcome. (2020, January 15). Retrieved December 3, 2021, from https://bit.ly/3OR06Gv.

10 Stephan, P. (2013, January 23). Too many scientists? Chemistry World. Retrieved December 4, 2021, from https://bit.ly/3JmxCU8.

11 Larson, R. C., Ghaffarzadegan, N. & Xue, Y. Too many PhD graduates or too few academic job openings: the basic reproductive number R0 in academia. Syst. Res. Behav. Sci. 31, 745–750 (2014).

12 Galloway, S. (2020). Post Corona: From Crisis to Opportunity. United States: Penguin Publishing Group.

13 Loveday, V. (2018). The neurotic academic: Anxiety, casualisation, and governance in the Neoliberalising University. Journal of Cultural Economy, 11(2), 154–166. https://bit.ly/3oLUUcw.

Chapter 1: An Innocent Fraud is Born

14 Spottiswoode, R. (Director). (2000). The 6th Day [Film]. Phoenix Pictures, Columbia Pictures.

15 Ferriss, T. (Host). (2017, December 20). Terry Crews — How to Have, Do, and Be All You Want (No. 287) [Audio Podcast Episode]. In the Tim Ferriss Show. https://bit.ly/3bnpiXJ.

16 Mirror.co.uk. (2009, February 22). Kate Winslet: 'I still worry I'm a rubbish actress'. Retrieved December 6, 2021, from https://bit.ly/3Qa83aY.

17 Cooper, A., Vanderbilt, G. The Rainbow Comes & Goes: A Mother and Son on Life, Love, and Loss. (HarperCollins, 2016)

18 Imposter syndrome | Mike Cannon-Brookes | TEDxSydney - YouTube. (2017, August 1). Retrieved December 6, 2021, from https://bit.ly/2NUCX8e.

19 Gottlieb, A. (2016). The Dream of Enlightenment: The Rise of Modern Philosophy. United Kingdom: Penguin Books Limited.

20 Nast, C. (2019, May 5). Emma Watson talks turning 30, working with Meryl Streep, and being happily single. British Vogue. Retrieved December 6, 2021, from https://bit.ly/3oQBi7g.

21 Gaiman, N. (2017, May 12). The Neil Story (with additional footnote). Retrieved December 7, 2021, from https://bit.ly/3d0RErd.

22 Sinek, S. (2019). The Infinite Game. United Kingdom: Penguin Books Limited.

Chapter 2: It's Not a Syndrome

23 Dawkins, R. (2012). The Magic of Reality: How We Know What's Really True. United Kingdom: Transworld Publ. Limited UK.

24 Clance, P.R., NIH Graduate Student Research Symposium (2016). "The Face of Tomorrow's Science".

25 Clance, P. R., Imes, S. A. (1978). The imposter phenomenon in high achieving women: Dynamics and therapeutic intervention. Psychotherapy: Theory, Research & Practice, 15(3), 241–247. https://bit.ly/3bmW2jE.

26 Caselman, T. D., Self, P. A., Self, A. L. (2006). Adolescent attributes contributing to the imposter phenomenon. Journal of Adolescence, 29(3), 395–405. https://bit.ly/3zqJbFb.

27 Langford, J., Clance, P. R. (1993). The imposter phenomenon: Recent research findings regarding dynamics, personality and family patterns and their implications for treatment. Psychotherapy: Theory, Research, Practice, Training, 30(3), 495–501. https://bit.ly/3Jw2L7B.

28 Josa, C. (2019). Ditching Imposter Syndrome: How To Finally Feel Good Enough And Lead With Courage, Confidence And Passion. Beyond Alchemy Publishing.

29 Lane, J. A. (2015). The imposter phenomenon among emerging adults transitioning into professional life: Developing a grounded theory. Adultspan Journal, 14(2), 114–128. https://bit.ly/3QfeDgi.

30 Badawy, R. L., Gazdag, B. A., Bentley, J. R., Brouer, R. L. (2018). Are all impostors created equal? Exploring gender differences in the impostor phenomenon-performance link. Personality and Individual Differences, 131, 156–163. https://bit.ly/3oOCFmI.

31 Clance, P. R. (1985). The Impostor Phenomenon: Overcoming the Fear that Haunts Your Success. United States: Peachtree Publishers.

32 Tavris, C., 'Success - Time Is On Your Side', Vogue Magazine, December 1982 (107/1).

33 Oxford English Dictionary, Draft Additions ("impostor syndrome" and "impostor phenomenon"), June 2018. See also: 'Oxford English Dictionary adds 1,000 old-new words', The Standard (Hong Kong), 22 June 2018. Retrieved 2 August 2022,

from https://bit.ly/3zoq4LT.

34 Calvo, F., Karras, B. T., Phillips, R., Kimball, A. M., Wolf, F. (2003). Diagnoses, syndromes, and diseases: a knowledge representation problem. AMIA. Annual Symposium proceedings. AMIA Symposium, 2003, 802.

35 Chrisman, S. M., Pieper, W. A., Clance, P. R., Holland, C. L., Glickauf-Hughes, C. (1995). Validation of the Clance Imposter Phenomenon Scale. Journal of Personality Assessment, 65(3), 456–467. https://bit.ly/3bmT8f0.

36 Reed, R. (2016). If I Could Tell You Just One Thing...: Encounters with Remarkable People and Their Most Valuable Advice. United Kingdom: Canongate Books.

37 Woolston, C. (2016). Faking it. Nature, 529(7587), 555–557. https://go.nature.com/3d0UiNF.

38 de Beauvoir, S. (1959). Memoirs of a Dutiful Daughter. Kirkup, J. (translator). United Kingdom: World Publishing Company.

39 Clark, M., Vardeman, K., Barba, S. (2014). Perceived Inadequacy: A Study of the Imposter Phenomenon among College and Research Librarians. College & Research Libraries, 75(3), 255–271. https://bit.ly/3PSdTOs.

40 Reisz, M., (2018). California scheme to get ex-prisoners into HE ripe for imitation. Times Higher Education.

41 Henning, K., Ey, S., Shaw, D. (1998). Perfectionism, the impostor phenomenon and psychological adjustment in medical, dental, nursing and pharmacy students. Medical Education, 32(5), 456–464. https://bit.ly/3JowLCd.

Chapter 3: No Longer Alone

42 Kelly, R. (2001). Donnie Darko [Film]. Newmarket Films.

43 Malhotra, R., Tareque, Md. I., Saito, Y., Ma, S., Chiu, C., Chan, A. (2021). Loneliness and health expectancy among older adults: A longitudinal population-based study. Journal of the American Geriatrics Society, 69(11), 3092–3102. https://bit.ly/3JoyOpT.

44 Levine, S. (2016). Belonging and Loneliness: A sense of belonging is a boon to life, while loneliness is the bane of life. Psychology Today.

45 Badawy, R. L., Gazdag, B. A., Bentley, J. R., Brouer, R. L. (2018). Are all impostors created equal? Exploring gender differences in the impostor phenomenon-performance link. Personality and Individual Differences, 131, 156–163. https://bit.ly/3PS7v9P.

46 Goleman, D. (1984). Therapists Find Many Achievers Feel They're Fakes. The New York Times.

47 Matthews, G. (1984). The impostor phenomenon: Attributions for success and failure. In G. Matthews (Chair), Impostor phenomenon: Research, assessment, and treatment issues. Symposium conducted at the 92nd Annual Convention of the American Psychological Association, Toronto, Canada.

48 Okoro, C. (2016). How colorism shapes our standards of beauty. TEDxStanford. Retrieved 2 August 2022, from https://bit.ly/3Q4quhk.

49 Kopelman, A., Roché, J. M. (2013). The Empress Has No Clothes: Conquering Self-Doubt to Embrace Success. United States: Berrett-Koehler Publishers.

50 Tom Hanks Says Self-Doubt Is 'A High-Wire Act That We All

Walk'. Movie Interviews. NPR. April 26, 2016.

51 Pennebaker, J.W., Boyd, R.L., Jordan, K., & Blackburn, K. (2015). The development and psychometric properties of LIWC2015. Austin, TX: University of Texas at Austin.

52 Goleman, D. Therapists Find Many Achievers Feel They're Fakes. New York Times. September 11, 1984.

Chapter 4: Genuine Imposters

53 Holmes, E. (2014). TEDMED Session Three: Achieving the Seemingly Impossible. [At the time of the book's 2022 release, this reference appears to have been pulled from the TED website.]

54 Carreyrou, J. (2018). Bad Blood: Secrets and Lies in a Silicon Valley Startup. United Kingdom: Pan Macmillan.

55 Klockars, C. B. (1980). The Dirty Harry Problem. The ANNALS of the American Academy of Political and Social Science, 452(1), 33–47. https://bit.ly/3OXXXZM.

56 Siegel, D. (1971). Dirty Harry. Warner Bros.

57 Hartmans, A., Leskin, P., Jackson, S. (2021). The rise and fall of Elizabeth Holmes, the Theranos founder who is now on trial for fraud. Business Insider. Retrieved 2 August 2022, from https://bit.ly/3oMiTbp.

58 Auletta, K. (2014). Blood, Simpler. Annals of Innovation. The New Yorker Magazine. Holmes quote from https://bit.ly/2PJxPDs.

59 Cramer, J. (2015). Theranos: A hot company takes fire. Mad Money. CNBC (USA). Retrieved 2 August 2022, from

https://cnb.cx/3PWwCIE.

60 From @eholmes2003 Twitter account. Direct link to tweet: https://bit.ly/3vzbxw1 (Still accessible at the time of writing, December, 2021).

61 Stripling, J., Zahneis, M. (2018). The Big Lie: A professor schemed to get a raise and win his department's respect. Instead, he wrecked his career. The Chronicle of Higher Education. Retrieved 2 August 2022, from https://bit.ly/3zTjwXj.

62 Battersby, M. (2014). The talented John Myatt: Forger behind the 'biggest art fraud of 20th century' on his criminal past - and how he went straight. Independent.

63 Landesman, P. (words), Edelstein, J. (photography). (1999). A 20th-Century Master Scam. The New York Times Magazine.

64 Con Man Case Files (2007). Season 1, Episode 1. Crime & Investigation Network.

65 'Arrest in bank robbery: Suspect's TV picture spurs tips'. (1996, April 19). Pittsburgh Post-Gazette.

66 Kruger, J., & Dunning, D. (1999). Unskilled and unaware of it: how difficulties in recognizing one's own incompetence lead to inflated self-assessments. Journal of personality and social psychology, 77(6), 1121-1134. https://bit.ly/2GNphtv.

67 Dunning, D. (2011). The Dunning–Kruger Effect: On Being Ignorant of One's Own Ignorance. Advances in Experimental Social Psychology, 44, 247–296. https://bit.ly/3zRd4jl.

68 Rosling, O., Rosling, H., Rönnlund, A. R. (2018). Factfulness: Ten Reasons We're Wrong About the World–and Why Things Are Better Than You Think. United Kingdom: Flatiron Books.

69 Henriques, D. B. (2011). The Wizard of Lies: Bernie Madoff and the Death of Trust. United States: Henry Holt and Company.

70 White, R. (Director). (2017). The Keepers [web series]. United States: Film 45 and Tripod Media.

71 Joost, H. & Schulman, A. (Directors). (2010). Catfish [documentary film]. United States: Relativity Media, Rogue Pictures, Hit the Ground Running, and A Supermarche.

Chapter 5: Finding Perspective

72 Eliott-Drake, L. (1911). The Family and Heirs of Sir Francis Drake, in Two Volumes. United Kingdom: Smith, Elder and Co.

73 Smith, J., Forbes, A. (2010). Tinderbox Heroes: Commemorating the Cheapside Street Disaster and the Extreme Challenges Faced by Glasgow's Postwar Fire Service. United Kingdom: Strathclyde Fire & Rescue Retired Employees Association.

74 Benzer, A. (2009). The Tao of Dating for Women: The Smart Woman's Guide to Embracing Your Inner Goddess and Finding the Fulfillment You Deserve. Elite Communications LLC.

75 Bays, C. (Executive Producer), How I met your mother. United States: Columbia Broadcasting System.

76 Dawkins, R. (Writer), Barnes, R. (Director) (2006). The God Delusion [television series episode]. In The Root of All Evil? United Kingdom: eyedoubleyousee for Channel 4.

77 Vaynerchuk, G. (2015, February 23). Monday Morning Motivational Video [video]. GaryVee. YouTube. Retrieved on 3 March 2022, from https://bit.ly/3Q7EQh6.

78 Clance, P. R. (1985). Chapter 9. In: The Impostor Phenomenon:

Overcoming the Fear that Haunts Your Success. United States: Peachtree Publishers.

79 Ferriss, T. (Host). (2018, June 6). Shep Gordon — The King Maker on His Best PR Stunts, Hugest Failures, and Practical Philosophies (No. 184) [Audio Podcast Episode]. In the Tim Ferriss Show. Retrieved on 9 February 2019, from https://bit.ly/3Qieysy.

Chapter 6: Failing Better

80 Jaremka, L. M., Ackerman, J. M., Gawronski, B., Rule, N. O., Sweeny, K., Tropp, L. R., Metz, M. A., Molina, L., Ryan, W. S., Vick, S. B. (2020). Common Academic Experiences No One Talks About: Repeated Rejection, Impostor Syndrome, and Burnout. Perspectives on Psychological Science, 15(3), 519–543. https://bit.ly/3QgozXa.

81 Lefcourt, H. M. (1991). Locus of control. In J. P. Robinson, P. R. Shaver, L. S. Wrightsman (Eds.), Measures of personality and social psychological attitudes (pp. 413–499). Academic Press. https://bit.ly/3oRoNbi.

82 Lukianoff, G., Haidt, J. (2018). The Coddling of the American Mind: How Good Intentions and Bad Ideas Are Setting Up a Generation for Failure. United Kingdom: Penguin Books Limited.

83 Flores, S. E. (2016). Facehooked: How Facebook Affects Our Emotions, Relationships, and Lives. United States: Reputation Books.

84 Whitcomb, N. (1952, June 14). Under the Counter. The Daily Mirror.

85 Russell, K. (1955). Zora, the unvanquished! [Photograph collec-

tion]. United Kingdom: TopFoto.

86 Whitcomb, N. (1954, December 16). The bulldog in old lace. The Daily Mirror.

87 Armitstead, C. (2013, December 17). How Beatrix Potter self-published Peter Rabbit. The Guardian. Retrieved on 2 August 2022, from https://bit.ly/3zQxQ2v.

88 Judkins, R. (2015). Chapter 76. In: The Art of Creative Thinking. United Kingdom: Hodder & Stoughton.

89 The Marilee Brothers. Famous Book Rejections. Retrieved on 26 January 2021, from https://bit.ly/3Sm49xB.

90 Stein, G. (1933). The Autobiography of Alice B. Toklas. New York: Harcourt, Brace and Company.

91 Golding, W. (1954). Lord of the Flies. United Kingdom: Faber & Faber.

92 Morris, S. (2014, September 17). Lord of the Flies milestone marked with archive loan to University of Exeter. The Guardian. Retrieved on 26 January 2021, from https://bit.ly/3oNKKYP.

93 Dawson, M. (2017, August 2). Editor who plucked 'Diary of Anne Frank' from rejection pile dies. New York Post. Retrieved on 26 January 2021, from https://bit.ly/3OXSgLk.

94 (2020, November 5). Famous authors who have been rejected multiple times. The Cultured Giraffe. Retrieved on 26 January 2021, from https://bit.ly/3Q5ttGi.

95 King, S. (2012). On Writing: A Memoir of the Craft. United Kingdom: Hodder.

96 Bach, R. (1973). Jonathan Livingston Seagull. United States: Scribner.

97 Bell, J.S. (2010). Rejecting Rejection. Retrieved on 29 January 2021, from https://bit.ly/3Qea0mJ.

98 Jesmyn Ward. National Book Foundation. Retrieved on 12 January 2022, from https://bit.ly/3JpDZG5.

99 Adams, R. (1972). Watership Down. United Kingdom: Rex Collings Limited.

100 Mitchell, M. (1936). Gone with the Wind. United Kingdom: Macmillan.

101 Jiang, J. (2015). What I learned from 100 days of rejection. TEDxMtHood. Retrieved on 7 December 2016, from https://bit.ly/3OVyuAi.

102 Jiang, J. (2015). Rejection Proof: How I Beat Fear and Became Invincible Through 100 Days of Rejection. United States: Harmony Books.

103 Jiang's Rejection Therapy company now owns an accompanying Rejection therapy card game, originally developed by Jason Comley, described in this podcast episode: Spiegel, A, & Miller, L. (2015). Disappearing Fear [Podcast Episode]. Invisibilia (Season 1, Episode 2, Part 2). https://n.pr/3vyY5bg.

104 Stefan, M. (2010). A CV of failures. Nature, 468(7322), 467. https://bit.ly/3Sob6hy.

105 Yoder, J. (2017, April 24). I Found a Tenure-Track Job. Here's What it Took. The Chronicle of Higher Education. Retrieved on 27 April 2017. https://bit.ly/3PYE06s.

106 Lord, S.J. Everyday Scientist: the Website of Sam Lord. Retrieved on 4 February 2021, from https://bit.ly/3vXRGXB.

107 CV of Failures. I'm Sara Rwye. An imperfect Venture Capitalist. Retrieved on 4 February 2021, from https://bit.ly/3JqTJJ4.

108 Voytek, B. VOYTEKlab. Retrieved on 4 February 2021, from https://bit.ly/3A1H6Bj.

109 Original tweet from @soragnilab account. Retrieved on 4 February 2021, from https://bit.ly/3JqU4vk.

110 (2016, April 30). CV of failures: Princeton professor publishes résumé of his career lows. The Guardian. https://bit.ly/3PWZe4B.

111 Swanson, A. (2016, April 28). Why it feels so good to read about this Princeton professor's failures. The Washington Post. https://wapo.st/3zPZbBY.

112 Fernandes, J. D., Sarabipour, S., Smith, C. T., Niemi, N. M., Jadavji, N. M., Kozik, A. J., Holehouse, A. S., Pejaver, V., Symmons, O., Bisson Filho, A. W., Haage, A. (2020). A survey-based analysis of the academic job market. eLife, 9, 1–30. https://bit.ly/3OPtMUt.

113 Heggeness, M. L., Carter-Johnson, F., Schaffer, W. T., Rockey, S. J. (2016). Policy Implications of Aging in the NIH-Funded Workforce. Cell Stem Cell, 19(1), 15–18. https://doi.org/10.1016/j.stem.2016.06.012.

114 The Bible. Matthew 25:29.

115 Altucher, J. (2021). Skip the Line: Ingenious, Simple Strategies to Propel Yourself to Wealth, Success and Happiness. United Kingdom: Ebury Publishing.

116 Duckworth, A. (2018). Grit: The Power of Passion and Perseverance. India: Scribner.

117 Nylund, J. (2018). Sisu: The Finnish Art of Courage. United
Kingdom: Octopus Publishing Group.

118 Jay, M. (2017, November 10). The Secrets of Resilience. The
Wall Street Journal. Retrieved on 14 November 2017, from
https://on.wsj.com/3oLs1gJ.

119 Seligman, M. E. (2011). Learned Optimism: How to Change
Your Mind and Your Life. United States: Knopf Doubleday
Publishing Group.

120 Taleb, N. N. (2012). Antifragile: Things that Gain from Disorder.
United Kingdom: Penguin Books Limited.

121 Haidt, J., Paresky, P. (2019, January 10). By Mollycoddling Our
Children, We're Fuelling Mental Illness in Teenagers.
Experience Stern. Retrieved on 2 August 2022, from
https://bit.ly/3vvBJYj.

122 Godin, S. (2011). The Dip. United Kingdom: Little, Brown Book
Group.

123 Kahneman, D. (2003). Maps of Bounded Rationality: Psychology for Behavioral Economics. The American Economic Review, 93(5), 1449–1475. https://bit.ly/3PXEQjK.

Chapter 7: Social Comparisons

124 François   Vatel.   Cook's   Info.   (2005,   July   13).
https://bit.ly/3blNhXm.

125 (2018, November 15). How to throw a medieval feast. History
Extra (BBC). https://bit.ly/3QdzXCT. See also: Chiquart (2010).

On Cookery of Master Chiquart (1420). United States: ACMRS.

126 Bowlin, B., Brown, N. Shame and Fish: The Embarrassing and Tragic Story of François Vatel [Podcast Episode]. Ridiculous History. (2019, August 20). Retrieved 30 March 2020, https://bit.ly/3vAR0qO.

127 Walker, M. Mme de Sévigné on Vatel's Death. Micheline's Blog ~ Art, music, books, history & current events. (2014, August 8). https://bit.ly/3OT16u2.

128 Chelminski, R. (2006). The Perfectionist: Life and Death in Haute Cuisine. United States: Gotham Books.

129 Clarke, B. (2019, May 15). The Michelin Guide, The Michelin Scars, The Michelin Lies [Podcast Episode]. Let's Talk About Chef (No. 8). Retrieved on 2 August 2022, from https://apple.co/3BAan70.

130 Michelin Guide. https://bit.ly/3oSsVYN.

131 Steinberger, M. Michelin and the Deaths of Two French Chefs. The New Yorker. (2016, February 5). Retrieved on 2 August 2022, from https://bit.ly/2KWahOh.

132 Muller, J. Z. (2019). The Tyranny of Metrics. United Kingdom: Princeton University Press.

133 Rémy, P. (2004). L'inspecteur se met à table. France: Éd. des Équateurs.

134 'They needed a scapegoat': Michelin Guide accused of hiding role in French chef's suicide. National Post. (2013, January 23). https://bit.ly/3JsMQqs.

135 Sitwell, W. (Presenter), Waldman, M. (Director). (2010). Miche-

lin Stars – The Madness of Perfection. United Kingdom: silver river (for the BBC).

136 Henley, J. (2016, February 1). Benoît Violier's apparent suicide highlights pressures on top chefs. The Guardian. Retrieved on 2 August 2022, from https://bit.ly/3zul74n.

137 Benedictus, L. (2019, July 20). 'I'm not a grieving widow, I'm a seething widow'. The Sydney Morning Herald. Retrieved on 2 August 2022, from https://bit.ly/3oQOkBs.

138 Garfield, E. What Is The Primordial Reference For The Phrase 'Publish Or Perish'? The Scientist. (1996, June 9). Retrieved on 3 February 2021, from https://bit.ly/3PWTXKe.

139 Acquisition of the Thomson Reuters Intellectual Property and Science Business by Onex and Baring Asia Completed. Cision PR Newswire. (2016, October 3). https://prn.to/2nSlGzZ.

140 Garfield, E. (1955). Citation indexes for science. Science, 122(3159), 108–111. https://bit.ly/3oMDU67.

141 Gallagher, R. (2017, February 27). Eugene Garfield – 1925-2017 – a life of impact. Annual Reviews News. https://bit.ly/3bm9rst.

142 Garfield, E. (2006). The History and Meaning of the Journal Impact Factor. JAMA, 295(1), 90–93. https://bit.ly/3bkVWt7.

143 Lawrence, P. A. (2007). The mismeasurement of science. Current Biology, 17(15), R583–R585. https://bit.ly/3JoQVvU.

144 Curry, S. Sick of Impact Factors [blog entry]. Reciprocal Space. (2012, August 13). Retrieved on 2 August 2022, from https://bit.ly/3oRFzHi.

145 Chemistry journal citation distributions [Blog entry]. Chemi-

cal Connections. (2015, December 10). https://bit.ly/3zrXWHP.

146 Cantrill, S. (2015, December 5). Nature Chemistry's 2014 impact factor citation distribution. Nature Chemistry. https://go.nature.com/3vzz3Jk.

147 Tregoning, J. (2018). How will you judge me if not by impact factor? world-view. Nature, 558(7710), 345. https://bit.ly/3BzmIbN.

148 Explainer: what is an H-index and how is it calculated? The Conversation. (2015, May 21). https://bit.ly/3QbntvG.

149 Ke, Q., Ferrara, E., Radicchi, F., Flammini, A. (2015). Defining and identifying Sleeping Beauties in science. Proceedings of the National Academy of Sciences of the United States of America, 112(24), 7426–7431. https://bit.ly/3OVEwRs.

150 Wildgaard, L., Schneider, J. W., Larsen, B. (2014). A review of the characteristics of 108 author-level bibliometric indicators. Scientometrics, 101(1), 125–158. https://bit.ly/3Qd5u7X.

151 The San Francisco Declaration on Research Assessment (DORA). https://bit.ly/3SpNFED.

152 Leiden Manifesto for Research Metrics. https://bit.ly/3JnPhLa.

153 Johnson, E. The Perils of Being Paul Ehrenfest, a Forgotten Physicist and Peerless Mentor. The MIT Press Reader. (2019, July 1). Retrieved on 5 May 2020, https://bit.ly/3JqhHnK.

154 van Delft, D. (2014). Paul Ehrenfest's final years. Physics Today, 67(1), 41. https://bit.ly/3d0U9tE.

155 Toby, J. (2019). Samuel Stouffer - Brief life of a skillful survey researcher: 1900-1960. Harvard Magazine.

156 The American Soldier, by Samuel A. Stouffer [and Others].
    (1949). United States: Wiley.

157 Pettigrew, T. F. (2015). Samuel Stouffer and Relative
    Deprivation. Social Psychology Quarterly, 78(1), 7–24.
    https://bit.ly/3zpDXtf.

158 Festinger, L. (1954). A theory of social comparison processes.
    Human Relations, 7, 117–140. https://bit.ly/3vz4F1s.

159 Davis, J. A. (1966). The Campus as a Frog Pond: An Application
    of the Theory of Relative Deprivation to Career Decisions
    of College Men. American Journal of Sociology, 72(1), 17–31.
    https://bit.ly/3ONRSz6.

160 Marsh, H. W., & Parker, J. W. (1984). Determinants of stu-
    dent self-concept: Is it better to be a relatively large fish
    in a small pond even if you don't learn to swim as well?
    Journal of Personality and Social Psychology, 47(1), 213–231.
    https://bit.ly/3zQ4HEG.

161 Marsh, H. W., & Hau, K.-T. (2003). Big-Fish-Little-Pond effect
    on academic self-concept: A cross-cultural (26-country) test of
    the negative effects of academically selective schools. Ameri-
    can Psychologist, 58(5), 364–376. https://bit.ly/3Qbnz6s.

162 Loyalka, P., Zakharov, A., Kuzmina, Y. (2018). Catching the
    Big Fish in the Little Pond Effect: Evidence from 33 Countries
    and Regions. Comparative Education Review, 62(4), 542–564.
    https://bit.ly/3BBGDqo.

Chapter 8: Questioning Your Brain

163 Freud, S., Riviere, J. (1943). A General Introduction to Psycho-
    analysis. United States: Garden City Publishing Company.

164 Paris, J. (2017). Is Psychoanalysis Still Relevant to Psychiatry? The Canadian Journal of Psychiatry, 62(5), 308–312. https://bit.ly/3Qgz1Oo.

165 Dewsbury, D. A. (1997). In celebration of the centennial of Ivan P. Pavlov's (1897/1902) The Work of the Digestive Glands. American Psychologist, 52(9), 933–935. https://bit.ly/3oVIL4F.

166 Pavlov, I.P. (1897). Lektsii o rabote glavnykh pishchevaritel'nykh zhelez [Lectures on the work of the principal digestive glands]. St. Petersburg, Russia: Typografiia Ministerstva Putei Soobsheniia; Pavlov, I. P. (1902). The work of the digestive glands (W. H. Thompson, Trans.). London: Griffin. (Original work published 1897).

167 Watson, J. B. (1913). Psychology as the behaviorist views it. Psychological Review, 20(2), 158–177. https://bit.ly/3SojmOT.

168 (2012). A Brief Biography of Dr. Albert Ellis 1913-2007. Retrieved 2 August 2022, from https://bit.ly/3znctVc.

169 Ellis, A. (2002). Overcoming Resistance: A Rational Emotive Behavior Therapy Integrated Approach, 2nd Edition. United States: Springer Publishing Company.

170 Leahy, R. L. (1996). Cognitive Therapy: Basic Principles and Applications. United States: Jason Aronson, Incorporated.

171 Spiegel, A, Miller, L. (2015, January 8). Dark Thoughts [Podcast Episode]. Invisibilia (Season 1, Episode 1, Part 1). https://n.pr/3br7OcM.

172 Pollard, C., Foreman, E. I. (2016). Cognitive Behavioural Therapy (CBT): Your Toolkit to Modify Mood, Overcome Obstructions and Improve Your Life. United Kingdom: Icon Books, Limited.

173 Mayo-Wilson, E., Dias, S., Mavranezouli, I., Kew, K., Clark, D. M., Ades, A. E., Pilling, S. (2014). Psychological and pharmacological interventions for social anxiety disorder in adults: a systematic review and network meta-analysis. The Lancet Psychiatry, 1(5), 368–376. https://bit.ly/3cQbZiI.

174 Vasile, C. (2020). CBT and medication in depression (Review). Experimental and Therapeutic Medicine, 20(4), 3513–3516. https://bit.ly/3QboKms.

175 Kearns, M. C., Ressler, K. J., Zatzick, D., Rothbaum, B. O. (2012). Early Interventions for PTSD: A Review. Depression and Anxiety, 29(10), 833–842. https://bit.ly/3BydufJ.

176 Gloster, A. T., Wittchen, H. U., Einsle, F., Lang, T., Helbig-Lang, S., Fydrich, T., Fehm, L., Hamm, A. O., Richter, J., Alpers, G. W., Gerlach, A. L., Ströhle, A., Kircher, T., Deckert, J., Zwanzger, P., Höfler, M., Arolt, V. (2011). Psychological treatment for panic disorder with agoraphobia: A randomized controlled trial to examine the role of therapist-guided exposure in situ in CBT. Journal of Consulting and Clinical Psychology, 79(3), 406–420. https://bit.ly/3Sm4xwg.

177 Kolubinski, D. C., Frings, D., Nikčević, A.V., Lawrence, J. A., Spada, M. M. (2018). A systematic review and meta-analysis of CBT interventions based on the Fennell model of low self-esteem. Psychiatry Research, 267, 296–305. https://bit.ly/3bkXAuN.

178 Szentagotai, A., David, D. (2009). The Efficacy of Cognitive-Behavioral Therapy in Bipolar Disorder: A Quantitative Meta-Analysis. The Journal of Clinical Psychiatry, 70(1), 5997. https://bit.ly/3oNTr5p.

179 Hazell, C. M., Hayward, M., Cavanagh, K., Strauss, C. (2016). A systematic review and meta-analysis of low intensity

CBT for psychosis. Clinical Psychology Review, 45, 183–192. https://bit.ly/3d582ah.

180 Aurelius Antoninus, M. (2006). Meditations. London: Penguin Publishing Group.

181 Ferriss, T. (2017). Why you should define your fears instead of your goals [Talk]. TED. Retrieved 2 January, 2021. https://bit.ly/3PXK6E0.

182 Ware, B. (2019). Top Five Regrets of the Dying: A Life Transformed by the Dearly Departing. United States: Hay House.

183 Foer, J. (2012). Moonwalking with Einstein: The Art and Science of Remembering Everything. United Kingdom: Penguin Books.

184 Sagan, C. (Presenter and Producer), Soter, S., Druyan, A. (Co-producers), Malone, A. (Director). (1980). Cosmos (Documentary). United States: PBS.

185 Sagan, C. (1978). The Dragons of Eden. United States: Ballantine Books.

186 Newman, J. D., Harris, J. C. (2009). The scientific contributions of Paul D. MacLean (1913-2007). The Journal of Nervous and Mental Disease, 197(1), 3–5. https://bit.ly/3zuo98y.

187 MacLean, Paul D. (1952). Some psychiatric implications of physiological studies on frontotemporal portion of limbic system (visceral brain). Electroencephalography and Clinical Neurophysiology 4 (4): 407-418. https://bit.ly/3JocyfX.

188 Peters, P. S. (2012). The Chimp Paradox: The Acclaimed Mind Management Programme to Help You Achieve Success, Confidence and Happiness. United Kingdom: Ebury Publishing.

189 Freud, S. (1923). Das Ich und das Es. Austria: Internationaler Psychoanalytischer Verlag.

190 (2008). A theory abandoned but still compelling. Yale Medicine Magazine. https://m.yale.edu/twd7.

191 Northcutt, R. G. (2002). Understanding Vertebrate Brain Evolution. Integrative and Comparative Biology, 42(4), 743–756. https://bit.ly/3BCsoBH.

192 Toker, D. (2018). You Don't Have a Lizard Brain. The Brain Scientist. Retrieved 2 August 2022, form https://bit.ly/3zSrgZv.

193 Thomas, B. (2012). Revenge of the Lizard Brain. Scientific American. https://bit.ly/3d1ldIW.

194 Barrett, L. F. (2017). How Emotions Are Made: The Secret Life of the Brain. United Kingdom: Pan Macmillan.

195 Epstein, D. (2019). Range: How Generalists Triumph in a Specialized World. United Kingdom: Pan Macmillan.

196 Asch, S.E. (1955). Opinions and Social Pressures. Scientific American. https://bit.ly/3PXkS91.

Epilogue: The Responsibility of Leaders

197 Black, J. Lectures on chemistry. Archived scans taken prior to final book edit. Retrieved 2 August 2022, from https://bit.ly/3p8owRL.

198 Shepherd, P. (2019). What if Imposter Syndrome is a good thing? [Talk]. TEDxUniMelb. Retrieved 2 August 2022, https://bit.ly/3QjNbhH.

199 Pope, A. (1999). The Dunciad: in four books. Kiribati: Longman.

200 Rilke, R. M. (2021). Letters to a Young Poet. United States: Dover Publications.

201 Yates, D. (2007). Harry Potter and the Order of the Phoenix. Warner Bros.

Printed in Great Britain
by Amazon

11161387R00165